COLLADA

COLLADA

Sailing the Gulf of 3D Digital Content Creation

Rémi Arnaud
Mark C. Barnes

CRC Press
Taylor & Francis Group
Boca Raton London New York

CRC Press is an imprint of the
Taylor & Francis Group, an **informa** business
AN A K PETERS BOOK

First published 2006 by A K Peters, Ltd.

Published 2019 by CRC Press
Taylor & Francis Group
6000 Broken Sound Parkway NW, Suite 300
Boca Raton, FL 33487-2742

© 2006 by Taylor & Francis Group, LLC
CRC Press is an imprint of Taylor & Francis Group, an Informa business

First issued in paperback 2019

No claim to original U.S. Government works

ISBN 13: 978-0-367-44629-1 (pbk)
ISBN 13: 978-1-56881-287-8 (hbk)

Visit the Taylor & Francis Web site at
http://www.taylorandfrancis.com

and the CRC Press Web site at
http://www.crcpress.com

Library of Congress Cataloging-in-Publication Data
Arnaud, Rémi.
    COLLADA : sailing the gulf of 3D digital content creation / Rémi Arnaud,
Mark C. Barnes.
        p. cm.
    Includes bibliographical references and index.
    ISBN-13: 978-1-56881-287-8 (alk. paper)
    ISBN-10: 1-56881-287-6 (alk. paper)
    1. Computer games--Programming. 2. Computer graphics. I. Barnes, Mark C.,
1963-   . II. Title.
    QA76.76.C672A82 2006
    794.8'1526--dc22

                                                                2006012625

Cover design: Skye Design (www.skyedesign.info).

Contents

Foreword

by Tim Sweeney

In 1963, Ivan Sutherland wrote Sketchpad [57], the world's first real-time computer graphics application. In that breakthrough effort, he defined the basic techniques for structuring scene data that are still present in today's 3D applications.

In one way, though, Sutherland had it easy. He didn't have to grapple with the problem that has frustrated every subsequent developer: interchange, the process of transporting 3D data between applications.

For more than 40 years, developers have implemented interchange using ad-hoc data formats and proprietary interchange techniques. Every new 3D modeling program defines its own proprietary scene data format and also implements partial support for importing data from other proprietary formats.

For example, in developing the Unreal Engine, my company has written importers for five scene file formats, and export plug-ins for the three major 3D applications. Each required significant development and testing effort. What's worse, every time we wanted to add a new feature, we had to update five import modules and three export plug-ins.

This is one of those classic software problems that makes a developer scream: "There must be a better way!"

Finally, there is a better way: **COLLADA**.

Developed in a cooperative effort between the industry's leading developers of applications, games, and platforms, COLLADA is the industry's first standard interchange format for digital content. It is an XML-based file format supporting the transfer of common types of 3D data between applications: 3D models, vertices, polygons, textures, shaders, transformations, lights, cameras, and much more. Just as importantly, it is an extensible format that will grow to support increasingly sophisticated 3D features as they evolve.

Given that 3D interchange is a decades-old problem, one might wonder why a solution is emerging only now. To answer this, we can look to three industry trends.

- First, since the advent of the Web and the XML standard in the 1990s, there has been a growing realization across the computing industry that standard interchange formats benefit all users and application vendors. XML has provided a unifying force because it eliminates the need for debate about the syntactic nuances of a file format, enabling industry groups to instead focus on defining the high-level content and data types in an XML Schema.

- Second, there has been a blossoming of innovative new 3D tools in recent years. Where previously an artist would work in one all-compassing modeling package such as 3D Studio Max, Maya, or Softimage, it is now common to use many specialized tools every day. For example, artists working on 3D games frequently use ZBrush for crafting organic objects, SketchUp for architectural modeling, and Modo for polygon modeling— as well as Max, Maya, and Softimage for scene composition. This workflow entails frequently moving data between applications.

- Finally, the growth of 3D game development means that hundreds of thousands of developers now must frequently move data between modeling applications and real-time game engines. The growing sophistication of the datasets has further stressed the need for an interchange format.

And now, thanks to COLLADA—and to the many people and companies whose efforts made it possible—industry-standard 3D interchange is now a reality, and developers and users of 3D software are already starting to benefit.

For example, my team is replacing the Unreal Engine's (see Plates XI and XII) many ad-hoc file importing modules and our proprietary content-export plug-ins with a single, unified COLLADA pipeline. From now on, when we implement a new feature or data format, we will only have to implement it once, using industry-standard XML tools, instead of multiple times in different code paths. At long last, there is a better way!

More importantly, many new kinds of 3D applications and tools will develop around the COLLADA standard over the coming years, and COLLADA will evolve as developers further the state of the art. It is wonderful to see that, more than 40 years after Sketchpad and the invention of real-time computer graphics, the industry is continuing to leap forward with such innovations.

Tim Sweeney
Founder, Programmer, CEO
Epic Games

Preface

Who Should Read this Book?

COLLADA is an advanced 3D asset description that was created through the collaboration of many partner companies and was adopted as an official industry standard by the Khronos Group in January 2006. It is supported by many commercial and noncommercial tools and is already used by thousands of developers.

COLLADA technology is freely available. It consists of the following:

- the formal specification document written in a specialized computer language representation: the COLLADA schema;
- a human-readable specification document, created from the schema, that describes each element one by one and provides additional guidelines.

This book was created as a guide to the COLLADA 1.4 specification with the goal of providing readers with all the information that will help them understand the concepts, learn how the technology is already implemented by various tools, and provide guidance for using COLLADA in their applications.

In addition, the authors wanted to provide insight into the design of COLLADA so that readers could better understand how the design decisions were made and how this standard may evolve. Since COLLADA covers such a wide spectrum, this information supplements the basic specification material to help developers understand how this technology is intended to be used.

Content developers interested in exchanging data between several tools will find valuable information in this book. Application developers planning to take advantage of COLLADA in their tool chain and tool providers wanting to add COLLADA compatibility will find this a very useful guide.

In addition, this book provides readers with a good review of current asset pipeline technology and can be used as academic material.

Why Is COLLADA Important?

The quantity, complexity, and expected quality of content is growing exponentially with each revision of hardware. Most of the focus so far has been on providing APIs and programming languages to help with the growing complexity and cost of software development, but little effort has been made providing technology to help with content development.

COLLADA's goal is to foster the development of better content tools by standardizing a common intermediate representation that encourages better content quality as well as facilitates the inclusion of many advanced features. A standard, freely available content description technology such as COLLADA liberates the content from proprietary formats, empowering developers to improve the quality and feature set of the content that digital content creation (DCC) and middleware tools are providing.

COLLADA also provides a metric that developers can use to evaluate the best tool for their needs (conformance test) and to validate content against the specification (schema validation).

Being a standard ratified by many companies, COLLADA also ensures the permanence of the availability of the content. It is particularly important in the current context of market consolidation where companies and tools can cease to exist without warning.

The reliance on a particular DCC tool's proprietary format forces developers to store the entire DCC tool and operating system along with the proprietary data for archival purposes. Games created 20 years ago are resurfacing today as classics, not unlike classic motion picture revivals. Game data was a perennial asset then, but the open-source nature of COLLADA and its Unicode data encoding helps to alleviate this problem.

Unfortunately, for vendors who dominate the market, there is a clear business advantage in having an opaque storage format and exposing it only through a limited, proprietary interface, because their customers' data is captured in the proprietary format of the tools they use. Since most of the data is stored in this format, competitors will not have access to all of it, and the cost of changing tools becomes proportional to the amount of content that the developer has already developed. This also makes it impossible for other vendors to provide innovative technologies easily. Even if another vendor added advanced features to their own tools, those features could not and would not be used by most developers until they became available in the main vendor's access interface and storage format. As time passes, customer innovation and creativity is compromised as well because they cannot author content that their DCC tool doesn't support. Luckily there is a counterbalance: since developers have to be able to access the data they need, a tool that would enable them to create content without providing access to it would not be useful for this market. DCC vendors have created application frameworks that enable their customers to plug in custom tools to compensate for the lack of features and to enable content import and export. This has become a large secondary market that diverts time and energy away from the true goals of advancing the features and capabilities of DCC tools. However, the tremendous cost of this market dynamic is becoming too great for the market to bear. A new approach is needed.

Why We Wrote This Book

The idea of writing a book on COLLADA to help with the adoption of the technology has been slowly germinating, but what really triggered this book happened during the Dublin Eurographics conference in 2005. At the end of a presentation about COLLADA, several questioners asked about the availability of additional material in order to use the technology in the professional or academic world.

Alice and Klaus Peters were also attending the conference, where they encouraged one of the authors to work on this project. Their trust, professionalism, knowledge of the business of technical publishing, and respect for the author's work are the main reasons this book has been written.

We hope you have as much fun reading this book as we had writing it.

About the Authors

Rémi Arnaud joined Sony Computer Entertainment US R&D in January 2003 as the graphics architect for the PlayStation®3 graphics API. Rémi has a wide range of experience in designing application interfaces, software tools, and runtimes for real-time graphics applications. He obtained his PhD in real-time image synthesis while working in the R&D department of Thomson Training and Simulation (Paris, France) designing visual systems for custom hardware and high-end workstations. He then moved to the US and worked for Silicon Graphics, where he was in charge of adding high-end features to IRIS Performer, a multiprocessor optimized scene-graph application. During this time, one of the features added through a hardware and software extension was the calligraphic light point capability mandatory for the most advanced civil aircraft training simulators (FAA Level D). The necessity to add this capability to content creation tools brought Rémi to collaborate with Mark Barnes for the first time. Rémi and one of his colleagues, Christopher

Tanner, soon caught the Silicon Valley start-up virus and created Intrinsic Graphics and codesigned the respected Alchemy cross-platform middleware solution for game development.

Mark Barnes joined Sony Computer Entertainment US R&D in July 2003 as a member of the graphics team where he is leading the effort on COLLADA. Mark's experience and knowledge in the field of visual simulation includes database tools, distributed processing, and real-time graphics. Mark was a member of the system software team supporting the Vertical Motion Simulator (VMS) laboratory at NASA Ames Research Center for several years, developing and improving real-time software for graphics, data acquisition, and simulation execution. The VMS lab was also the first customer of an innovative 3D modeling tool called Multigen. Mark eventually accepted a position at Multigen-Paradigm, Inc. (then Software Systems), where he became responsible for the OpenFlight database format and IRIS Performer tools and integration. He was also an engineer on the innovative SmartScene project. During this period of time, Mark established close working relationships with the Performer team at Silicon Graphics (SGI) that was soon to include Rémi Arnaud. Subsequently, Mark was an engineering manager of Muse Communications, Inc., developing advanced virtual environment software for the Internet. He also worked as a staff engineer at IVAST, Inc., developing MPEG-4 client systems.

Acknowledgments

Several contributors have helped the authors to create this book.

Daniel Horowitz from NVIDIA, in addition to his role of chairman of the COLLADA FX sub-working group, has been very generous to contribute the entire content for Chapter 5, "COLLADA Effects."

Christian Laforte from Feeling Software has provided 3 appendices to this book: "COLLADA Plug-In for 3ds Max," "COLLADA Plug-In for Maya," and "COLLADA FX Plug-In for Maya."

Alexandre Jean-Claude from Avid/Softimage has provided the "SOFT-IMAGE|XSI 5.1 Plug-In" appendix.

Special thanks to Altova GmbH for putting together a wonderful application called XMLSpy that we used to create many of the illustrations in this book.

The authors are deeply grateful to Sony Computer Entertainment (SCE) for accepting and financing this R&D project. In particular, we extend our thanks to Dominic Mallinson, Director of US R&D, and to Senior Manager Attila Vass, who have given their trust and support to this project and encouraged the authors to create this book in their free time. Ken Kutaragi,

CEO/President of SCE, Masayuki Chatani, Corporate Executive and CTO of SCE, and Teiji Yutaka, Vice President, R&D Division of SCEI, are to be thanked for having accepted the COLLADA strategy and inclusion in the PlayStation®3 software SDK.

The COLLADA team at SCE has provided many hours of hard work to create several revisions of the specification and sample software. Gàbor Nagy has participated in many aspects of the design, chaired the Physics sub-working group, created many demonstrations, and integrated COLLADA in his own modeler, Equinox 3D. Lilli Thompson created the first COLLADA conformance test, relentlessly tracked issues, and created a good deal of COLLADA content. Richard Stenson led the effort of delivering COLLADA to PS3 developers. Andy Lorino edited the COLLADA schema and developed the COLLADA DOM API. Robin Green wrote the first COLLADA FX specification, the largest single part of COLLADA, and chaired the sub-working group. Greg Corson worked on the COLLADA RT and the COLLADA DOM libraries, tracking and fixing many bugs. Three interns also helped with the COLLADA project: Daniel Horn helped implement the first viewer, Fabien Goslin created sample code, and Philippe David created the Refinery asset conditioner.

Many people at Sony Computer Entertainment provided help and support to this project: Lia Adams, Geoff Audi, Michael Budwig, Guy Burdick, David Coombes, Erwin Coumans, Mark Deloura, Nat Duca, Jason Doig, Ellen Finch, Richard Forster, Roy Hashimoto, Alan Heirich, Masatomo Ito, Tatsuya Iwamoto, Vangelis Kokkevis, Antoine Labour, Dmitri Makarov, Bruno Matzdorf, Axel Mamode, Care Michaud-Wideman, Ed Owen, J. Patton, Amy Pilkington, Sébastien Rubens, Aoki Sachiyo, Vlad Stamate, Pip Stuart, Gregg Tavares, Andrew Walker, Yoshinori Washizu, Mike Weiblen, Rob Withey, and Mason Woo.

COLLADA design would not have been possible without the participation of many people from several other companies.

Jeff Yates, now working at Havok, believed in the project since its inception, participated in the design, and created the first 3ds Max plug-in when he was working at Discreet. Jean-Luc Corenthin and his management, Michel Kripalani and Marc Petit, have since managed this project at Autodesk/Discreet.

Gordon Bradley working at Autodesk/Alias participated in the design and wrote the initial plug-in for Maya. Joyce Janczyn, Jérôme Maillot, Michel Besner, Kevin Tureski, and Steven Roselle have provided support for the project.

Alexandre Jean-Claude from Avid/Softimage created the plug-in for XSI and is still working on this project and providing help with the design. Many other people helped at Softimage: Gareth Morgan, Marc Stevens, James Rogers, Alain Laferrière, Simon Inwood, Luc Bolduc, and Takashi Umezawa.

The team at Feeling Software (Christian Laforte, Guillaume Laforte, Zhang Jian, Antoine Azar, Alfred Leung and Misako Matsumoto) provided COLLADA with fantastic, professional-grade plug-ins for 3ds Max and Maya, as well as extensions such as COLLADA FX and COLLADA Physics for Maya and are now working on the COLLADA 1.4 conformance test.

The Emdigo team (Christopher Tanner, Cédric Perthuis, Steve Gleiztmann, and Rory Mather) participated in the design, created the first version of the COLLADA DOM, and took the risk of using COLLADA as the core of their technology for their start-up.

The AGEIA team (Stan Melax, Andy Hess, Emmanuel Marquez, Grady Hannah, John Ratcliff, Mikael Skolones, and Greg Stoner) helped tremendously with the design of COLLADA Physics.

The NVIDIA team (Sébastien Dominé, Ignacio Castano, Daniel Horowitz, and Chris Maughan) really embraced COLLADA for their software tools strategy and is providing COLLADA with great tools and design contributions.

The Khronos Group is doing a wonderful job, particularly Neil Trevett (President), Elizabeth Riegel (marketing), Andrew Riegel (events), and Tony DeYoung (webmaster).

There are many other people involved and supporting COLLADA. Our deepest apologies for any not included here: Farshid Almassizadeh (Electronic Arts), Karthic Bala (Vicarious Vision), Adam Billyard (Criterion Software), Steven Collins (Havok), David Burke (Epic Games), Mark Daly (NVIDIA), Patrick Doane (XLGames), Jerome Durand (EkoSystem), Cass Everitt (NVIDIA), Chris Grimm (ATI), Jason Hoerner (THQ), Chas Inman (NVIDIA), Chris Keogh (Havok), Mark J. Kilgard (NVIDIA), Bill Licea-Kane (ATI), Mikael Lagré (Blender), Kathleen Maher (Peddie Research), Bryan Marshall (Codemasters), Nathan Martz (Double Fine Productions), Jay Moore (GarageGames), Kari Pulli (Nokia), Callan McInally (ATI), Tom McReynolds (NVIDIA), Kevin Norman (Maxis/EA), Bruno Patatas (ViaRender Systems), Jon Peddie (Peddie Research), Nicholas Perret (Omegame), Mark Rein (Epic Games), Randi Rost (3Dlabs), Tim Sweeney (Epic Games), Kevin Thacker, Stephen Wilkinson (Nokia), Chris Wynn (NVIDIA), Jenny Zhao (Vicarious Vision/Emdigo).

Rémi Arnaud would like to give a very special thanks to his wife, Cécile, and his two kids, Melody and Nicolas, for enduring many hours alone while he worked on this book, and for their love and support.

Mark Barnes gives a heartfelt thanks to Amy Arreola for her love, compassion, and inspiration.

Trademarks

In alphabetic order:

3ds Max is a registered trademark of Autodesk, Inc.

AGEIA, *PhysX*, and *NovodeX* are trademarks of AGEIA Technologies, Inc.

COLLADA is a trademark of Sony Computer Entertainment, Inc.

FX Composer is a trademark of NVIDIA Corporation.

Glide is a trademark or registered trademark of 3dfx Interactive, Inc., and NVIDIA Corporation.

Google and *Google Earth* are trademarks of Google, Inc.

Havok, *Havok Physics*, *Havok Animation*, and *Havok Complete* are registered trademarks of Havok and Telekinesys Research Limited.

Half-Life is a registered trademark of Valve Corporation.

HOOPS is a trademark or registered trademark of TechSoft America or its subsidiaries in the United States and in other countries.

Intrinsic Alchemy is a trademark of Intrinsic Graphics, Inc.

IRIS GL is a trademark of SGI, Inc.

Khronos is a trademark of the Khronos Group, Inc.

Maya is a registered trademark of Autodesk, Inc.

Modo is a trademark of Luxology, LLC.

OpenFlight is a trademark of Multigen-Paradigm, Inc.

OpenGL and *OpenGL ES* are registered trademarks of SGI, Inc.

DirectX is a registered trademark of Microsoft Corporation.

RenderMan is a registered trademark of Pixar Animation Studios.

RenderWare is a trademark or registered trademark of Criterion Software Limited in the U.S. and/or other countries.

Softimage is a registered trademark of Avid Technology, Inc.

Unreal is a registered trademark of Epic Games, Inc.

W3C is a registered trademark of the Massachusetts Institute of Technology (MIT), European Research Consortium for Informatics and Mathematics (ERCIM), or Keio University (Keio) on behalf of the W3C.

XMLSpy is a registered trademark of Altova GmbH.

Zbrush is a registered trademark of Pixologic, Inc.

All other trademarks, service marks, trade names, or product names mentioned are the property of their respective owners.

1 Introduction to COLLADA

Overview

This chapter explains why the COLLADA technology has been developed. It provides a global view, defines the problems addressed by the technology, the main actors, and the goals and perspectives for this new technology. It provides an historic overview and information on how COLLADA is being designed and adopted. The goal is to give the reader an insight into how the design choices are made and how this technology might evolve.

Problem Domain

An interactive application is composed of two major components:

1. the application, which provides information in real time to the user and the means to interact with it;
2. the content, which contains the information through which the application navigates and provides a view to the user.

COLLADA focuses on the domain of interactive applications in the entertainment industry, where the content is three-dimensional and is a game or related interactive application. Therefore, the user of the application will be referred to as the *player*.

The types of information that can be provided to the player depend on the output devices available. Most games use one or several screens to display the visual information, sometimes a system with stereo visualization, and a set of speakers for the audio information. Often, some physical sensation can be rendered, as simple as a vibrating device embedded in the joystick, or as sophisticated as a moving cabin in arcade settings.

The application may output, or *render*, several *sensors* at the same time, often in different places. An *observer* is a term that defines a group of sensors that move together. For example, an observer in a (virtual) car may have at least two visual sensors to represent the out-of-the-windows view (in this case, the view through the windshield) and the rear-mirror view. Several observers, which may be simultaneous users, can be displayed together by the same application, for example, in split-screen games where two or more players are sharing the same screen.

The content must include all data required by all the sensors that the application wants to use. The content can have multiple representations stored, partially sharing some of the elements. For example, if the content represents a landscape, different materials may be needed to represent the four seasons. The different representations of the data are called *scenes*.

Another type of interactive application is a training simulator in which the goal is to teach the user how to behave in real situations. These applications are not games, and the trainees' reactions when they make a deadly mistake in a simulation make this quite clear. COLLADA does not focus on simulation applications, but it could certainly be used in this domain as well [1].

The computer-generated animation movie industry is also very interested in COLLADA. This application is completely scripted, not interactive. That industry's goal is to be able to produce previsualization of scenes that look as final as possible, in a very small amount of time, which is why they are interested in integrating game technology in their production process.

Other types of applications may also profit from COLLADA, but its goal is to concentrate on interactive game applications, not to expand the problem domain. Other applications that require the same type of technologies will indirectly benefit from it.

Separation between Content and Runtime

The first interactive real-time applications rendering three-dimensional graphics required very expensive dedicated hardware and were used mainly in training simulation. Physical separation between content and runtime did not exist in the early applications (such as in the GE Apollo lunar landing trainer) [2]. The content was embedded in the code, or more specifically, some subroutine was coded to render a specific part of the content. Eventually, effort was made to store the embedded content as data arrays, and the code became increasingly generic so it could render all kinds of data.

The next logical step was to separate the data physically from the code. This allowed creating several products with the same application, but with different data. More products were defined by the data itself, and content creation soon became a completely separate task.

The real-time application was then referred to as the *runtime*, and the content for the runtime was stored in the *runtime database*. In the game industry, the runtime is called the *game engine*.

Digital content creation (DCC) tools were created, but the data structures and algorithms used for modeling did not match with the data that can be processed in real time by the application. DCC tools were also used by the movie industry for the production of computer-generated movies in which an advanced rendering engine was attached to the tool to produce a set of still images that compose the frames of the movie.

DCC tools and advanced rendering techniques, such as ray tracing [3] or shader languages such as RenderMan [4], required more advanced concepts than a real-time application could handle. Mathematical descriptions of surfaces such as splines and Bézier surfaces became necessary in the computer-aided design (CAD) market [5].

Interactive applications needed both the advanced modeling techniques and the simpler representation usable in real time. Because of this, compilation techniques, used to create binary executable code from high-level languages, were adapted for the content processing. The database used in the DCC tool was therefore called the *source*. The data compiler takes the source data and creates the runtime data.

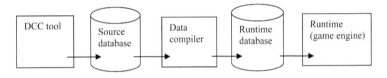

Figure 1.1. Content pipeline synopsis.

The runtime database soon became too large to fit in the memory of the target system. The content had to be sliced and paged in real time, depending on where the observers were. This quite challenging problem sometimes required specific hardware assistance and necessitated a very specific encoding of the content. Specific algorithms had to be developed for terrain paging [6] and texture paging [7].

Because of economic constraints, severe limitations exist in hardware targeted by the game industry. The data must be organized in the most optimal way possible. For performance optimization, many game applications use their own file system and combine the various elements in a single file. Some developers run optimization programs for hours to find the best placement of the elements for better interactivity. The idea is to optimize seek time and place data accordingly. This is very similar to the optimization section of a compiler, with a complexity similar to the NP-complete salesman optimization problem [8].

Another example of paging technology used outside the game industry is the Google Earth application [9]. This application enables the user to look down on the planet from any altitude and render a view based on satellite altimetery and imagery information. It is the result of generalizing the terrain- and image-paging technology developed for high-end simulation applications [10].

Such applications handle only static data and have limited interactivity for the user to move around in the environment. However, most applications, especially in the entertainment industry, require the content to be highly dynamic. For example, animated objects are needed, either objects moving independently in a scene (moving object) or prescribed animations controlled by various parameters, such as a windsock depending on the direction and speed of the wind, or a feature like a bridge that can have different representations depending on whether or not it has been destroyed.

The objects in the runtime database are often organized in a graph, where each branch represents the relative position of the objects or different choices of multiple representations. This data organization is commonly referred to as the *scene graph*, and several runtime technologies have been developed to exploit this [11].

Some early rendering techniques used a particular organization of the scene graph to determine how the objects hide each other in the view, such as the BSP method [12]. Early hardware accelerator performance was greatly affected by the objects sent outside of the camera's field of view, so scene graphs were organized with a container-type relation. All the "children" bounding volumes are enclosed in the "parent" bounding volume; therefore a culling operation can cut entire branches if the parent is not in the field of view.

More complex dynamic behavior is now required for interactive applications. The content needs to evolve following direct interaction with the user. This can be physical interaction with the virtual representation of the user in the application, or it can be indirectly linked to user interaction, such as when a pile of boxes collapses if one of the boxes is removed. Very complex control systems are developed to combine scripted animation, artificial intelligence (AI), physical simulation, and user control.

In other words, the content must be designed for interactivity, not only for the interaction with the user but also for the interactivity between the different elements of the content. The relationship between objects is much more complex, and the scene-graph technology is reaching its limit in capacity, because the graph becomes too complex and overloaded with many interdependent relationships. The dynamic nature of the entertainment application is such that the scene-graph technology is not sufficent to manage all of the content. Instead, hybrid techniques are developed, often targeting a specific game genre. Fortunately, modern rendering hardware performance is less impacted by sending objects outside the field of view, so the main rendering optimization that the scene-graph technology required is no longer an issue.

The process of creating the runtime database from the source database has become more complex and resource-intensive over time. The simple link between the content creation and the runtime is now an entity of its own, called the *content pipeline*. With the need for larger and more interactive content, game developers have to spend substantial resources on this technology.

The Content Pipeline

The content pipeline is composed of the following elements:

- digital content creation (DCC) tools used by artists to create the source data;
- the exporter, a program written for a given DCC tool that permits the content to be extracted from the DCC tool;
- the conditioning pipeline, a set of programs that apply several transformations to the content, such as geometry cleaning and optimizing for fast rendering;
- the runtime database, specifically encoded for a given runtime and often for a given target platform.

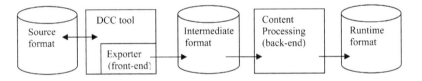

Figure 1.2. The content pipeline.

A novice may ask why it is necessary to write an exporter, since the DCC tool already saves the data in the source database, or why an importer couldn't be created as part of the conditioning pipeline tools. There are, in fact, many difficulties that make these solutions impractical.

The main problem is that the format used by the DCC tool is often proprietary, so it is not possible to write an importer. Even when the format is available, it may be very complex to read and require knowledge of the DCC tool algorithms that are not available to users.

In practice, the exporter is an integral part of the pipeline, since it is already doing some processing on the source data, utilizing the DCC built-in functions to convert internal representation to a more usable format. From the point of view of compiler technology, the exporter is actually the front end of the data compiler, and the data produced by the exporter is the intermediate format.

To enable users to extract the data, DCC tools typically offer a software development kit (SDK) that provides an application programming interface (API) to interact with the internal representations. Some DCC tools provide different APIs, depending on the type of data most often needed by the application. For instance, a game SDK is sometimes provided specifically to help game developers.

DCC tool vendors prefer providing and supporting SDKs rather than publishing the details of their internals and supporting developers tinkering with reading their proprietary files directly. The main reason for DCC tools to do this is that they need to be able to provide new releases. If there were applications depending on a given internal structure, this would make major improvements very difficult. It is thus much easier to hide the internals and provide stability at the SDK level.

Therefore, application developers are forced to create exporters. Even with the relative stability of the SDK, developers must still continuously update their exporters if they want to keep up with new releases of tools. Experience shows that developers often decide to stick to one specific release of a particular DCC tool for a given production, since the cost and risk associated with constantly updating the content pipeline is too intensive. This also affects the development of advanced technology by DCC vendors for game developers who are in the middle of a game-development cycle.

Interestingly, there is also a business advantage since this locks developers into using given vendors and restricts the window of time in which competitors can have a chance at acquiring a new customer. Retooling often happens only when new hardware is introduced, whether it is a new-generation console or a new type of hardware such as a mobile phone. Even then, switching from one DCC tool to another is problematic because of the artists' familiarity with a given DCC tool interface.

Exporter development is not an easy task, but it is forced upon developers. All game developers agree that creating and maintaining an exporter is very time consuming. Nevertheless, they also understand that the content pipeline is a piece of technology they have to master and cannot depend on pieces that are not perfect.

Not only is the resulting game content limited by the game developer's capacity in developing a good content pipeline, but more often, better tools or technologies cannot be introduced because of the lack of flexibility in the design of content pipelines.

COLLADA was created to address this worrisome situation.

Problem Description

To export the data, developers have to design a format in which to export it. This is no simple task, especially because the format must be flexible enough to withstand changes in requirements during the development process, such as introducing new data types.

Once the data is exported, developers still have to write an importer for this data into their content processing facility. Some developers try to solve the problem by having the entire content pipeline contained in the exporter code, so that the output of the export process is directly in the format needed by the runtime. This approach is often problematic since the plug-in interface is not designed to handle such complex applications. It is also the cause of major maintenance problems when the DCC application SDK is evolving and because of the complete lock-in to a given DCC tool and often to a specific version of this tool.

Another approach developers take is to limit the input data to the simplest data, such as geometry, texture mapping, images, and animation curves, and to create a set of integrated tools to create the remaining data, often including the game engine as the means to visualize the data. This proves to be a quite successful approach for developers whose goal is to concentrate on a specific subset of game applications and who can create their content with a relatively small team. Such a tool, if well designed and implemented, provides artists and game designers with a very short feedback loop between content creation and its visualization in the runtime. On the other hand, this approach has several limitations. For example, the edits made in the tool cannot be pushed up the pipeline; therefore, if the input data needs to be modified, all the edits have to be done again. Another drawback is that it is impossible to use external technologies without integrating those directly into the tool itself.

These approaches are in fact contrary to the improvement of the situation, which should be to require an opening up of the tool pipeline to enable developers to use a variety of independent tools, easing the introduction of new technologies, and making possible the adaptation of the content pipeline to be used by larger teams and for all genres of games.

The Zoo

Content pipelines often use more than one intermediate format, since each tool may have its own export format or may not provide an SDK or plug-in facilities for developers to use their own format. In other words, this is a zoo!

The data is exported from the modeler in a given format. An independent tool is used to adjust some properties that the DCC tool does not understand, then another tool is used to gather several assets into a game level, which is then sent to the final optimizer that will create the game-specific runtime format. Each of those tools may very well use independent and incompatible formats since it is difficult to create one format for all. It is so much more convenient for individuals to create their own tools rather than having to collaborate and spend valuable time on making compromises.

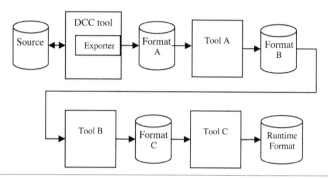

Figure 1.3. A typical zoo.

This process has several limitations.

- The content pipeline is one-way. Therefore, changes cannot be saved back into the source database. When changes need to be done from the source, the data must go through the entire processing of the content pipeline before they can be seen in the level-editor tool. This process takes time, thus impacting productivity.

- The tools are not interchangeable, which often creates situations where data have to be propagated through "back doors" when a change occurs in the process.

- There is no easy way to create shortcuts in the process to enhance productivity.

Artists need to see their work running in the runtime. Ideally, they need to be able to do so without having to go through the entire content pipeline process. Therefore, a separate path, called the *fast-path*, needs to be created in parallel. To maintain the highest possible performance, only the data that is modified will go through the fast-path; the rest of the data will be loaded in the optimized runtime format. During production, it is necessary for the game engine to be capable of loading both the optimized data and the intermediate format.

A Common Intermediate Format

Everything would be much simpler if all the tools in the content pipeline could export and import a well-defined common format. Developers would not need to write and maintain their own exporters, and the data would be available directly to the content pipeline.

COLLADA's goal is to foster the development of a more advanced content pipeline by standardizing a common intermediate representation, encouraging better quality content, and bringing many advanced features to the standard. COLLADA should be the transport mechanism between the various tools in the content pipeline.

But is it possible to establish such a common format?

DCC tools have been developed independently and may have very different ways of describing the data. Some tools have very specific attributes that some developers want to use in their pipeline but which would be impossible to export from other DCC tools. Defining a set of common representations that can be exported by all the tools and making sure that the tool-specific parameters can still be represented is a hard task.

The DCC Vendors

In the entertainment industry, there are three major DCC tools:

- 3ds Max;
- Maya;
- XSI.

All vendors understand the value of a common format, but for a different reason. They are seeking not only an intermediate format but also an interchange format.

The goal of an interchange format is to enable the data to move freely from one tool to another. The main idea is to enable several DCC tools to be used by developers in the same production or to enable developers to switch easily from one main DCC vendor to another DCC vendor. Of course, a DCC vendor who has a much larger market share than the others may not be interested in risking it and may not want a common interchange format to exist, or at least not one that is not under his control.

Recently, Autodesk, who owned 3ds Max, acquired Maya. This consolidation of the market creates a difficult situation for game developers since Autodesk may use its strong position to reduce the interchangeability of data with external tools. At the same time, the need for interoperability between Maya and 3ds Max is growing, unless one of the tools is to be scavenged and merged into the other one. This recent move makes it both more important and more difficult for the existence of a common interchange format.

Most of the time, developers use a single DCC tool in their production pipeline. Another product may have a set of functionalities that would improve developer productivity, but the only way for the new tool to be usable would be to have it inserted in the current content pipeline. The new tool has to be able to interchange data with the primary tool.

Softimage had long ago developed the dotXSI format and SDK to enable interchangeability between tools. They have published the format publicly and have created exporters and importers for the other DCC tools available in open source [13].

The problem is that even if freely available, dotXSI is designed and owned by one of the DCC vendors and therefore competing vendors cannot be expected to fully support it.

The main drawback from the user's point of view for one single company to own the intermediate format is that they are then in the position to define exactly what features are to be represented in the format, thus making it impossible for the other vendors to innovate since any advanced features they might add would not be used by developers until available in the interchange format.

Smaller tool companies have the same problem and have to interface with all of the major tools. Most partner with the DCC vendors and create importers and exporters or embed their application as a plug-in.

A Collaboration Model

Other industries have experienced a similar problem. COLLADA design methodology has been modeled from the experience in the 3D graphics accelerator industry. There used to be many 3D APIs, such as PHIGS, GKS-3D, Doré, HOOPS, Glide, and IrisGL, promoted by various vendors, but the industry really took off only when standard APIs were adopted. The two current mainstream APIs—Direct3D and OpenGL—were established as standards and created in 1992 and 1995, respectively [14].

The OpenGL proposition was to create a committee, the OpenGL Architecture Review Board (ARB), regrouping all the providers who would collaborate to design a common API. This approach proved successful despite serious competition among the vendors.

Direct3D was created by Microsoft and became a de facto standard in the PC market simply because of the large share of the market that Microsoft operating systems have.

One major difference between OpenGL and Direct3D is the opportunity for hardware vendors to provide exclusive extensions to the API, enabling them to innovate and better serve their specific customer needs. This advantage can also be a disadvantage because if too many vendor-specific extensions are created, each vendor ends up with a different API, thus weakening the standard. Therefore, there is a significant interest for the companies belonging to the OpenGL ARB to compromise and offer a common API.

Since the lack of a standard intermediate format is hurting interactive industry developers, it ultimately hurts the major platform vendors in this industry, in particular, the game-console vendors.

Each generation of game consoles exponentially adds to the demand for interactive content, in quantity as well as in quality. The cost and quality of content production is directly proportional to the quality of the content pipeline, and especially the quality of the exporters.

The authors of this book, both working in the US R&D department of Sony Computer Entertainment (SCE), started the project of a standard intermediate format that would be designed in partnership with the major tool vendors. During SIGGRAPH '03, the first meetings took place, and thanks to the dominant position of SCE in the entertainment industry, the three main DCC vendors agreed to participate in this project.

This project became known as COLLADA, an acronym for COLLAborative Design Activity [15].

Intermediate or Interchange Format?

Similarly, the design goal for COLLADA has been to enable not only exporting data from the DCC tools but also reimporting it. The main reason for this is to enable a large variety of tools to be able to interact with the primary DCC tool chosen by the game developer, using COLLADA as a conduit. This is to answer the growing need for developers to be able to use (or create) utilities that will fit in their content pipeline without having to learn how to embed their utility inside the main DCC. It also enables the middleware industry to create external utility tools with specific tasks, such as triangulating, cleaning up the geometry, and remapping texture coordinates. Potentially, the open-source community could be involved in this, although the game community is currently not inclined to use or participate in open-source projects, mostly due to the risk of patent infringement.

In the model shown in Figure 1.3, the source database is stored in the DCC tool binary format, and COLLADA is used as the intermediate format

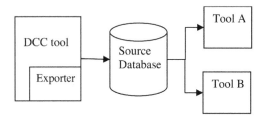

Figure 1.4. Content pipeline with a DCC tool and external utilities.

between the various tools. The communication between tools can be direct, but most often it is done using a file system.

Since one of the external tools can be another DCC tool, can COLLADA be used as an interchange format? It certainly is an interchange format, but it is limited to the content that can be stored in COLLADA and the capability for the DCC tools to recognize this content.

COLLADA includes the notion of techniques and profiles (see "Techniques, Profiles, and Extras," page 34). Each COLLADA-compatible tool has to correctly interpret the data in the "common" technique; this is mandatory to make sure COLLADA has a subset that is universally recognized.

The purpose of profiles is to enable tools or game developers to extend the format by creating a specific section in the content that is clearly marked by a label indicating the nonstandardized part of the content. Although the application-specific techniques cannot be interpreted by other tools, it is still written using the same syntax rules, so it can still be loaded by all the applications.

Ideally, a COLLADA document going through the process of importing and then exporting from a given tool should keep all the extra data. This rule is fundamental to enable developers to extend the format in the way they need without having to change the exporter and importer code for all the tools they are using [16].

The goal for an interchange format is to be able to transport all the data from one DCC tool to another without any loss and then to reverse the operation. This is not the primary design goal for COLLADA. This would be equivalent to having a compiler be able to recreate the source from the intermediate representation.

On the other hand, it is possible that eventually some of the tools may not have their own format and may use COLLADA as their native format. In that case, COLLADA would become the source format. Although this is not the current goal for COLLADA, much attention has been put in the design to enable this possible usage.

This approach would have the benefit of solving the data archival issue. Currently the only way to archive the source assets of an application is to store all the tools, including the DCC tools, with the assets in order to be able to reuse the asset later. Even if the DCC tools can be retrieved, it is not guaranteed that they can be run again on future development systems, since they often rely on a specific version of an operating systems and/or hardware configuration. In addition, it may be impossible to find a proper license for those applications in the future. Storing all the source data in an open standard such as COLLADA would significantly raise the possibility of using the assets in the future.

Another unexpected usage of COLLADA by some companies is to utilize this format, or a binary equivalent representation, directly as a runtime format. COLLADA is definitely not designed as a target format, but it turns out that it can be suitable for being used directly by the runtime. This is mostly due to the massive deployment of the XML technology on many devices, which makes it easier to interface directly with COLLADA documents. This does not mean that the content pipeline would be reduced to nothing; it just means that the conditioning of the data can be done directly in the COLLADA format.

COLLADA: A Short History

It is important for the graphics community to participate in the design of a standard intermediate format, in order to avoid the situation where one single vendor dictates what features should be included and then uses their position to eliminate competition.

Following SIGGRAPH '03, Sony Computer Entertainment did a thorough analysis of all the existing formats and, in the process, involved several other companies in the game industry, notably Criterion Software, which was at the time the most successful independent middleware company with their product RenderWare [17].

Many other companies became involved in the project:

- Vicarious Vision, a game developer that also was a middleware provider with the product Alchemy, which they acquired with the purchase of Intrinsic Graphics [18];
- Emdigo, a start-up in the mobile space, using COLLADA for 3D graphics on cellular phones [19];
- Novodex, a real-time game physics company [20];

- Discreet, representing 3ds Max [21];
- Alias, representing Maya [22];
- Softimage, representing XSI [23].

An informal working group was established, and after a year of weekly meetings, the COLLADA 1.0 specification was produced. The goal was that every partner would be satisfied with the specification so that DCC vendors would create importer/exporter plug-ins for the format. SCE insisted that the specification and plug-ins source code would be made public. It was not an easy task to get agreement on even the most basic definitions. More than one company pushed their current format to be adopted instead of creating a new one, which was not possible because of the highly competitive industry, and because a completely open format was needed without any intellectual property (IP) issues.

The work paid off. At SIGGRAPH '04, the first public presentation of COLLADA 1.0 was made in a sponsored Tech Talk [24]. Even though the presentation was about a public open source project, SIGGRAPH organizers looked at the COLLADA presentation as a commercial project and requested sponsorship for it.

The presentation included numerous demonstrations of COLLADA content exported by one DCC vendor and then loaded back into another, modified and saved back, and loaded again into another DCC tool or into a middleware content pipeline. COLLADA content was also demonstrated running simultaneously on Xbox® and PlayStation®2 on the same screen with a video split-screen mechanism. In addition, a reduced version of the same content was created and demonstrated on a mobile phone.

This presentation surprised a lot of people and annoyed some. The audience was amazed at seeing the DCC vendors helping each other to make sure the data was correctly exchanged between their tools.

Why was SCE sponsoring an interchange format? The audience expected SCE to focus only on the PlayStation® platforms and avoid cross-platform capabilities by developing only proprietary technologies.

Many developers reported they needed a common intermediate format and thanked the partners for working on it, but it was so sudden that they said they would wait before embracing it, since it could go away as fast as it appeared!

Some complained that the COLLADA group was defining yet another format and instead should have embraced an existing format. The most upset crowd was from the X3D community that has worked to create a format for 3D content visualization for the Web [25], which used some of the same basic constructs used in COLLADA. The main difference between the two formats is the result of the fact that X3D is derived from the VRML scene graph concept for Web browsing of 3D assets, while COLLADA is targeting advanced game applications.

The COLLADA 1.0 specification concentrated on putting together the basic elements of the format. It was missing some fundamental features to be usable by game developers, such as animation. The main goal was to get the community excited about this project and gather feedback.

Overall, the presentation was quite successful, since it produced more involvement from the game and middleware community and gathered a large amount of feedback, which resulted in several revisions of the format (1.1, 1.2, 1.3, 1.3.1, and 1.4) [26].

More companies joined the COLLADA working group: ATI [27], NVIDIA [28], 3Dlabs [29], and Nokia [30].

The design committee work progressed with the objective to bring to COLLADA all the features required by the game industry.

A lot of work was needed to improve the quality of the plug-ins and refine the specification. At SIGGRAPH '04, the only way a plug-in was tested was by using the content for the demonstration. It quickly became clear that this was not sufficient, since all the early adopters encountered so many problems that it made the technology usable only for very basic applications.

SCE started to put in place a conformance test, a really complex task. Once the early version of the conformance test was put in place and early adopters had provided feedback, a bug database was put in place, revealing some fundamental issues with the plug-ins, sometimes revealing aspects of the specification that were too loosely defined.

The speed at which bugs were fixed was slow because the amount of resources available at the DCC vendors for this project was limited and directly related to the number of customers requesting it—a typical "chicken and egg" problem. If the quality of the plug-ins was not improved significantly, developers would not use the technology; if developers were not using the technology, the plug-ins would not improve.

The situation progressed slowly, but in the right direction. One favorable event was the fact that SCE announced that COLLADA would be the official format for the PlayStation®3 SDK, which was a target for the DCC vendors [31]. Another big push came from the hardware vendors who were suffering from the problem of a lack of standard format. They have to develop numerous plug-ins and deal with the fact that each of their customers has a different format, which makes it expensive and complex to support. In addition, hardware vendors are already accustomed to collaborations for standardization.

With the addition of features required by game developers, such as animation and skin and bones, early adopters started to use COLLADA in their tool chain, putting more pressure on DCC vendors to do a good job on their exporters/importers.

Another lesson learned during this year was that, in order to be adopted, COLLADA would need to provide an API for developers to load, modify, and save COLLADA content easily. This was something we wanted to avoid, first because it is more work, but also because there are several commercial tools already available for this task that could be adapted for COLLADA. However, many developers were waiting for an official API to access COLLADA content from their application.

SCE then decided to start working on the COLLADA DOM, a source code providing a C++ object model that reflects the COLLADA elements in the application memory. The first version was subcontracted to Emdigo and was limited to a sample code to load and save COLLADA documents, but it lacked the capability to edit the data in place. After delivery of this sample code, SCE dedicated resources to improve this code and add the missing features to make it really useful. The COLLADA DOM was finally released as open source in January 2006 (see "The COLLADA DOM," page 167).

Another direction of improvement was to determine what the most important features were for the next-generation (PlayStation®3, Xbox® 360) content and to add those to the specification and the plug-ins. The decision was to focus on adding shader effects and physical properties to COLLADA.

At SIGGRAPH '05, the first anniversary Tech Talk presentation was made. In addition, COLLADA presentations were made in in September 2005 in Europe at Eurographics '05 and in Japan at CEDEC '05.

These presentations were a sneak preview of COLLADA 1.4 features, described in this book, which include shader effects (COLLADA FX) and real-time physics and collisions (COLLADA Physics). Once again, numerous demonstrations were made by many partners, showing more tools.

- Softimage demonstrated XSI supporting both the shader effects and physics. They also demonstrated the new version of their viewer (the XSI viewer), a fast-path visualization tool capable of displaying all the new features simultaneously.

- Alias demonstrated how the COLLADA external reference system can be used to improve productivity.

- Discreet demonstrated work-in-progress of their shader and physics implementation.

- Nokia and Emdigo demonstrated COLLADA content running on mobile phones.
- NVIDIA demonstrated an alpha version of FX Composer 2.0, a shader-effect tool based on the COLLADA FX specification. The files created by FX Composer were then loaded back into DCC tools and assigned to several objects before being saved back and visualized with external viewers.
- Feeling Software demonstrated Nima, a plug-in based on AGEIA's PhysX that enables authoring and exporting of COLLADA Physics content inside Maya.

The technologies demonstrated were very advanced. Never before had there been a shader-effect format capable of using the Cg, HLSL, and GLSL languages. Never before had shader effects been exchanged back and forth between DCC tools and external tools. Never before had common physical parameters been exchanged between several tools and viewers. Although COLLADA 1.4 was to be delivered publicly months later, the presentations were very successful, and hundreds of developers were impatient to have access to this new release.

COLLADA: An Industry Open Standard

An important announcement at SIGGRAPH '05 was that the Khronos Group had accepted COLLADA as an industry standard [32], along with OpenGL ES and several other real-time APIs. This was a very important step for COLLADA since its specification had been ratified by the Khronos Group promoters, a significant group of companies, and had finally reached an official industry-standard status.

COLLADA now has a life of its own (and will survive even if the original partners change their minds in the future), providing the stability that is necessary for the majority of developers, tool vendors, and middleware companies to invest in it. In addition, the Khronos Group provides the necessary IP protection, since ratification from the Khronos Group means that all the members have agreed that COLLADA did not infringe on any IP they owned, or, if that was the case, they agreed to provide an IP license to anyone using COLLADA.

Getting COLLADA to be accepted by the Khronos Group was no easy task. The major difficulty was that COLLADA was not an API, and the Khronos Group had only dealt with APIs in the past. Much convincing was necessary for the members to accept that common APIs were not enough, but that they also had to make sure that content was available in a standard format.

On the other hand, the original partners were balancing the benefit of having COLLADA as a formalized open standard, with the perception that SCE was abandoning the project to the Khronos Group. Because of this, SCE decided to become a Promoter member of Khronos, the highest rank of partnership. This was necessary for SCE to affirm their continuous involvement in the project, which was key in its development.

Only two years after the project started, and one year after being publicly announced, COLLADA partners were successful in creating an industry standard targeted for the entertainment industry.

The authors want to thank all the partners and congratulate them for this exceptional result.

2 COLLADA Document

Overview

This chapter explains COLLADA core technology choices such as XML, XML Schema, URI, and addressing mechanism. Then it presents the COLLADA document and its core elements: `<COLLADA>`, `<asset>`, and libraries. It ends with a discussion about XML text versus binary encoding.

XML Language

COLLADA is primarily a technology that encodes both the content and the information on how to use the content (semantics). It needs to have a well-defined structure in order to organize complex content into manageable units.

Second, COLLADA needs to allow encoding of international character codes so that it is readily usable in different countries around the world.

As a technology, COLLADA could have been developed simply as an application programming interface (API) targeting the software developers who would be the early adopters. The goal, however, was a higher-level description of COLLADA that would enable a wide range of adopters to leverage it using well-established technologies. For this approach to work, we needed to develop COLLADA using a high-level language that provided the principal features of structure and internationalization.

Extensible Markup Language (XML) was chosen for COLLADA because it met the development language requirements. XML is well defined by the World Wide Web Consortium (W3C®) [33] and is supported by a large number of tools and applications. It provides a standard language to describe the structure, semantics, and content of a document. XML provides a very well-defined framework for creating and storing structured information.

Issues such as character sets (ASCII, Unicode, Shift_JIS) are already covered by the XML standard, making any document written in XML internationally useful. XML is also fairly easy to understand given a sample instance document alone, without documentation, something that is rarely true for other formats. There are XML parsers for nearly every language and locale on every platform, making the files easily accessible to almost any possible application.

COLLADA therefore shares some of its vocabulary and definitions with XML.

- **Document.** The information represented using XML is embodied in a document. An XML document can be a file, a webpage, a database query, or a entire database.

- **Element.** An XML document consists primarily of elements. Elements can be nested, producing a hierarchical structure of information. The outermost encapsulating element of the document is called the root element. Each element is bounded by a start tag and an end tag. The start tag is the name of the element surrounded by < and >. The end tag is the same identifier surrounded by </ and >. The data in between the two tags is called the content of the element. The content may consist of character data and child elements. The character data (text) comprises the value information of the element. The child elements contribute structure to the information.

  ```
  <tag> content </tag>
  ```

  An element that does not have any content is called an empty element. In that case, there is no need for an end tag, and the start tag is changed to indicate an empty element by using /> instead of >.

  ```
  <empty_tag/>
  ```

- **Attributes.** An element can also contain attributes. An attribute is a name-value pair separated by an equal sign that follows the name of the element in the start-tag. The value is always enclosed in quotation marks. Each attribute is separated from the next and the start-tag by spaces. An attributes typically contains metadata about the element itself and is orthogonal to the element's content.

  ```
  <tag attr1="value1" attr2="value2"> content </tag>
  ```

- **Comment.** A comment is an entity that is bounded by <!-- and -->.

  ```
  <!-- this is a comment -->
  ```

  An XML comment can appear anywhere an element can appear in a document. A comment is not considered part of the element content and is only there to provide information to the reader of the document.

XML Schema

XML is a language used to create all kinds of documents. When a set of documents shares the same rules of structure and content constraints, the documents are said to conform to the same schema. To facilitate the use of XML in the creation of schemata, the W3C defined the XML Schema definition language. XML Schema language provides the means to describe the structure and constraints of a family of XML documents that follow the same rules for syntax and content. XML Schema documents are also XML documents using a set of elements defined by the W3C. A single document, within a family of documents that share the same schema, is called an *instance document.*

XML Schema uses other XML technology as part of its own specification by the W3C, among them the XML Information Set, Namespaces in XML, and XML Path Language specifications. These XML technologies provide a solid foundation for the development of a database schema.

XML tools that support XML Schema are able to provide enhanced features to XML authors who are creating XML documents. The schema contains metadata about the structure of the document for editing tools so that they can present the author with context-sensitive content suggestions. It also provides content constraint information that enables the author to validate the document as it is being written or, perhaps more importantly, long after the document has been in distribution.

The XML document describing the structure and constraints of a COLLADA document is called the COLLADA schema; it is unique and publicly accessible. The XML documents that conform to the COLLADA schema are called COLLADA instance documents.

Document Validation

An XML Schema language document provides the descriptive information required to validate an instance document. By applying the rules and constraints contained within the schema to an instance document, an application can check the correctness and conformance of the instance document. Validation is the process of determining if a value abides by all the constraints that apply to it. If any one constraint is not met, the value is invalid and quite probably in error as well. Any content in the instance document that is not declared in the schema is implicitly invalid.

The degree to which a schema constrains the data of an instance document varies from schema to schema. An independent constraint is one that is independent of application or business logic (context) and is the simplest to describe and implement. A dependent constraint, on the other hand, depends on one or more business rules that must be accessed during validation processing. If the business rule cannot be accessed, that constraint cannot be checked, and the value cannot be validated.

For example, a schema can independently constrain a value to be an integer type. This independent constraint is valid for all uses of the value. To further constrain this value, for example, so that it is also a billing account number in a corporate database requires access to that database; this is an example of a *dependent constraint*. The XML Schema language provides syntax that describes primarily independent constraints, although it is possible to describe some dependent constraints as well by capturing at least part of the business logic rule in the schema.

An XML parser, which supports the XML Schema, reads the instance document to determine the schemata (if any) that the document declares. The parser locates and loads the schemata and compares the content and structure of the instance document against the rules within the schema. If there are no errors in the checks and comparisons, the instance document is a valid document.

Let's look at an example of validation using the XML Schema language and an XML instance document. The main points to understand are the following.

- You must have an instance document.
- You must have a schema document.
- The instance document must declare its schema.
- The XML parser must be aware of the XML Schema language and be able to access both documents.

The XML parser reads the instance document (see Figure 2.1) and learns that it declares the schema namespace (xmlns) of http://www.collada. org/2005/11/COLLADASchema, which is for COLLADA 1.4.0. In this

```
<?xml version="1.0" encoding="utf-8"?>
<COLLADA
  xmlns="http://www.collada.org/2005/11/COLLADASchema"
  version="1.4.0">
  <!--
  This is a partial COLLADA instance document. The
  COLLADA schema includes constraints that require that
  the version attribute must be present and must have a
  value of "1.4.0" in order to validate.
  -->
</COLLADA>
```

Figure 2.1. An example instance document.

example schema (see Figure 2.2), we show a partial declaration for the
<COLLADA> element, and it has one attribute named `version`.

The XML Schema language lets us declare that the version attribute has a
type of "`xs:string`", meaning that it is an unbounded character string as
far as encoding is concerned.

```
<xs:attribute name="version" type="xs:string"
```

Furthermore, the schema declares that the use of the attribute is required.
As a result, it would be a validation error if the instance document was missing this attribute.

```
<xs:attribute name="version" use="required"
```

Finally, the schema declares that the value of the version attribute is fixed
as "`1.4.0`". It would be a validation error if the value of the version was
anything else.

```
<xs:attribute name="version" fixed="1.4.0"
```

Putting these few constraints together, the schema provides enough information to the parser to enable it to check the instance document and confirm

```
<?xml version="1.0" encoding="utf-8"?><xs:schema
  xmlns="http://www.collada.org/2005/11/COLLADASchema"
  xmlns:xs="http://www.w3.org/2001/XMLSchema"
  targetNamespace=
    "http://www.collada.org/2005/11/COLLADASchema">
<!--
  This is a partial COLLADA schema document. The
  COLLADA element is shown with one attribute
  called "version" and constraints regarding its
  occurrences and value.
-->
<xs:element name="COLLADA">
  <xs:complexType>
  <xs:attribute name="version" type="xs:string"
    use="required" fixed="1.4.0">
  </xs:attribute>
  </xs:complexType>
</xs:element>
</xs:schema>
```

Figure 2.2. An example schema document.

that it does indeed have a <COLLADA> root element that also has a version attribute whose value is exactly "1.4.0".

This example passes validation:

```
<?xml version="1.0" encoding="utf-8"?>
<COLLADA
 xmlns="http://www.collada.org/2005/11/COLLADASchema"
 version="1.4.0">
</COLLADA>
```

This example fails validation because the version attribute is missing:

```
<?xml version="1.0" encoding="utf-8"?>
<COLLADA
 xmlns="http://www.collada.org/2005/11/COLLADASchema">
</COLLADA>
```

This example fails validation because the version attribute has a value of "invalid":

```
<?xml version="1.0" encoding="utf-8"?>
<COLLADA
 xmlns="http://www.collada.org/2005/11/COLLADASchema"
 version="invalid">
</COLLADA>
```

This example fails validation because the COLLADA element has an attribute not declared in the schema:

```
<?xml version="1.0" encoding="utf-8"?>
<COLLADA
  xmlns="http://www.collada.org/2005/11/COLLADASchema"
  version="1.4.0" unknown="invalid">
</COLLADA>
```

COLLADA Document

COLLADA documents are, therefore, XML instance documents. The COLLADA schema document defines the valid structure and contents of a COLLADA document. The schema document explicitly declares what must or may be present in a valid instance document. Content present in the instance document that is not so declared in the schema is implicitly invalid.

A COLLADA document is the unit of storage or transmittal for the content. When a COLLADA document is stored as a file, the recommended file extension is ".dae" (Digital Asset Exchange). Since a COLLADA document is also an XML document, it is possible, but not recommended, to use the file extension ".xml" to indicate a generic XML instance document.

As a transmission unit, a COLLADA document can be the result of a database query or a network data transfer request. A Structured Query Language (SQL) query made to a relational database management system (RDBMS) can return a COLLADA document in the result transaction. A HyperText Transfer Protocol (HTTP) "GET" request issued to a network server can return a COLLADA document in the response message.

The document may be stored in the database or created in response to the query. For example, if the entire geometric surface of the Earth is stored in a database and a query is made to access the geometry of the state of Hawaii, then the database will create a transaction that contains only the information requested as a COLLADA document. Likewise, a World Wide Web (WWW) server can create a COLLADA document and transfer it to an XML browser as an HTTP message.

Therefore, COLLADA is the language of communication between applications and does not mandate the data storage format, although it can be used for that purpose as well. COLLADA can be used to enable or enhance the interoperability of two systems both as a storage format and as a message format ("COLLADA is your asset in motion" [34]).

As another example, consider a computer's file system. A file system is the most pervasive method of storing data on a computer. In fact, the file system is a simple database system that stores information in individual files accessible by name. In this case, you can store a COLLADA document as a file. The only query possible with the file system is to retrieve the file that contains the entire contents of the document.

With a more sophisticated database system, COLLADA documents transmitted to the database can be merged into a global dataset. Partial updates can be done by the database system, rather than having the client application load the entire document, make the changes, and save the entire document back. In this case, the entire dataset does not have to live in a COLLADA document.

From this explanation, it should be clear that COLLADA is not imposing a particular organization of stored data. Tools and applications can manage the organization of data into relational database systems, Web servers, directories of files, or as a single file.

Document Navigation

We have already explained that COLLADA documents are structured XML instance documents, which means that this structure is hierarchical and properly nested. In XML terms, the documents are "well formed." Within a document, elements relate to each other along canonical axes: hierarchical and referential. The document hierarchy creates a parent-child relationship. The parent element contains the nested child element exhibiting aggregation or composition of information. Document elements can also refer to other elements using an addressing scheme. There are two such addressing schemes used by COLLADA documents: Uniform Resource Identifier (URI) and Scoped Identifier (SID). In this section, we will briefly explain both of these mechanisms.

Uniform Resource Identifier

World Wide Web (WWW) navigation is based on the Uniform Resource Identifier (URI) Internet standard. The URI standard describes syntax for resource names and locations that identify those resources. A URI that describes the name of a resource is called a Uniform Resource Name (URN). A URI that describes the location of a resource is called a Uniform Resource Locator (URL).

The URL is the most familiar URI syntax, as it is widely used by Web browsers to navigate the World Wide Web. Users are presented with a URL in the form of document links to select, copy, and type quite often while using those applications. The canonical format of a URI includes several parts.

URI Part	Example
scheme	http + ":"
authority	"//" + www.collada.org
path	"/" + example/directory/file
query	"?" + constraint
fragment	"#" + identifier

The *scheme* part defines the connection protocol such as "http" or "file." The *authority* part defines the server and credentials used to initiate the connection. The *path* part defines the location of the resource on the server. The *query* part defines additional constraints that identify the resource. The *fragment* part defines a portion of the resource. When all the parts are present, the URL is considered an absolute URL, disregarding the fragment part for this purpose. When some of the parts are not specified, the URL is considered a relative URL and must be resolved against the base URL of the document.

Scoped Identifier

COLLADA defines the Scoped Identifier (SID) addressing mechanism to locate and target elements and values within an instance document. The SID syntax uses familiar hierarchical path separated expressions. The SID syntax includes several parts.

SID Part	Example
base	MyLeg
path	"/" + knee
selector	"." + ANGLE

The *base* part defines the unique ID of the element that establishes the scope of the navigation. The *path* part defines the hierarchical list of identifiers that are unique within the scope of the base identifier. These are scoped identifiers. The *selector* defines the value member of the element that is addressed.

COLLADA Element

The <COLLADA> element is the root of the COLLADA document. A <COLLADA> element must contain one <asset> element. The other child elements are optional, so it can contain zero or more library elements, zero or one <scene> element, zero or more <extra> elements. All the child elements must be in this order. The library elements may occur in any order among themselves. No other child elements may occur.

The schema indicates that the <COLLADA> element is a complex element that contains both child elements and attributes. The elements are in a sequence, indicating that the order must be respected.

- The first child element is an <asset> element that must occur one time.
- Several optional library elements may occur next. Each type of library has a specific name as shown in Figure 2.3. The libraries are an optional choice set. The subscript $0 . . \infty$ indicates that this choice may occur a minimum of zero times with a maximum occurrence that is unbounded.
- An optional <scene> element may occur next. It may occur zero or one time only.
- An optional <extra> element may occur next. It may occur zero or more times. The subscript $0 . . \infty$ indicates that this choice may occur a minimum of zero times with a maximum occurrence that is unbounded.

In addition, the <COLLADA> element has a mandatory version attribute, which is a string. For COLLADA 1.4.0, the version string must be "1.4.0".

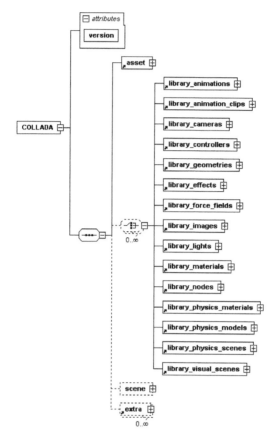

Attribute	Type	Fixed
version	VersionType	"1.4.0"

Figure 2.3. The <COLLADA> element.

The <COLLADA> element requires the <asset> in order to provide at least the creation and modification date for the COLLADA document. The <asset> and <library_...> elements are described below. The <scene> element indicates the default scene to be used for this document, and it is described in Chapter 3, "COLLADA Geometry."

Figure 2.4 is an example of a <COLLADA> element.

COLLADA Assets

A COLLADA document contains many pieces of information that the content developer considers as individual assets. Assets need to have additional

```
<?xml version="1.0" encoding="utf-8"?>
<COLLADA
 xmlns="http://www.collada.org/2005/11/COLLADASchema"
 version="1.4.0">
  <asset>
    <contributor>
      <author>lthompson</author>
      <authoring_tool>Maya 7.0.1 COLLADA exporter
      </authoring_tool>
      <source_data>file://C:/ ... /cube_I-Maya.mb
      </source_data>
    </contributor>
    <created>2005-07-28T18:12:59Z</created>
    <modified>2005-07-28T18:12:59Z</modified>
    <unit name="centimeter" meter="1.e-002"/>
    <up_axis>Y_UP</up_axis>
  </asset>
  <library_materials>  ... </library_materials>
  <library_geometries>  ... </library_geometries>
  <library_lights>  ... </library_lights>
  <library_cameras>  ... </library_cameras>
  <scene>  ... </scene>
</COLLADA>
```

Figure 2.4. A <COLLADA> element.

information attached to them, such as the author, date of creation, date of the last modification, and so forth. The <asset> element serves this purpose. In short, if an element has an <asset> child element, it is an asset. Assets are hierarchical by nature, therefore <asset> can be found in child elements of an element that has an <asset> element itself. The problem is how to define what element can be an asset and what element needs to be part of an asset.

In COLLADA 1.4, it has been decided to allow the <asset> element to be a child element of any element that can be referenced by a URL fragment expression. The reasoning is that everything that can be referenced can also be separated from the rest of the document and therefore needs to contain all the extra information, so that it stays with the asset even when singled out.

The content creator decides how to organize and manage the assets. Therefore, the <asset> element is an optional child element for nearly every element that has an ID attribute. But the <asset> element itself has some mandatory attributes. Only two attributes have been made mandatory in COLLADA 1.4: the creation date and last modification date. As stated previously, the `<asset>` element is also a required child element of the `<COLLADA>` element. This is the only case where it is required, since by definition a document is the unit of packaging of COLLADA and therefore it must contain this additional information.

Asset management is a very important issue that needs to be addressed in the near future, since it is becoming a huge issue for the entertainment industry. The COLLADA design committee initially focused on making sure all the necessary features existed. Now that this task has been almost completed, more attention will be focused on the content pipeline as described in Chapter 8, "COLLADA Content Pipeline."

The `<asset>` element also enables multiple representations of the same data within one element. It contains the extra data that will be used by the application to decide which representation to use.

The `<asset>` element contains metadata that provides information regarding its parent element (see Figure 2.5). It does not have attributes, but it does have many child elements.

- `<contributor>`—Optional. The `<contributor>` element contains information about an author of the document. This information includes the name, copyright, authoring tool, and links to the source data, as well as comments. There can be more than one contributor.

- `<created>`—Required.

- `<modified>`—Required. These two elements contain the dates when the document was first created or last modified. Most of the time, documents are the result of an export process, so this will indicate when the export process was made. In a COLLADA document, dates are always represented in an ISO 8601 format.

  ```
  <created>2005-07-28T18:12:59Z</created>
  ```

  The example above shows the date format. The year, month, and day, followed by the literal uppercase `T`, followed by 24-hour, minutes, and seconds, followed by the time zone (`Z` is Coordinated Universal Time, or UTC).

- `<source_data>`—Optional. The `<source_data>` element contains the URI to the source data from which the parent element was created. Most of the time, this will indicate the source data that was exported to COLLADA.

- `<unit>`—Optional. The `<unit>` element contains descriptive information about the unit of measure, expressed in meters. It is an empty element (no content) and has attributes for the name of the unit and the measurement with respect to the meter. The unit element may appear zero or one time.

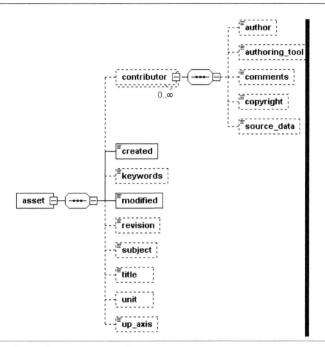

Figure 2.5. The `<asset>` element.

The default value for the name attribute is "meter". The default value for the meter attribute is "1.0".

```
<unit name="nautical_league" meter="5556.0" />
```

- `<up_axis>`—Optional. The `<up_axis>` element contains descriptive information about the coordinate system of the geometric data. All coordinates are right-handed in a COLLADA document. This element specifies which axis is considered up. The default is the positive *Y*-axis. The `<up_axis>` element may appear zero or one time.

The `<up_axis>` element can contain one of the following three possibilities:

- Y_UP, the default value, indicates that the positive *Y*-axis points up and, by convention, the positive *X*-axis points to the right.

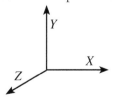

- Z_UP indicates that the positive Z-axis points up and, by convention, the positive X-axis points to the right.

- X_UP indicates that the positive X-axis points up and, by convention, the positive Z-axis points inward.

- `<revision>`—Optional. The `<revision>` element contains the revision information for the parent element. It is not a date but a string, usually in the form of "Major.Minor.Patch," such as "`1.4.0`", but it could be "`Alpha1`" or "`RC2`".

- `<title>`—The `<title>` element indicates the name of the project for which this data has been created. For example, for a game, this is the game title.

- `<subject>`—Optional. The `<subject>` element contains a description of the topical subject of the parent element. It could be "`Marcus's house`" or "`Rémi's car`".

- `<keywords>`—Optional. The `<keywords>` element contains a list of words used as search criteria for the parent element.

- `<comments>`—Optional. The `<comments>` element contains descriptive information about the parent element.

COLLADA Libraries

COLLADA does not impose any specific organizational requirements on a project's data but instead tries to accommodate the organization chosen by the project developer. A COLLADA document is the fundamental unit of such an organization. Each document is organized as a sequence of libraries. One document could contain only data of a specific type or contain all the data that is necessary to completely describe an entire game level. In any case, the document data is organized into libraries of a specific type.

A COLLADA document can contain several library elements. The various library elements can contain one optional <asset> element and zero or more <extra> elements. Each library can contain only one type of child element that contains content in accordance with the type of library. For example, the <library_animations> element can contain <animation> elements, and the <library_cameras> element can contain <camera> elements. Each library can have an ID attribute and a name attribute. Both attributes are optional.

The complete list of library elements includes:

Library	Contains
<library_animations>	<animation>
<library_animation_clips>	<animation_clip>
<library_cameras>	<camera>
<library_controllers>	<controller>
<library_geometries>	<geometry>
<library_effects>	<effect>
<library_force_fields>	<force_field>
<library_images>	<image>
<library_lights>	<light>
<library_materials>	<material>
<library_nodes>	<node>
<library_physics_materials>	<physics_material>
<library_physics_models>	<physics_model>
<library_physics_scenes>	<physics_scene>
<library_visual_scenes>	<visual_scene>

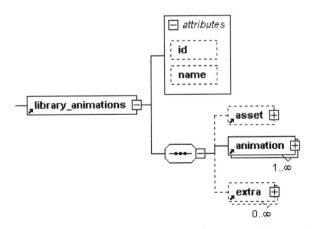

Figure 2.6. `<library_animations>` **element.**

The different elements contained in a library are described in detail in later chapters.

Techniques, Profiles, and Extras

A true separation between source content and target content would mean that all the data for any target platform can be computed from the data in the source. Unfortunately, this is not the case. Indeed, it is unfortunate because this means that the content itself must be authored for each platform. In practice, a developer will regroup the platforms per category; for example, a split could be made between consoles and PDA-type devices.

In the past, the platforms were so different that very little content could be shared. This trend is changing as more devices have real-time 3D graphics capabilities. The possibility for sharing content is now there, but it still is a complex problem because of fundamental technological differences between devices, even those in the same category. For instance, in the mobile space, OpenGL ES 1.1 is fundamentally different from OpenGL ES 2.0. The OpenGL ES 1.x interface is a fixed pipeline only, whereas the OpenGL ES 2.0 interface defines a programmable pipeline and requires the use of shaders. An application that was targeted for OpenGL ES 1.x will have to be rewritten for OpenGL ES 2.0, and the content will have to be changed to include shaders.

The trend is toward more devices with 3D graphics capabilities. However, despite the standardization effort, the capabilities will still be very disparate to enable the necessary market flexibility. Technically, this means that standards are considered more often as an exchange language and less often as a fixed list of features that everyone has to implement. This is indeed what generated the big change between OpenGL ES 1.x and OpenGL ES 2.0.

When creating content, developers cannot always know every target platform on which the content will be used. Who could have predicted that many arcade games created 20 years ago for special hardware would now be available on so many platforms (mobile phones, PDAs, hand-held consoles, PCs, etc.)? Fortunately, the content was quite simple, and sometimes it is cheaper and faster to recreate the content than to try to recover the old source content. However, this is not going to be possible with the quantity and complexity of the content created today.

COLLADA as a content description language must allow for this flexibility and enable several representations of the same piece of content to be stored under one element. Each piece of alternative content is marked by the `<technique_common>` or `<technique>` element (see Figure 2.7).

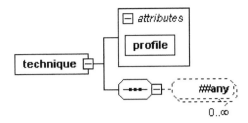

Attribute	Type	Default
profile	xs:NMTOKEN	required

Figure 2.7. The `<technique>` element.

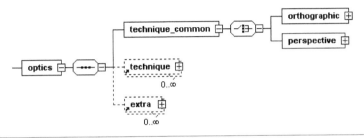

Figure 2.8. `<camera>` `<optics>` element.

The `<technique_common>` and `<technique>` elements can be found in many COLLADA elements where alternative representations are supported. The representation of the `<technique_common>` element for a particular parent element is well-known and fixed, whereas the content model of the `<technique>` element is variable and extensible. Therefore, the `<technique>` element requires a profile attribute that differentiates each technique from other alternatives in the same scope.

When a common representation for an element is well-known, the `<technique_common>` element is a required child element, and the `<technique>` element is an optional child element. When there is no common representation, the `<technique>` element is a required child element. In this way, multirepresentation is supported, and a common representation is required when it is defined in the schema. Let's look at the structure of the `<camera>` `<optics>` element as an example.

In Figure 2.8, we see that the common technique is defined as a choice between `<orthographic>` and `<perspective>` child elements, one of which is required. The extensible `<technique>` element is optional in this case and can occur more than once.

In a COLLADA document, it will have the following structure:

```
<camera>
 <optics>
  <technique_common>
   <perspective/>
  </technique_common>
  <technique profile="Maya"/>
  <technique profile="XSI"/>
 </optics>
</camera>
```

Profiles represent several sets of functionality for a specific platform. When the runtime content has to create data structures from the source content for a particular target platform, the various profiles can be used as a filter on the COLLADA document. For instance, a given platform may want to have all the content from techniques that match its capability but exclude content that is not compliant with a specific rule. The set of available profiles depends on the production methodology defined by each developer.

Once the data has been compiled and optimized for a given target platform, it is still possible to use COLLADA to store such data in the same document as the source data. In that case, the `<technique>` element is used to supply the information about the target platform for which the content was compiled, as well as potentially all the information required to recreate the compiled data.

Whereas the `<technique>` element embodies alternative data representation, the `<extra>` element embodies additional data representation (see Figure 2.9). The `<extra>` element has been in the COLLADA specification

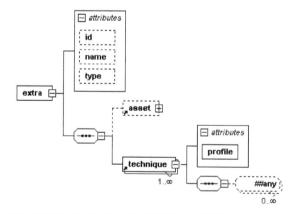

Figure 2.9. The `<extra>` element.

since its first version and has undergone changes as the design of user metadata has been refined. In COLLADA 1.0, the `<extra>` element was arbitrary text data. In COLLADA 1.1, the `<extra>` element was a container of `<param>` elements. The `<param>` element provided the data mapping capabilities that were most often needed by users, but it lacked the ultimate extensibility arrived at in COLLADA 1.4. In COLLADA 1.4, the `<extra>` element represents an asset of well-formed XML content contained in a `<technique>`.

This schema definition enables the `<extra>` element to contain any type of information, categorized by technique and profile. The extra information can also be managed as an asset.

Binary versus Text Encoding

Developers have to face larger and increasingly complicated content, with higher expectations of quality. Since the content pipeline is not very fast for most developers and is already seen as a bottleneck for the productivity of the artists, many developers are concerned about using UTF-8 or ASCII encoded XML content rather than binary encoded content.

These concerns have not been clearly articulated in many cases. A developer may simply say, "We should do a binary format because it is better than a text format" or "I don't want to deal with importing a text format in my game engine." From these general sentiments, the design group has asked questions and done research to identify exactly what the concerns are and whether they are valid concerns.

The design group learned from this investigation that the three primary concerns are: processing time, storage space, and numeric precision. Because a large part of the content is integer or floating-point numbers stored in arrays, these concerns should be addressed.

Many developers have been concerned by the time it takes to load and save a number using XML rather than a binary format. Typically, they view data import processing time as an unwanted overhead. Any extra time to bring data into the application should be minimized or eliminated. Developers have solved this problem by exporting their data in raw binary form directly from their application data structures so that no additional time is needed to import that data. The stored data exactly matches the in-memory data. This solution works best when the processor is truly the bottleneck for data transfer. It is a solution that trades space for speed as the binary data is not compressed in any way. However, on systems where the processor has plenty of spare cycles, it is actually wise to spend extra time encoding and compressing data so that it requires less storage and bandwidth. Therefore, it is clear that one approach isn't always best, and any irrational bias toward a binary format must be overcome with an enlightened design discussion.

Other developers are just as concerned about the storage size required for XML encodings. They believe that text encodings are less efficient than binary encodings. They also see the verbose markup of XML and think that it adds extra "bloat." Some developers also fear that any text encoding will result in a loss of accuracy compared to the binary encoded number. The design group determined that a proper encoding implementation need not lose any precision and even cited a research paper that proved this to be true [35]. Because of these concerns, some developers wanted to depart from the XML standard and embed binary data directly within the COLLADA document or drop XML altogether. The design group rapidly pushed back on this idea, since the choice of leveraging XML was essential to COLLADA. The main hurdle to explain to developers was that a robust data import system must be able to encode, decode, compress, and encrypt data to satisfy the requirements of various applications and platforms. Some time must be allocated to import processing, and some of that time can be spent decoding and swizzling values into data structures. COLLADA is designed to be used as a transfer language between two applications, but it does not define how the data is to be represented within the memory of the target platform. This is why the XML encoding of content matches the needs of COLLADA, because XML libraries that can process the content are available on all platforms. It is sufficient to have access to the source code of such libraries and recompile them on the given platform, and the compiler will create the right conversion code.

COLLADA does provide mechanisms to store external binary data and reference it from a COLLADA element. This is already done most of the time for image data. In this way, COLLADA does take advantage of the existing formats supported by developers. Although it is possible to store an image within the XML file, this is not particularly practical in the common case.

Binary data by definition is not designed to be shared between all platforms. Of course, there are binary encoding standards, such as IEEE for floating-point numbers, but not all platforms have a full implementation of this standard. Most graphic processors do not fully implement this standard for performance issues. Some devices do not have floating-point numbers at all, and some processors do not fully implement this standard on their vector processing units. Clearly, use of a binary encoding will limit the portability of data, and developers must understand this in order to embrace other solutions.

Because the concern is mostly about the storage of floating-point and integer arrays, why not reference an external file that contains those arrays in a binary format? Why not save the file in a compressed format if the real concern is the storage space? For several reasons, this solution, which is applied almost universally to image data, is not even discussed by developers for the other data-intensive parts of the file. The main reason is that this will create many files and will be impossible to manage. Asset management is indeed a major issue for developers, and it is becoming an increasing challenge for developers. Therefore, their first reaction is to reject anything that makes this problem worse by creating more files.

The easiest way to store a COLLADA document is just to use a file system and store the data directly into a text file, but COLLADA is not limited to this. A COLLADA document can be the result of a database query, for example, transmitted in XML format. Developers may have to accept this change, though, because some experiments have shown that this process is necessary to correctly handle the ever-increasing number of assets.

One important feature is that COLLADA can be organized in many different files. It is possible to separate the data into various libraries and also create a COLLADA root that contains only references to other COLLADA files. Those files, in turn, contain references to other files. This creates a tree that can rapidly split a huge amount of data into many files whose size can then be handled easily by the tools. Using the multiple representation capability of COLLADA, it is possible to have a very simplified version of the data at a higher level in the content tree. This even enables manipulation (translation and rotation) of the data in its simplified form without the need to load the entire content in the digital content creation (DCC) tool. If needed, it is possible to select the other representation and have the full resolution data loaded in the DCC tool [36].

This methodology represents a huge leap forward in tool-chain acceleration from the current methodology used by game developers. However, it will take some time before all the tools can move from the current paradigm that processes a single file into a real content-management system, manipulating a tree of files. The next step is an even better paradigm shift to a tool chain based on a real database system rather than a file system.

In the meantime, it is important to understand what the size and speed difference actually is between using COLLADA XML as a file and using a DCC tool binary format. It turns out that most DCC tools are using a 64-bit IEEE encoding, which uses the same space as eight characters. It is difficult to make an exact measurement of the difference in sizes. The worst case is when all the numbers require all the digits to be represented accurately in the XML format. In that case, the XML format can be two to three times larger than the binary data.

On the other hand, some numbers are much smaller to encode in text than in IEEE binary encoding. For instance, all the numbers from 0 to 9 can be encoded in two bytes (one for the number, one for the space), and yet they still require four bytes when encoded in binary.

Measurement on real data and experimentation is the best way to compare the two approaches. It turns out that the size of the data is very similar in either case. This is surprising to many developers who are proponents of binary formats, since they expected that the COLLADA file would be much larger.

Another issue to consider is the speed at which the data is exported from a DCC tool. Partial export and update of the data is certainly a good answer to this performance issue, with an order of magnitude speed improvement over the text versus binary aspect alone. It is indeed generally faster to output four bytes of binary data for a float, rather than using a more complex algorithm to encode and possibly compress the value first.

Actually, most of the time spent in the exporter is not in data conversion but in accessing the data through the DCC SDK or API. The DCC tool is generally organized to be very generic and enable all kinds of operations but not necessarily the fastest method. Therefore, almost no actual speed improvement is seen when using a binary file rather than a standard XML file in existing DCC applications [37].

3 COLLADA Geometry

Overview

This chapter explains how to assemble geometry in COLLADA. The data model for COLLADA geometry is a stream-processing model [38] in which data sources are assembled into data sinks. In COLLADA, the data sinks are <mesh> elements, and the data sources are, oddly enough, <source> elements. A coherent data set is contained within a <geometry> element. Assembling the data streams into a geometry mesh involves several elements, including <float_array>, <int_array>, <accessor>, <source>, <mesh>, and <input>. These elements are used as data-stream building blocks within the <geometry> element.

Arrays

The vast majority of data is represented by arrays of values, without semantics. In the original design, array data was weakly typed and required extra metadata in the instance document to describe the contents fully. Unfortunately, XML Schema–aware parsing tools could not validate this data because the schema did not contain enough information. The designers considered this a problem because the array elements contained the bulk of the data in the document. After much discussion, the decision was made to replace the weakly typed arrays with strongly typed arrays where all of the required information resided in the schema [39]. This design leverages XML Schema language features and enables far better document validation. It also makes it easier for schema-aware or schema-based software to decode the data and directly it directly in the internal format that corresponds with the schema type. There are five types of arrays:

- <float_array> to store floating-point numbers;
- <int_array> to store signed integers;
- <bool_array> to store Booleans;

- `<IDREF_array>` to store references to IDs;
- `<Name_array>` to store names and SIDs.

Each array element has a mandatory `count` attribute, providing the number of items in the array. This was added to enable parsers to preallocate memory to store the data. Without this information, a program would have to count the number of items before being able to allocate the necessary memory.

Since arrays are referenced by other elements in the document, an `id` attribute has been added. A `name` attribute is also available, not for referencing but to provide a convenient name for the data. The `id` value has to be unique within the document, but `name` values do not.

It is noteworthy that COLLADA arrays can contain a wide range of values. The reason behind this design decision is one of evolution and controversy and deserves a little background. One of COLLADA's original design requirements was to be human-readable and, therefore, a text-encoded data format. This was controversial enough for game developers who rely almost exclusively on what they call "binary formats." In fact, COLLADA was summarily rejected by many developers learning this one single design fact. For them, a text format was simply out of the question, as described in Chapter 2. That controversy is the subject of another time. For now, let's discuss the current topic—familiar type name exceptions.

As a text-encoded format, COLLADA is not overly concerned about the representation of numbers on the target platform. COLLADA was designed to not use platform details like floating-point format, register size, or memory address space. Expressing this goal in the COLLADA schema meant choosing schema types with arbitrary precision, such as `<xs:integer>`, that are able to describe data sets that scale from resource-constrained mobile devices to high-end workstations. Over time, the schema has evolved and refined its view of the high-end target platform to 64-bit systems. This is a practical compromise short of the ideal while still encompassing all the implementations for the current and next generation of computer-game platforms. Hence, the COLLADA schema now uses XML Schema language 64-bit numeric types for all numbers.

The COLLADA numeric types for integers and floating-point numbers are called "`int`" and "`float`", respectively. Because these are familiar names to C language programmers, some game developers believe that they should map directly to C language data types of the same name. COLLADA does not adhere to this as a design goal, which leads to some controversy over the type names.

`<float_array>`

The `<float_array>` element is derived from an internal type called `<ListOfFloats>`, which is actually a list of XML Schema Language double-precision floating-point type (`<xs:double>`).

```
<xs:simpleType name="ListOfFloats">
    <xs:list itemType="xs:double"/>
</xs:simpleType>

<xs:element name="float_array">
  <xs:complexType>
    <xs:simpleContent>
      <xs:extension base="ListOfFloats"/>
    </xs:simpleContent>
  </xs:complexType>
</xs:element>
```

`<float_array>` has the following attributes:

Attribute	Type	Default
count	uint	required
digits	xs:short	6
magnitude	xs:short	38
id	xs:ID	—
name	xs:NCName	—

The `digits` attribute indicates the number of significant decimal digits of the float values that can be contained in the array. The default value is "6".

The `magnitude` attribute indicates the largest exponent of the float values that can be contained in the array. The default value is "38".

Those two optional parameters indicate the accuracy of the data. The default values correspond to a standard 32-bit IEEE 754 floating-point number. If the array contains values of higher precision or greater magnitude, the attributes should be changed accordingly.

`<int_array>`

The `<int_array>` element is very similar to the `<float_array>` element. It is derived from the internal type called `<ListOfInts>`, itself a list of the XML Schema language 64-bit signed integer type (`<xs:long>`).

```
<xs:simpleType name="ListOfInts">
  <xs:list itemType="xs:long"/>
</xs:simpleType>
```

```
<xs:element name="int_array">
  <xs:complexType>
    <xs:simpleContent>
      <xs:extension base="ListOfInts"/>
    </xs:simpleContent>
  </xs:complexType>
</xs:element>
```

<int_array> contains the following attributes:

Attribute	Type	Default
count	uint	required
maxInclusive	xs:integer	"2147483647"
minInclusive	xs:integer	"−2147483648"
id	xs:ID	—
name	xs:NCName	—

The minInclusive and maxInclusive attributes indicate the minimum and maximum values that can be present in the array. By default, the values are constrained to the range of signed 32-bit integers. If the array contains values outside this range, the attribute values need to be changed accordingly. It is possible to indicate a smaller range or limit the range to positive or negative values using these optional attributes.

<bool_array>

The <ListOfBools> is a list of the XML Schema language Boolean type (<xs:Boolean>).

```
<xs:simpleType name="ListOfBools">
  <xs:list itemType="xs:boolean"/>
</xs:simpleType>

<xs:element name="bool_array">
  <xs:complexType>
    <xs:simpleContent>
      <xs:extension base="ListOfBools"/>
    </xs:simpleContent>
  </xs:complexType>
</xs:element>
```

<bool_array> contains the following attributes:

Attribute	Type	Default
count	uint	required
id	xs:ID	—
name	xs:NCName	—

<bool_array> has the usual optional id, name, and required count attributes. A Boolean value indicates the logical sense of true or false. This value can be stored using the literal values "true" or "1" for true and "false" or "0" for false. Other values are not permitted and will cause a validation error, including such obvious variations as "TRUE" or "T".

<IDREF_array>

<IDREF_array> is a list of ID references defined by the XML Schema language type <xs:IDREFS>. This type defines values that are references to ID values of type <xs:ID> elsewhere in the document.

```
<xs:element name="IDREF_array">
 <xs:complexType>
  <xs:simpleContent>
   <xs:extension base="xs:IDREFS"/>
  </xs:simpleContent>
 </xs:complexType>
</xs:element>
```

<IDREF_array> contains the following attributes:

Attribute	Type	Default
count	uint	required
id	xs:ID	—
name	xs:NCName	—

This array type also has the attributes of id, name, and count.

<Name_array>

<Name_array> is derived from the internal type called <ListOfNames>, itself a list of the XML Schema language type <xs:NCName>.

```
<xs:simpleType name="ListOfNames">
  <xs:list itemType="xs:NCName"/>
</xs:simpleType>

<xs:element name="Name_array">
  <xs:complexType>
    <xs:simpleContent>
      <xs:extension base="ListOfNames"/>
    </xs:simpleContent>
  </xs:complexType>
</xs:element>
```

<Name_array> contains the following attributes:

Attribute	Type	Default
count	uint	required
id	xs:ID	—
name	xs:NCName	—

The <xs:NCName> type describes XML name values that cannot have colon characters ("NC" stands for non-colon) to indicate a name in an alternative name space. COLLADA uses names such as these primarily for scoped ID (SID) attribute values and also for user-defined names.

Sources

The <source> elements represent the raw data streams that are then accessed through the <input> elements. These are described in the discussion of the various geometry supported natively in COLLADA. In addition to the raw data, the <source> element provides access methods to the information. These access methods implement various techniques according to the representation of the information.

The raw data can be embedded in the <source> element within the COLLADA document as the content of an array element (see Figure 3.1). It can also be a reference to an external resource in another format. Allow-

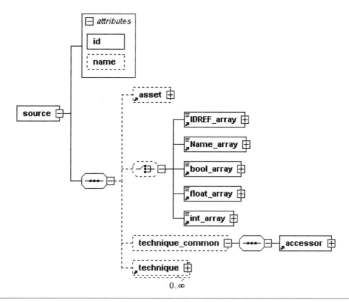

Figure 3.1. The <source> element.

ing the raw data to be embedded within the COLLADA document is ideal for portability and for packaging. The external data can be in any format. However, if it is not in COLLADA format, it will only be recognized by the applications that can understand that format. Depending on their particular use case, developers can decide to use either or both approaches to create an optimal data flow within their content pipeline [40].

Within the <technique_common> element, the <accessor> element describes the output of the <source> element. Otherwise, the output is described by the <technique> element and recognized only by applications that understand that particular technique's profile.

<accessor>

The <accessor> element describes the common or well-known representation of the outputs of a <source> element. The <accessor> provides the parameter-binding information that forms the data source's output interface, or "plug." The inputs of the primitive collation elements connect to the sources via these access interfaces and complete the data stream model of geometric information (see Figure 3.2).

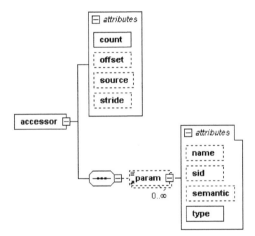

Attribute	Type	Default
count	uint	required
offset	uint	0
source	xs:anyURI	—
stride	uint	1

Figure 3.2. The <accessor> element.

The `<accessor>` element provides a level of abstraction over the sources so that they can store data without any semantics. This approach enables exporters within the tool chain to optimize storage within the data sources as much as possible. This was an original design goal for the data-streaming model within COLLADA, although existing implementations have not taken full advantage of it. Often when an export tool is created, it does not transform or optimize the structure of the data, as its primary purpose is to write out the data from the DCC tool. Therefore, data exported from DCC tools usually mirror the structure of the artist's tools. As tool chains built around COLLADA become more robust and sophisticated, we can expect more optimizations paid to the COLLADA documents, resulting in even smaller and more efficient content within the documents as they move through the content pipeline.

Through a combination of attributes and child `<param>` elements, the `<accessor>` element provides a flexible interface to its `<source>` element. The `count` attribute indicates the number of items that the source's array contains from the point of view of the `<accessor>` element. The array may contain more values, but those values outside this range are not accessed, at least not from this context. The `offset` attribute provides the index of the first value in the array that is accessed. Therefore, the `<accessor>` element may start gathering data from some point midway within the array, although the default and most common `offset` value is zero.

The number of values to sample per iteration of the `count` attribute is defined by the `stride` attribute. The `stride` indicates how many values to access each time; the default is one. As a corollary to this, the value of `stride` must also be greater than or equal to the number of parameters specified. It is acceptable to have fewer parameters resulting in unbound data values being discarded, but it is not acceptable to have the reverse situation of undefined parameter values. The values' type is determined by the data type of the source array.

The `source` attribute contains a URI pointing to the array resource. It is possible for the actual data to be located in an external document. If the external data is in an alternative storage format, the application must map the data to conform to the outputs described by the `<accessor>` element. This brings us to the parameter bindings described by the child `<param>` elements.

Most of the information needed to bind the output of the data source to the input of the geometric primitive is defined by the child `<param>` elements. There can be one parameter for each value represented in the output. If the `<param>` element has a name, it can be bound by name as an output parameter. Otherwise, the value is read as part of the sample, but it is not passed on as output because it is unbound. In this way, values in the data source can be effectively skipped.

The ordering of <param> elements is important as well. The output values from the <accessor> element are bound in the order that the parameters are specified. It is important to note that shuffling of the source data does not occur no matter how the parameters are ordered. This may seem odd, but remember that the source array has no semantics. Therefore, switching the order of parameters only changes what names are bound to the values that are sampled from the array.

For example, if you have an array of values referenced by two different <source> elements, it is possible to bind the values differently as follows:

```
<source id="time">
  <float_array id="raw_data" count="3">
  11.0 12.0 13.0
  </float_array>
  <technique_common>
    <accessor source="#raw_data" count="3">
      <param name="TIME" type="float"/>
    </accessor>
  </technique_common>
</source>

<source id="angles">
  <technique_common>
    <accessor source="#raw_data" count="3">
      <param name="ANGLE" type="float"/>
    </accessor>
  </technique_common>
</source>
```

One source supplies the values as "TIME"; the other source supplies the same values as "ANGLE". The following is another example of scalable usage in which one <source> element accesses the values as two-dimensional coordinates while another interprets them as three-dimensional values.

```
<source id="xyz">
 <float_array id="raw_data" count="3">
  11.0 12.0 13.0
 </float_array>
 <technique_common>
  <accessor source="#raw_data" count="1">
   <param name="X" type="float"/>
   <param name="Y" type="float"/>
```

```
   <param name="Z" type="float"/>
  </accessor>
 </technique_common>
</source>

<source id="xy">
 <technique_common>
  <accessor source="#raw_data" count="1">
   <param name="X" type="float"/>
   <param name="Y" type="float"/>
   <param type="float"/>
  </accessor>
 </technique_common>
</source>
```

Flexibility exists to interleave and repurpose the values of a data source. As content pipeline tools continue to analyze and optimize COLLADA documents, they should produce smaller, more efficient documents for subsequent stages of the pipeline.

Geometry

In the COLLADA schema, the `<geometry>` element is the container for all the information that describes a geometric shape. When we consider geometry as a digital asset, it is the `<geometry>` element containing the asset metadata that defines the asset (see Figure 3.3). The application then translates, or instantiates, the `<geometry>` element onto a visual representation.

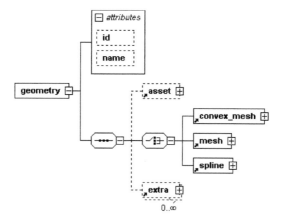

Figure 3.3. The `<geometry>` element.

Many possible representations of three-dimensional objects are used when creating digital assets. Some of the more common forms of geometry are listed below, although this is definitely not an exhaustive list:

- B-spline;
- Bézier;
- polygonal mesh;
- NURBS;
- patch;
- subdivision surfaces.

Until recently, COLLADA only supported the polygonal mesh because this was the only primitive that was deemed necessary by game developers. In COLLADA 1.4, the `<spline>` element was introduced because most of the prerequisite information was already being used to support animation function curves. Also added was the `<convex_mesh>` primitive created for COLLADA Physics that can also be visualized.

Meshes

COLLADA 1.4 supports only a simple subset of the polygon-based geometric description models for rendering: lines and polygons. It would be simple to add more, but few game developers have requested it so the COLLADA design group has not made it a priority. Artists can use any type of technique in their digital content tools to create geometry, but when that content is transported by COLLADA, the data must be converted into a supported type of geometry description (see Figure 3.4).

Since several representations of the same object can be stored within the COLLADA document, some tools may export the model used internally as `<extra>` metadata as an extension to one of the polygonal representations standardized for COLLADA. In future releases, more geometric descriptions may be part of COLLADA, but most game-content pipelines are currently not designed to accept more than a restricted set of polygonal geometries.

The `<mesh>` element has no attributes as it is designed to be managed from its parent `<geometry>` element. The raw data used for the mesh is stored in the `<source>` element. A source contains the array elements and also the semantic information for accessing its data. A complete description of `<source>` is given in a later section.

The schema for `<mesh>` uses the XML Schema language `<choice>` element (`<xs:choice>`) to allow great flexibility in the order of primitive collation elements. In general schema usage, the choice is made once

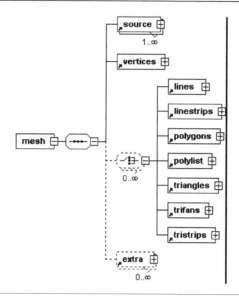

Figure 3.4. <mesh> elements.

from the given set of possibilities listed. However, in this particular case, the <choice> element is modified with the minOccurs="0" and maxOccurs="unbounded" attribute values. This means that the choice can be made zero or more times. With these extra qualifiers, the choice indicates that a mesh can contain any number of primitives, in any order. A mesh can contain lines and polygons, all referencing the same set of sources declared within the mesh. A mesh may not have any child elements, except for a cloud of points without lines or polygons.

The child elements of the <mesh> element must appear in a prescribed sequence, as follows:

- one or more <source> elements;
- exactly one <vertices> element;
- zero or more of the primitive collation elements that are available, in any order:

  <lines>

  <linestrips>

  <polygons>

  <polylist>

  <triangles>

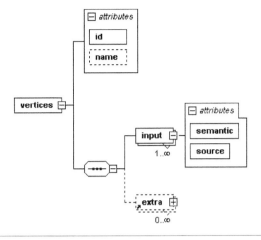

Figure 3.5. The `<vertices>` element.

```
<trifans>
<tristrips>;
```
• zero or more `<extra>` elements.

Each of the collation elements follows the same data-streaming model with certain optimizations or generalities particular to the primitive it represents. This is discussed later in this chapter.

The `<vertices>` element is a special element that groups all the vertex attribute data, contained in the `<source>` element, that is used by all the primitives in the mesh regardless of primitive collation (see Figure 3.5). In other words, the `<vertices>` element contains all the mesh vertex information that is invariant to primitive winding and assembly. The `<vertices>` and `<source>` elements are the only required child elements of the `<mesh>` element, because that is all that is needed to represent a cloud of points.

The `<vertices>` element represents all of the vertices of the mesh. It makes it possible to directly access all the vertices of a mesh and apply a given transformation to all of the vertices at the same time, without having to browse all the primitives.

The `<vertices>` element can be referenced internally by the mesh primitives' `<input>` elements. It has a mandatory id attribute and can also have a name attribute. It is useful to be able to store extra parameters with the vertices, such as game-specific data, so an optional `<extra>` element is available.

The role of the `<input>` element is to assign a semantic to a data source, explaining what the raw data is going to be used for in the current context. This enables the raw data to be organized however the developer wishes. Either the data are spread over multiple sources or interleaved in relatively fewer arrays. The `<input>` element, therefore, has a `source` attribute that references a `<source>` element. It also has a `semantic` attribute that contains a well-known value. Both of these attributes are mandatory.

The `semantic` attribute is a symbolic token that can take several values defined as common profile enumerations in the COLLADA schema. Most of the time, the `<vertices>` element will have a single `<input>` with a "POSITION" semantic and a reference to the `<source>` element that contains the values representing the *N*-dimensional (often 3D *x, y, z*) positional coordinate of each mesh vertex. It is also possible to have other input and semantics in the `<vertices>` element so that more than just the position information can be associated with a mesh vertex. The "POSITION" semantic is strongly correlated with the identity of individual mesh vertices and the `<vertices>` element.

A `<mesh>` describes two types of geometries: line and polygon. The triangle, a special case of polygon, is also supported since this is the most common type of polygon. The polylist is another more compact representation of a polygon. In addition, these optimized versions for hardware acceleration are also supported: line strips, triangle strips, and triangle fans.

All of the different types of primitive collation elements also share the following child elements:

`<input>`

The role of the `<input>` element is similar to the `<vertices>` element, associating a semantic to a data source and declaring an input to the collation element. This element is the child element of the geometric primitives described below.

Attribute	Type	Default
offset	uint	required
semantic	xs:NMTOKEN	required
source	URIFragmentType	required
set	uint	—

Within a geometric primitive, the `<input>` element has a mandatory `source` attribute, which is a reference to a `<source>` element, as well as a `semantic`, an `offset`, and a `set` attribute.

The `offset` attribute indicates which indexes, contained in the `<p>` element, are to be used to index into the referenced source element. Multiple inputs can share the same index, and this is indicated by shared `offset` values between them. The `offset` attribute is therefore mandatory.

The `set` attribute is optional. It is used to associate several inputs into a coherent set of information. For example, you would assign the same `set` value to multiple inputs that have related semantics, such as texture coordinates and texture tangents, when they must be processed together.

The `semantic` attribute is a token that can take several values. The following is a list of the values used in the context of geometry. The other possible values are described in subsequent chapters as they correspond to other specific usage of the `<input>` element.

- "VERTEX"—Vertex attribute data principally containing the position of each vertex. This semantic is used to reference the `<vertices>` element. This is an indirection into the global definition of the mesh vertex attribute data described previously. Recall that the "POSITION" semantic cannot be used within a primitive collation element.
- "COLOR"—Color coordinate vectors (RGB colors).
- "NORMAL"—Normal vectors, defined in a direct coordinate system.
- "TEXCOORD"—Texture coordinate vectors.
- "TEXTURE"—Texture objects.
- "TANGENT"—Tangent vectors.
- "BINORMAL"—Bi-tangent (often called bi-normal) vectors.
- "UV"—Generic parameter vectors.

Note that the input data streams are scalable from one-dimensional data to *N*-dimensional data. The most common uses involve 2D texture coordinates and 3D geometric coordinates.

A collation element may have any number of `<input>` elements. The "NORMAL" and "TANGENT" information is usually not supplied for lines, only for polygons. The "TEXCOORD" is used to position textures on the geometry. Several "TEXCOORD" semantics are present in the case of multitextured geometry. In addition, the "TEXTURE" semantic is used to supply the image data and parameters associated with a texture object. Finally, the "UV" semantic supplies generic information that can be used according to vertex information for arbitrary purposes.

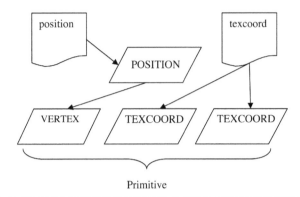

Primitive

Figure 3.6. `<mesh>` geometry elements.

`<p>`

The `<p>` element contains indexes that reference into the `<source>` elements, using the semantic described by the `<input>` elements. It is defined as a list of unsigned integers and contains values between 0 and $N-1$ *(N* is the number of values in the associated source).

```
<xs:element name="p" type="ListOfUInts"/>
```

A geometric element contains a sequence of `<p>` elements, where "p" stands for primitive. Each `<p>` element describes the vertex attributes for an arbitrary number of individual geometric primitives (see Figure 3.6).

Since the `<input>` elements can share the same `offset`, the number of indexes per geometric primitive is given by the largest `offset` value plus one.

Let's look at the following `<mesh>` example:

```
<mesh>
 <source id="position" />
 <source id="texcoord" />
 <vertices id="vx">
  <input semantic="POSITION" source="#position"/>
 </vertices>
 <lines count="1">
  <input semantic="VERTEX" source="#vx" offset="0" />
  <input semantic="TEXCOORD"
     source="#texcoord" offset="1" />
  <input semantic="TEXCOORD"
     source="#texcoord" offset="1" />
  <p>0 0 1 1</p>
 </lines>
</mesh>
```

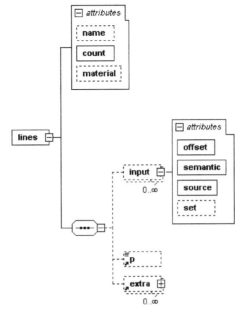

Attribute	Type	Default
count	uint	required
material	xs:NCName	—
name	xs:NCName	—

Figure 3.7. The `<lines>` element.

The `<mesh>` element contains one line, as the `<lines count="1">` indicates. There are three `<input>` elements. Two of them share the same offset so the number of indexes per vertex is two. Since a line has two end-points, there are four indexes total within the `<p>` element.

A complete sampling of a single vertex is accomplished by gathering one value from each input using the associated index in the `<p>` element.

All the geometry collation elements (`<lines>`, `<polygons>`, etc.) need to include a mandatory `count` attribute. The `<count>` attribute indicates how many geometric primitives are contained in the primitive collation element. The optional `material` attribute indicates the visual material associated with the geometric primitives. They may also have an optional `name` attribute to store a user-defined name for the primitive. Mesh elements

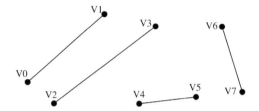

Figure 3.8. Two vertices are required for each line.

can also have optional `<extra>` elements that contain additional application-specific data, which may be added on a per-mesh basis.

Lines

Each line is defined by its start point and its end point. The `<lines>` element can contain any number of line segments (see Figure 3.7). Every two vertices comprise an individual line.

The count attribute is required; it indicates the number of individual lines. Here is a simple example describing four individual lines.

```
<lines count="4">
 <input semantic="VERTEX"
     offset="0" source="#Vtx"/>
 <p> 0 1 2 3 4 5 6 7 </p>
</lines>
```

Figure 3.8 shows a visual representation of the preceding `<lines>` element.

Line Strips

Line strips are a collection of connected line segments (see Figure 3.9). They represent connected lines in a more compressed manner than disconnected lines would to describe the same set of line segments. In a line strip, the first two vertices comprise the first line segment. Each additional vertex completes another line segment saving the cost of a vertex for each segment, as shown in Figure 3.10.

The count attribute is required; it indicates the number of line strips. The number of lines per line strip is not specified. Here is a simple example describing four connected lines within a single line strip.

```
<linestrips count="1">
 <input semantic="VERTEX"
     offset="0" source="#Vtx"/>
 <p> 1 2 3 4 5 </p>
</linestrips>
```

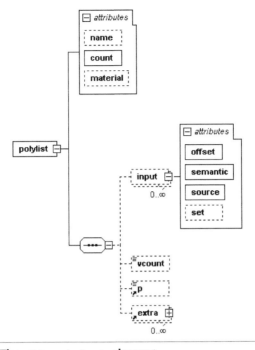

Figure 3.9. The `<linestrips>` element.

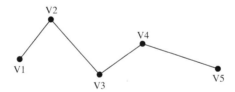

Figure 3.10. Only five vertices are required for four connected lines.

Polygons

A polygon is defined by its edges. It is therefore very similar to a closed line strip, in which a line segment is automatically added between the first and the last point and the resulting contour outline is considered a solid surface.

As far as COLLADA is concerned, there are no additional constraints. This enables the user to create all kinds of polygon primitives.

First, if the vertices are not in the same plane, the polygon is nonplanar. In fact, because of the limitation in numerical accuracy for the value of each vertex, every polygon with more than three vertices is actually nonplanar. Many of the algorithms used in a typical content pipeline will not be able to deal with nonplanar polygons, so it is important for the DCC tools or the COLLADA exporter to make sure the <polygons> are in fact planar.

Planar polygons can be simple or complex. A complex polygon has intersections (a multiple of two) within its own edges. Simple polygons can be convex or concave [41]. In addition, polygons may have holes.

Polygons are described by either a <p> element, as with the other collation elements, or by a <ph> element (see Figure 3.11). The <p> element represents the external contour. The <ph> element, as its name implies, contains both <p> and <h> elements. It contains one <p> element and one or more <h> elements, describing the inner hole contours. This organization enables

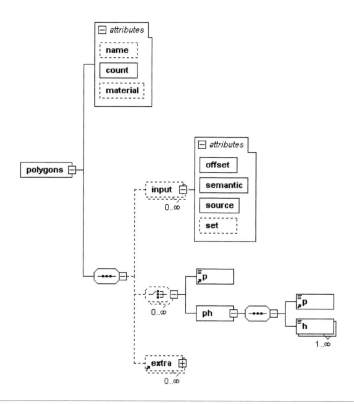

Figure 3.11. The <polygons> element.

applications that do not need to understand holes to simply ignore the <h> element and use the external contours of the <p> elements and the <ph> elements. <polylist> elements cannot represent holes since only the external boundary of each primitive is provided.

Here is a <polygons> example, describing a box that is composed of six quads:

```
<polygons material="Blue" count="6">
  <input semantic="VERTEX" offset="0" source="#box-Vertex"/>
  <input semantic="NORMAL" offset="1" source="#box-Normal"/>
  <p>0 0 2 1 3 2 1 3</p>
  <p>0 4 1 5 5 6 4 7</p>
  <p>6 8 7 9 3 10 2 11</p>
  <p>0 12 4 13 6 14 2 15</p>
  <p>3 16 7 17 5 18 1 19</p>
  <p>5 20 7 21 6 22 4 23</p>
</polygons>
```

Polygon Lists

The <polylist> element describes almost the same information as the <polygons> elements but in a slightly compressed syntax that can greatly reduce the XML parsing overhead (see Figure 3.12). Most of the cost savings is due to the elimination of all but one of the <p> elements.

The <vcount> element describes the number of vertices per primitive. As with the <polygons> element, the <p> element contains the indexes to the vertices that form the edges of the primitives. In this case, there is only one <p> element containing all the edges of all the primitives. To assemble a single primitive, you sample one value from the <vcount> element and then sample the indicated number of values from the <p> element, keeping track of where you leave off after each sampling iteration.

Here is an example describing a box identical to that shown in the previous <polygons> example.

```
<polylist material="Blue" count="6">
  <input semantic="VERTEX" offset="0" source="#box-Vertex"/>
  <input semantic="NORMAL" offset="1" source="#box-Normal"/>
  <vcount>4 4 4 4 4 4</vcount>
  <p>
   0 0 2 1 3 2 1 3   0 4 1 5 5 6 4 7
   6 8 7 9 3 10 2 11   0 12 4 13 6 14 2 15
   3 16 7 17 5 18 1 19   5 20 7 21 6 22 4 23
  </p>
</polylist>
```

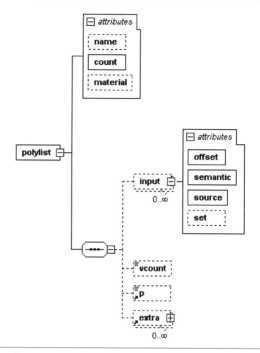

Figure 3.12. The `<polylist>` element.

Most content pipelines are not designed to deal with anything other than simple convex polygons consisting of triangles and quadrilaterals. It is therefore recommended that you have a tool at the beginning of the content pipeline to check the topology of the `<polygons>` and `<polylist>` elements. This tool chain constraint leads us to the family of `<triangle>` elements.

Triangles

Triangles avoid all the geometric issues that can arise in generic polygons. By nature, triangles are planar, simple, and convex. However, triangles can degenerate into lines or a single point, which can also create problems for tools. Triangles are defined by exactly three vertices.

Since triangles have a constant number of vertices, they are organized like the `<polylist>` element but without the need to supply a primitive count (see Figure 3.13). In this case, each `<p>` element contains a list of individual triangles. The first triangle is formed from the first, second, and third vertices. The second triangle is formed from the fourth, fifth, and sixth vertices, and so on.

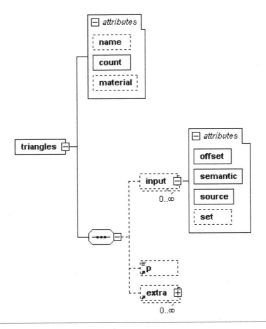

Figure 3.13. The `<triangles>` element.

Once again, the `count` attribute is mandatory and indicates the total number of triangles. The number of indexes is therefore three times the product of the number of unique `<input>` elements and the `count` value.

Here is an example describing four individual triangles.

```
<triangles material="Blue" count="4">
 <input semantic="VERTEX" offset="0" source="#box-Vertex"/>
 <p> 0 1 2 3 4 5 4 6 7 0 9 10 </p>
</triangles>
```

Triangle Strips

A triangle strip is a set of triangles that share one edge (see Figure 3.14).

It is interesting to note that the schema definition of `<tristrips>` is almost identical to that of `<triangles>`. A `<tristrips>` element can contain several triangle strips, or t-strips, each represented by a `<p>` element (see Figure 3.15). The `count` attribute indicates the number of triangle strips.

The first triangle in a strip is defined by three vertices. Each successive triangle is defined by a single vertex, since it shares the last two vertices of the previous triangle. The `<tristrips>` representation is therefore more

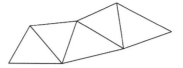

Figure 3.14. A triangle strip.

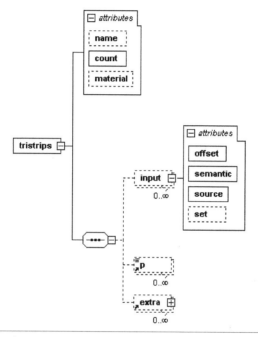

Figure 3.15. The `<tristrips>` element.

compact than the `<triangles>` representation. If N is the number of triangles in a triangle strip and I is the number of unique `<input>` elements, the number of indexes in the `<p>` element is given by the formula $I*(2+N)$, which can be significantly smaller than the formula for individual triangles, $(I*3*N)$.

The triangle strip also has a significant role in the content generation for graphics, since all the graphics accelerators are optimized for this particular representation. One of the criteria used to judge how adequate the content is for real-time rendering is to divide the number of triangles by the number of indexes and compare it with three. This measure is used by many game developers as a criteria of quality for some of the content.

Early adopters have questioned the need for the `<tristrips>` element in the COLLADA schema, since the `<triangles>` element represents exactly the same data. The reason for its inclusion is the importance of `<tristrips>` to the targeted users. Every content pipeline has a t-strip stage, which computes the triangle strips that are optimized for a particular platform. Since each platform has a different set of constraints, the triangle strips can be fairly different. For example, there is generally a hardware limitation on the length of the t-strip where it has to be split to fit into the input buffer. So if a t-strip is just one triangle too long, there is a very abrupt performance drop.

Again, the multirepresentation capabilities of COLLADA can be used to store the optimized triangle strips for each platform as separate assets. It is important to note the value of the `<asset>` element as it applies to multi-representation. Each t-strip can store the time stamp when it was computed, making it possible for the content pipeline to detect if the original data is newer. If the original data is newer, the triangle-stripping process must be applied again. Triangle-stripping is a time-consuming process, so doing it only when and where it is needed is a great advantage for tool chains.

Since this computation is an optimization process, it is sometimes preferable not to create the t-strips or perhaps to use a quicker, less optimal algorithm. This is done to shorten the time needed for the artist to see the result on the target platform, at the cost of full performance. This is a desirable feature because the ability to view intermediate results quickly may have a great impact on artist productivity. Again, the `<asset>` element on the geometry can be used to detect that the optimized version of the mesh has not been computed and should not be used for preview.

Triangle Fans

Triangle fans, or t-fans, are a variation of triangle strips (see Figure 3.16).

Instead of connecting the triangles with the two last vertices of the previous triangle, these triangles are connected by the two first vertices. Therefore, all the triangles of a triangle fan share the same first vertex, which creates the shape of a fan.

The schema for `<trifans>` is again very similar to the `<tristrips>` schema (see Figure 3.17). The only difference is how the indexes are used to compose the geometry. The number of indexes in the `<p>` element is given by the same formula as for t-strips, providing a potential size reduction factor of three compared to a triangle list.

Most of the geometry in the content is a set of closed three-dimensional shapes, which in turn should be converted into an optimized t-strip. Unfortunately, it is often not possible to create a single strip to represent a surface.

Figure 3.16. Triangle fan.

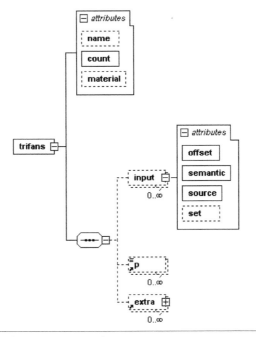

Figure 3.17. The `<trifans>` element.

The t-fan is then required to enable the strip to make a sharp turn to continue growing in length.

Since using a t-fan still produces a discontinuity, the improvement seems minimal compared to simply creating a new t-strip from that point in the computation. This issue has been alleviated by current hardware accelerators that allow t-strips and t-fans to be connected in the same primitive. Enabling both a t-strip and a t-fan in COLLADA makes it is possible to create the optimal representation for next-generation hardware. It is also possible to use a modeling trick to obtain a similar result with degenerate triangles. If the same vertex is repeated at the end of a t-strip, this creates a triangle that degenerates into a line, which will be trivially rejected, and the t-strip can continue, effectively sharing the first and second vertices, instead of the second and third vertices.

Clearly, it is difficult to create an ideal triangle stripper. That task is left as an exercise to the reader! The important part to understand is that COLLADA has all the elements to enable this process and store the optimized result once it is computed.

Convex Mesh

The `<convex_mesh>` element shares all the schema structure and attributes of the `<mesh>` element with the added constraint that all polygonal primitives in the mesh are convex.

There is one aspect of `<convex_mesh>` that is distinct from the `<mesh>` element. The `<convex_mesh>` element does not have to supply all of the mesh data itself. The convex hull of an arbitrary geometric shape can be computed and used instead. The `convex_hull_of` attribute indicates the geometry from which the convex hull should be computed by the application. This geometry type was added to the COLLADA schema during the design of the physics portion of the schema. The ability to derive convex hulls from a preexisting geometry was considered an important feature that is supported by the popular physics engines available to the industry [43].

Spline

The `<spline>` element represents a multisegment spline curve with control vertex and segment information. By default, the curve is open but can be closed using the `closed` attribute. This element has been added to enable representation of curves, rather than surfaces, in COLLADA.

Describing a 3D Cube in COLLADA

This chapter described the COLLADA elements that are involved in the representation of mesh geometry. There are several high-level concepts to understand as well as several bits of supporting infrastructure. Summarizing from the top, we have the concept of geometry represented by polygonal meshes. A mesh is assembled from data streams that comprise the vertex data for each point in the mesh. The data streams are accessed using indexes, and this level of indirection enables some optimizations such as the elimination of redundant values in the stored data arrays.

Now, let's take a look at an example of a three-dimensional cube as it is represented in COLLADA. First, we declare a library element to contain the information; in this case, it is a `<library_geometries>` element. This is followed by a <geometry> element. The <geometry> element is given an id attribute with the value "box" so that it can be instantiated into the scene.

```
<library_geometries>
  <geometry id="box">
```

Next, we declare an <asset> element so that the geometry can be managed by asset management tools. The only information required by the <asset> element is <created> and <modified> child elements. These supply the date and time the <geometry> element was created and last modified.

```
<asset>
  <created>2006-02-06T23:00:00Z</created>
  <modified>2006-02-06T23:00:00Z</modified>
</asset>
```

Following the asset information (if any) is the <mesh> element that contains all the geometric information for the geometry. The mesh contains one or more <source> elements that contain the raw data arrays and an access description for them. In the example, the first source contains the vertex position information within a <float_array> element.

```
<mesh>
  <source id="position">
    <float_array id="position-array" count="24">
    -0.5 0.5 0.5
    0.5 0.5 0.5
    -0.5 -0.5 0.5
    0.5 -0.5 0.5
    -0.5 0.5 -0.5
    0.5 0.5 -0.5
    -0.5 -0.5 -0.5
    0.5 -0.5 -0.5
    </float_array>
```

The <accessor> element declares that the source's output is three-dimensional coordinates (X, Y, and Z). This is declared as the common technique for accessing the array. In this example, there is no user-defined technique so there is no optional <technique> element.

```
    <technique_common>
      <accessor source="#position-array" count="8"
          stride="3">
        <param name="X" type="float" />
```

```
        <param name="Y" type="float" />
        <param name="Z" type="float" />
      </accessor>
    </technique_common>
  </source>
```

The second `<source>` element in the example contains vertex-normal information.

```
<source id="normal">
  <float_array id="normal-array" count="24">
  1.0 1.0 1.0
  0.7 0.7 0.7
  -1.0 -1.0 1.0
  1.0 -1.0 1.0
  -0.7 0.7 -0.7
  1.0 1.0 -0.0
  -1.0 -0.7 -0.7
  0.0 -1.0 -1.0
  </float_array>
  <technique_common>
    <accessor source="#normal-array" count="8" stride="3">
      <param name="X" type="float" />
      <param name="Y" type="float" />
      <param name="Z" type="float" />
    </accessor>
  </technique_common>
</source>
```

After the data sources are declared, the mesh vertices are declared with the `<vertices>` element. Here the mesh vertices are declared to have only positional information, which is the minimum amount of information.

```
<vertices id="vertex">
  <input semantic="POSITION" source="#position"/>
</vertices>
```

Finally, we declare the actual geometric primitives that will represent the geometry. In this case, we are using *N*-sided polygons that are described in the `<polygons>` element. Besides using the mesh vertices as one of its inputs, the polygons also have an `<input>` element with a `semantic` attribute value of "NORMAL". This means that the vertex normal for these primitives depends on the polygon collation. Otherwise, it would be possible, and likely more efficient, to include that normal information as an input to the `<vertices>` element.

Note also that this set of polygons indicates, with a `material` attribute, that it should be bound to a material associated with the symbol "`Blue`" when it is instantiated by the application.

```
<polygons material="Blue" count="6">
 <input semantic="VERTEX" idx="0" source="#vertex"/>
 <input semantic="NORMAL" idx="1" source="#normal"/>
 <p>0 0 2 1 3 2 1 3</p>
 <p>0 4 1 5 5 6 4 7</p>
 <p>6 4 7 6 3 0 2 1</p>
 <p>0 2 4 3 6 4 2 5</p>
 <p>3 6 7 7 5 0 1 2</p>
 <p>5 0 7 1 6 2 4 3</p>
</polygons>
</mesh>
</geometry>
</library_geometries>
```

This long example ends with the closing end tags for the elements in the reverse order of their start tags so that the example is well-formed XML.

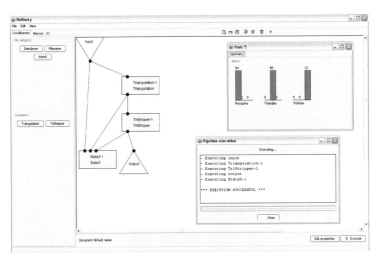

Plate I. Refinery execution of a content pipeline. This is a screen shot of Refinery executing a sample content pipeline, transforming all geometries to triangles, and then all triangles to triangle strips. The stats box produces the windows with three drawings, the number of <polygons>, <triangles>, and <tristrips>. Each drawing has three values plotted, one for each input. The lower-right window is the text output from the execution of the pipeline. (Image courtesy of Sony Computer Entertainment © 2005-2006)

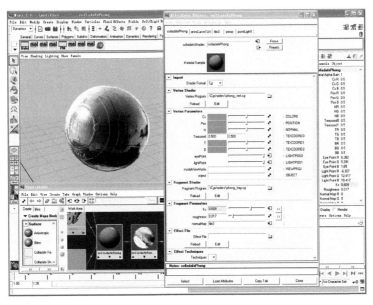

Plate II. Environment reflection shader. This is a screen shot of the COLLADA FX plug-in for Maya, demonstrating a shader with an environment reflection effect, implemented using Cg vertex and fragment shaders. (Image courtesy of Feeling Software © 2005-2006)

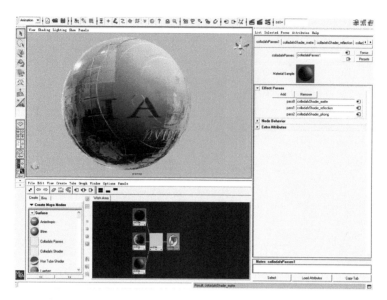

Plate III. Multi-pass material. This is a screen shot of the COLLADA FX plug-in for Maya, demonstrating a material with matte, phong, and reflection passes. On this interface, the user can click the "Add" button to create a new pass that can then be connected to a material. Alternatively, a click on the "Remove" button will delete the last pass and disconnect it if appropriate. (Image courtesy of Feeling Software © 2005-2006)

Plate IV. Layered material. This is a screen shot of the COLLADA FX plug-in for Maya, demonstrating the usage of several passes in layers. (Image courtesy of Feeling Software © 2005-2006)

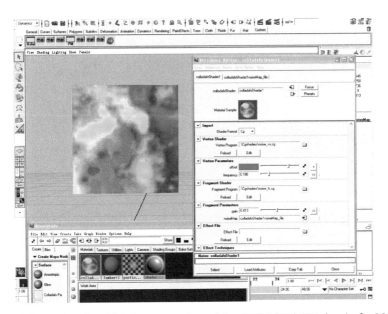

Plate V. Fractal noise. This is a screen shot of the COLLADA FX plug-in for Maya, demonstrating an effect using a fractal noise generated from a random texture. (Image courtesy of Feeling Software © 2005-2006)

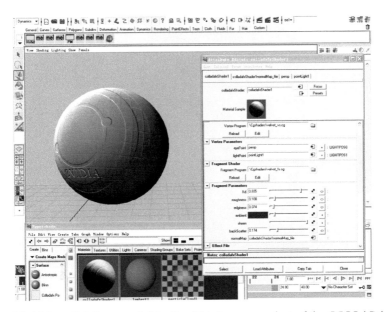

Plate VI. Velvet lighting model in Cg. This is a screen shot of the COLLADA FX plug-in for Maya, demonstrating a velvet lighting model using Cg shader language. (Image courtesy of Feeling Software © 2005-2006)

Plate VII. Car crash. This is a screen shot from the Nima plug-in, illustrating collisions between convex and non-convex rigid bodies. A non-convex rigid body car slides along a ground plane and ramp. In front of it, a wall of bricks is "bouncing" in expectation. The car goes through the brick wall. (Image courtesy of Feeling Software © 2005-2006)

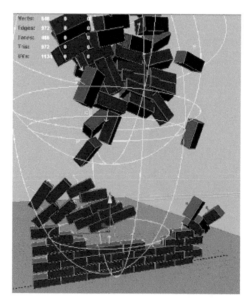

Plate VIII. Tornado. This is a screen shot from the Nima plug-in, illustrating how a brick wall is affected by a tornado made from two force fields (an attraction field in the bottom and a vortex field on top), using the interactive playback to try it out. (Image courtesy of Feeling Software © 2005-2006)

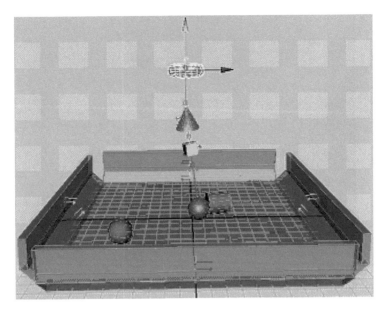

Plate IX. Constraints. This is a screen shot from the Nima plug-in, illustrating a six degrees of freedom rigid constraint. A series of rigid bodies are connected in a chain. The top rigid body (torus) is passive and can therefore be interactively manipulated to demonstrate constraints. (Image courtesy of Feeling Software © 2005-2006)

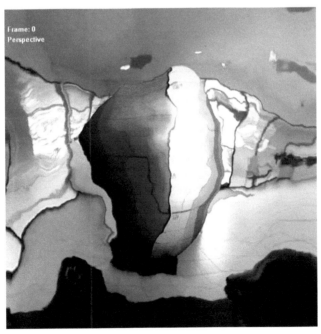

Frame: 0
Perspective

Plate X. Distortion filter. This is an example of a COLLADA full screen shader effect. (Image courtesy of NVIDIA © 2005, 2006)

Plate XI. Unreal Engine—warrior. This image is extracted from a real-time demonstration of the Unreal Engine running on a Playstation 3. This particular demonstration was unveiled at the E3 2004 press event. The Unreal Engine, one of the most successful game engines, has adopted the COLLADA technology for their content pipeline. (Image courtesy of Epic Games © 2005-2006)

Plate XII. Unreal Engine—robot captor view. This image is extracted from the same real-time demonstration on the Playstation 3 mentioned in Plate XI. This view shows a full screen shader effect. (Image courtesy of Epic Games © 2005-2006)

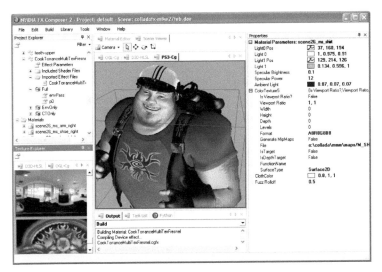

Plate XIII. FX Composer 2.0. FX Composer 2.0 is an application to create, debug, and tune shader effects. It is able to load entire COLLADA documents in order to see the effects on the real asset. It is a tool for cross platform development that supports Cg/OpenGL and HLSL/DX environment, as well as the PS3 specific target.(Image courtesy of NVIDIA © 2005-2006)

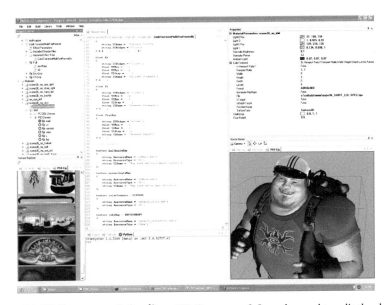

Plate XIV. FX Composer 2.0 editor. FX Composer 2.0 can be used to edit the shader programs as well as tune the parameters for any of the techniques. It is a very flexible tool that incorporates a Python script language that can also be used in order to apply the tool in batch mode in a tool chain. (Image courtesy of NVIDIA © 2005-2006)

Plate XV. PS3 Duck Demo. This is a screen shot that was taken directly from a demonstration running on the Playstation 3 during the E3 expo in May 2005. This technical demonstration was created to show off the numerical and graphical performance of the new console. It shows many advanced rendering techniques used to create realistic water and environment, as well as real-time physics, including rigid body and fluid dynamics. (Image courtesy of Sony Computer Entertainment © 2005-2006)

Plate XVI. This is a snapshot of COLLADA RT with CFX, identical to the demonstration used from the GDC 2006 presentation "COLLADA for PLAYSTATION® 3," presented by Richard Stenson. All the data and software necessary to create this image are included in the SourceForge COLLADA DOM distribution.

4 COLLADA Scenes

Overview

This chapter discusses COLLADA scene composition and object instantiation, including the concepts of materials, lights, cameras, and geometry within the visual scene.

Materials

Every computer graphics system has a concept of rendering and a methodology on how to represent that information in the object to be drawn or rendered on the display device. In the real world, we also have a notion of an object's visual appearance or what it looks like to us. When asked what a floor looks like, we answer, "It looks like concrete" or "It looks like redwood." Our response is to describe the material of the floor. This is a fairly abstract answer that relies on the questioner's own knowledge of "concrete" or "redwood" to visualize the floor's appearance. By identifying the material of the floor, we have given a high-level description of its appearance.

The COLLADA design also uses the concept of material to represent the appearance of geometry at the highest level [43]. The <material> element is the container for all the information that describes the visual appearance of a geometric object (see Figure 4.1). It is composed of three elements:

- an optional <asset> element that contains the asset metadata;
- an <instance_effect> element that declares the rendering effect that achieves the material's visual appearance;
- an optional <extra> element that contains additional user-defined or application-specific information.

COLLADA design relies entirely on COLLADA FX and the <effect> element to describe the rendering state for a material. The <instance_effect> element instantiates the effect within the <material> element.

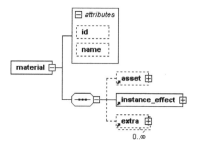

Figure 4.1. The `<material>` element.

As explained in the previous chapter, geometric primitives, such as the `<polygons>` element, have a `material` attribute that declares a symbolic name for a `<material>` element that will ultimately be bound to it during the instantiation process that is guided by the `<instance_material>` element. The `<instance_material>` element has a `symbol` attribute that defines the material's symbolic name for this purpose.

```
<polygons material="Blue" count="6">
...
<material id="Unique_Blue" name="My_Blue">
...
<instance_material symbol="Blue" target="#Unique_Blue"/>
```

The `id` attribute defines the material's identity so that it can be referenced and located using a URL reference. The `<instance_material>` element has a `target` attribute that references the material `id`. Materials also have a friendly `name` attribute that is not involved in the binding process.

Materials are instances of effects. Effects are shading algorithms that are written in a variety of shading languages, such as Cg or GLSL, and packaged with a variety of programmable state and other platform-specific configuration settings. Effects are executed on modern graphics processing units (GPUs) as a series of shader programs. To learn more about effects and shaders, please refer to Chapter 5, "COLLADA Effects," page 91.

When instantiating an effect, any parameter of the effect can be changed by the material. For example, a "`shiny_effect`" can be used to create a "`blue_shiny`" material and a "`gold_shiny`" material by adjusting the appropriate color parameter in the `<material>` element.

```
<effect id="shiny_effect">
 <profile_COMMON>
  <technique>
   <newparam sid="Diffuse_Color">
    <semantic>DIFFUSE</semantic>
```

```
    <float3> 0.8 0.8 0.8 </float3>
    </newparam>
    <newparam sid="Super_shiny">
     <semantic>SHININESS</semantic>
     <float> 0.2 </float>
    </newparam>
    <phong/>
   </technique>
  </profile_COMMON>
 </effect>

 <material id="blue_shiny">
  <instance_effect url="#shiny_effect">
   <setparam ref="Diffuse_Color">
    <float3> 0.0 0.0 1.0 </float3>
   </setparam>
  </instance_effect>
 </material

 <material id="gold_shiny">
  <instance_effect url="#shiny_effect">
   <setparam ref="Diffuse_Color">
    <float3> 0.8 0.6 0.2 </float3>
   </setparam>
  </instance_effect>
 </material>
```

The previous example shows a single <effect>, identified as "shiny_effect", which defines two new parameters. One of those parameters has a sid value of "Diffuse_Color". The "blue_shiny" material sets that parameter, using the <setparam> element, to a pure blue (RGB) color value. The "gold_shiny" material sets it to a gold color value. These settings take place when the material is bound to some geometry in the scene.

To encourage document modularity, materials are declared and defined inside <library_materials> elements. A COLLADA document that contains only a set of materials in a library can define a visual theme, such as "hardwood_floors", that is reused by many different documents that share the floor descriptions with each other, for example:

```
<COLLADA>
 <asset/>
 <library_materials id="hardwood_floors">
  <asset/>
  <material id="walnut" />
  <material id="oak" />
  <material id="mahogany" />
 </library_materials>
</COLLADA>
```

Lights

Lights are absolutely necessary for computing the visual representation of an object. Without a light source, everything in the scene will be rendered black on black for most geometry. Some lighting models include the concept of glowing or emissive geometry that do not require a light source to produce their color. Lights are not part of the geometry or material definition. Lights are independently defined and are important parameters to the rendering algorithm along with the given geometry and material.

The number of active lights is often limited in the graphics hardware or software due to the high cost associated with each additional light in the calculations. Even so, the quality of the rendering is directly proportional to the number of light sources in the scene, so artists are constantly striving to make the best use of all available lights. This is a major reason why lights are a distinct element in the design of COLLADA even though global illumination models enable any and all objects in the scene to emit light and contribute to the final rendering result [44].

To be active, a light must be instantiated into the visual scene. The directional, point, and spot lights take their position and orientation from the coordinate system of the parent <node> element in the scene (see Figure 4.2). The ambient light is not affected by such spatial transformations since it radiates omnidirectionally from everywhere in the scene equally.

The basic light source representation is defined by the light's <technique_common> child element (see Figure 4.3). It can contain one of four possible choices of light types that are common among graphics applications and fixed-function rendering implementations. The four choices are ambient, directional, point, and spot [45]. Each type of light has specific properties that artists use to create the visual lighting effects. The simpler ambient light requires fewer calculations than the complex spot light.

Ambient Light

Ambient light radiates energy from every direction equally. Its light appears to come from everywhere at once. The intensity of the light is not attenuated by distance or viewing angle. This is the simplest type of light and the cheapest way to add color to objects in the scene.

```
<xs:element name="ambient">
 <xs:complexType>
  <xs:sequence>
   <xs:element name="color" type="TargetableFloat3"/>
  </xs:sequence>
```

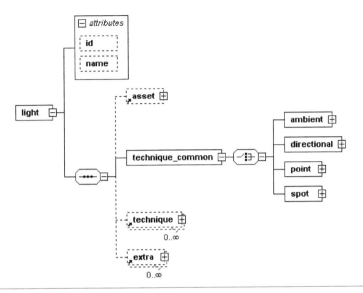

Figure 4.2. The `<light>` element.

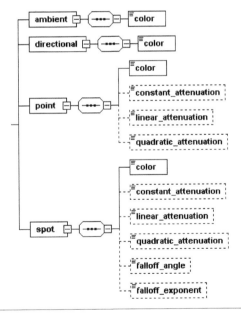

Figure 4.3. The `<light><technique_common>` element.

```
   </xs:complexType>
</xs:element>
```

As you can see from the schema for the `<ambient>` element, it defines a single `<color>` element that contains the RGB color value for the light. The ambient color value can be targeted for animation as discussed in Chapter 6, "COLLADA Animations," page 121.

Directional Light

Directional light radiates energy from one direction. The light source is always infinitely far away so the light rays are parallel to the direction everywhere in the scene. The intensity of the light is not attenuated. This type of light is often used to model the sun, moon, and stars.

```
<xs:element name="directional">
 <xs:complexType>
  <xs:sequence>
   <xs:element name="color" type="TargetableFloat3"/>
  </xs:sequence>
 </xs:complexType>
</xs:element>
```

The `<directional>` element is also relatively simple, defining only a `<color>` element. Its type implicitly means that it has a direction vector that shines the light down its local negative Z-axis. This direction can be reoriented by rotating the light when it is placed in the scene.

Point Light

Point light radiates energy from a single location in all directions equally. The intensity of this light can be attenuated by its distance from the viewer. This light is probably the most common light because it models most everyday light sources, such as candles and lamps.

```
<xs:element name="point">
 <xs:complexType>
  <xs:sequence>
   <xs:element name="color" type="TargetableFloat3"/>
   <xs:element name="constant_attenuation"
         type="TargetableFloat"
         default="1.0" minOccurs="0"/>
   <xs:element name="linear_attenuation"
         type="TargetableFloat"
         default="0.0" minOccurs="0"/>
   <xs:element name="quadratic_attenuation"
         type="TargetableFloat"
```

```
        default="0.0" minOccurs="0"/>
   </xs:sequence>
  </xs:complexType>
</xs:element>
```

The `<point>` element is noticeably more complicated than either the `<ambient>` or `<directional>` elements. Not only does it define a `<color>` element, but also three types of attenuation: constant, linear, and quadratic. Each attenuation element is optional and has a default value if it is not supplied. These elements define values for three terms in the attenuation formula:

$$\text{Attenuation} = A1 + A2 + A3$$
$$\text{where} \quad A1 = \textit{ConstAttenuation}$$
$$A2 = (\textit{Dist} \times \textit{LinearAttenuation})$$
$$A3 = (\textit{Dist}^2 \times \textit{QuadraticAttenuation})$$

The location of the point light is established when it is placed in the scene. For example, here we place a point light at the local coordinates $X=50$, $Y=30$, and $Z=20$ using a `<translate>` element.

```
<library_lights>
 <light id="lamp">
  <technique_common>
   <point>
    <color> 1.0 1.0 0.2 </color>
   </point>
  </technique_common>
 <light>
</library_lights>

<node>
 <translate> 50.0 30.0 20.0 </translate>
 <instance_light url="#lamp"/>
</node>
```

Spot Light

The spot light is similar to a point light that shines a beam of light along the direction it is facing. The beam expands wider, in a cone shape, as the distance from the light increases. This type of light source is used to model flashlights, searchlights, headlights, and, of course, spotlights.

A spot light's brightness is attenuated by its distance from the viewer, by its orientation, and also by the angle of the beam away from the light's direction. The attenuation due to distance uses the same formula as for point lights.

```
<xs:element name="spot">
 <xs:complexType>
  <xs:sequence>
   <xs:element name="color" type="TargetableFloat3"/>
   <xs:element name="constant_attenuation"
         type="TargetableFloat"
         default="1.0" minOccurs="0"/>
   <xs:element name="linear_attenuation"
         type="TargetableFloat"
         default="0.0" minOccurs="0"/>
   <xs:element name="quadratic_attenuation"
         type="TargetableFloat"
         default="0.0" minOccurs="0"/>
   <xs:element name="falloff_angle"
         type="TargetableFloat"
         default="180.0" minOccurs="0"/>
   <xs:element name="falloff_exponent"
         type="TargetableFloat"
         default="0.0" minOccurs="0"/>
  </xs:sequence>
 </xs:complexType>
</xs:element>
```

The <spot> element has an implied direction facing down the negative *Z*-axis, just like the <directional> element. The actual orientation is established when the light is placed in the scene, as with the other light types.

The shape of the spot light beam is defined by the <falloff_angle> and <falloff_exponent> child elements. The value of <falloff_angle> can range from 0 to 90 degrees, or it can have the special value of 180 degrees for a uniform distribution, just like a point light source. The value of <falloff_exponent> can range from 0 to 128. Higher exponent values focus the beam, making it brighter in the center and dimmer at the perimeter of the beam, as a function of the cosine of the angle between the light direction and the surface (normal) of the object it is shining on.

Camera

The <camera> element defines viewing parameters (see Figure 4.4). Like a real camera, it has optical and imaging properties that can be adjusted to suit the needs of the user. To change the field of view on a camera, you change the lens, assuming it's not a fixed-lens or disposable camera. More often, you change the film to match the lighting conditions, using a slow exposure film on a bright sunny day. Although analog film is on the decline with the advent of digital cameras, the comparison still holds. In COLLADA, the <optics>

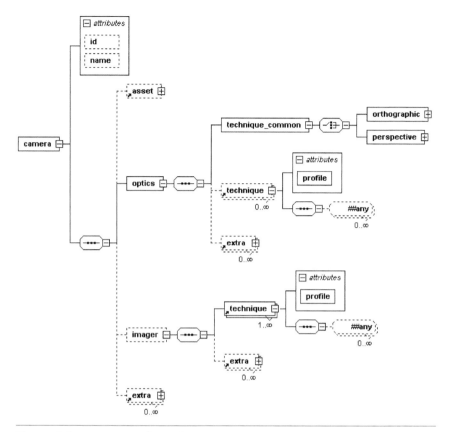

Figure 4.4. `<camera>` element.

element models the lens of the camera. The `<imager>` element models the film loaded into the camera.

A camera's position and orientation are established when it is placed in the scene. By convention, a camera's implicit orientation has it looking down its Z-axis, with its X-axis to the left and its Y-axis upward. As with other objects that can be placed in the scene, cameras are defined within a library module using the `<library_cameras>` element.

```
<library_cameras>

 <camera id="my_camera2">
  <asset/>
  <optics>
   <technique_common>
    <orthographic>
```

```
  <xmag>1000.0</xmag>
  <ymag>700.0</ymag>
  <znear>0.1</znear>
  <zfar>10000.0</zfar>
   </orthographic>
   </technique_common>
   <extra/>
  </optics>
  <imager>
  <technique/>
  <extra/>
  </imager>
  <extra/>
 </camera>
....

<camera id="my_camera1">
 <asset/>
 <optics>
  <technique_common>
   <perspective>
    <xfov>1000.0</xfov>
    <yfov>500.0</yfov>
    <znear>2.0</znear>
    <zfar sid="animated_far">100.0</zfar>
   </perspective>
   </technique_common>
   <extra/>
  </optics>
  <extra/>
 </camera>

</library_cameras>

<node>
 <translate> 100.0 0.0 -100.0 </translate>
 <instance_camera url="#my_camera2"/>
</node>
```

Optics

The `<optics>` element models the camera lens and is extensible. The properties most often needed are defined within the `<technique_common>`
element. Alternatively, artists can supply their own definition using the
`<technique>` element. In either case, additional properties can be given
using the `<extra>` element.

Within the common technique, two types of lens are provided by the `<orthographic>` and `<perspective>` elements. The orthographic lens projects the scene onto the plane of the film (`<imager>`) so that the lines of projection are parallel to the plane. The resulting image lacks any depth perspective. Conversely, the perspective lens preserves the eye's natural perception of objects using a projection where each line extends to its own vanishing point. The eye is able to discern three-dimensional perception of the resulting image and to retain a sense of geometric perspective, hence the name of this projection.

The schema for these two elements look more complicated than they really are, as they offer some choices in how the parameters are specified. Using the `<orthographic>` element's schema, we will explain the choices. First, the schema is as follows:

```
<xs:element name="orthographic">
 <xs:complexType>
  <xs:sequence>
   <xs:choice>
    <xs:sequence>
     <xs:element name="xmag" type="TargetableFloat"/>
     <xs:choice minOccurs="0">
      <xs:element name="ymag" type="TargetableFloat"/>
      <xs:element name="aspect_ratio"
            type="TargetableFloat"/>
     </xs:choice>
    </xs:sequence>
    <xs:sequence>
     <xs:element name="ymag" type="TargetableFloat"/>
     <xs:element name="aspect_ratio"
            type="TargetableFloat" minOccurs="0"/>
    </xs:sequence>
   </xs:choice>
   <xs:element name="znear" type="TargetableFloat"/>
   <xs:element name="zfar" type="TargetableFloat"/>
  </xs:sequence>
 </xs:complexType>
</xs:element>
```

To specify an orthographic projection, we need to know the *X*- or *Y*-axis magnification at a minimum (in conjunction with the display devices viewport size). We also want the option of providing both or either magnifications and the aspect ratio. Finally, we need to know the near and far clipping planes to complete the viewport viewing frustum.

```
<orthographic>
 <xmag> 1280 </xmag>
 <ymag> 1024 </ymag>
</orthographic>

<perspective>
 <yfov> 50.0 </yfov>
 <aspect_ratio> 0.88 </aspect_ratio>
</perspective>
```

The schema for these optical elements allows the artist to use these choices without needing to supply more information than is required. For example, it would be a validation error to supply all three elements of <xmag>, <ymag>, and <aspect_ratio> at once.

```
<orthographic>
 <xmag> 1280 </xmag>
 <ymag> 1024 </ymag>
 <aspect_ratio> 1.25 </aspect_ratio> <!-- validation error -->
</orthographic>
```

Imager

The <imager> element is like camera film and is fully extensible [46]. There are no common properties for this element because existing DCC tools do not have a consistent methodology for this aspect of rendering. The COLLADA design group considered using ASA/ISO film speed ratings, but the decision was made to leave it open to extension using the <technique> and <extra> elements.

Node

So far, this chapter has discussed placing items in the scene, such as the lights and cameras. The first step in this process is to create a node hierarchy of coordinate transformations. Each node in the hierarchy defines its own local coordinate system (see Figure 4.5). Any object contained in the node inherits these coordinates and therefore its placement. This is the primary job of the <node> element [47].

The node is an asset and can be extended with additional information in the <extra> element. The <node> element has several optional attributes, among them

- id and name attributes for identification;
- sid attribute for animation targeting;
- layer and type attributes as an aid to rendering and scene-graph software.

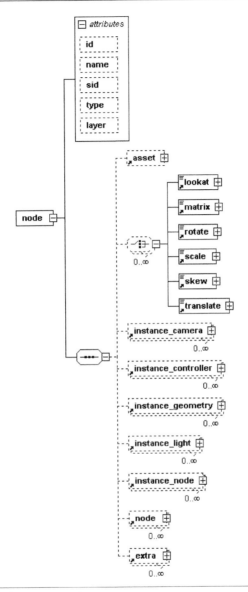

Figure 4.5. The <node> element.

The type attribute is useful when creating articulated characters and similar models. A type value of "JOINT" distinguishes a skeleton joint from other nodes in the hierarchy.

A `<node>` element has the following optional attributes:

Attribute	Type	Default
id	xs:ID	—
layer	ListOfNames	—
name	xs:anyURI	—
sid	xs:NCName	—
type	NodeType	"NODE"

The `layer` attribute is somewhat unique in that it contains a list of names and not a single value. This is because the node can belong to several rendering layers at once, and so more than one layer name can be supplied, separated by whitespace. For example, the following node has membership in three layers:

```
<node id="hill_0013" layer="ground mountains California">
<instance geometry url="#some_hill"/>
</node>
```

The `<node>` element represents the transformation hierarchy recursively, so it can have itself as a child element. The collection of nodes form a directed acyclic graph (DAG) or tree. It has the same structure as the scene graph that is often used in higher-level rendering software.

```
<node name="Earth">
  <node name="Europe">
    <node name="France">
      <node name="Paris"/>
      <node name="Grenoble"/>
    </node>
    <node name="UnitedKingdom">
      <node name="Wales"/>
      <node name="Scotland"/>
    </node>
  </node>
</node>
```

The relationship of the parent nodes to their child nodes is arranged spatially so that objects sharing the same coordinate system will have the same parent node. Traversing from the root of the tree to the object, node by node, enables software to process and render the scene efficiently. To define its own local coordinate system, each `<node>` element can have any number of three-dimensional transformation elements to translate, rotate, and scale it. The set of possible transformation elements are in the following list:

- `<lookat>` element represents a position and orientation;
- `<matrix>` element represents an accumulation of transformations;
- `<rotate>` element represents a rotation about an axis;
- `<scale>` element represents a nonuniform scale;
- `<skew>` element represents a shearing translation and rotation;
- `<translate>` element represents a translation.

These transformations can be combined in any number and ordering to produce the desired coordinate system for the parent `<node>` element. The COLLADA specification requires that the transformation elements are processed in order and accumulate their result as if they were converted to column-order matrices and concatenated using matrix post-multiplication. Therefore, import and export software must preserve the ordering at all times; otherwise, the coordinate systems will not remain correct between applications. To illustrate, here are some transformations injected into the previous node tree example.

```
<node name="Earth">
 <translate sid="T1"> 500.0 123456.0 0.0 </translate>
 <rotate sid="R1"> 36.0 0.0 1.0 0.0 </rotate>
 <node name="Europe">
  <matrix sid="M1"> 1 2 3 4 5 6 7 8 9 10 11 12 13 14 15
  </matrix>
  <node name="France">
   <lookat sid="L1"> 23000 10000 400 0 0 0 0 1 0 </lookat>
  </node>
  <node name="UnitedKingdom">
   <translate sid="T2"> -254 965 -22 </translate>
  </node>
 </node>
</node>
```

With this example, we have given each node the following coordinate systems:

- Earth = $(T1) \cdot (R1)$;
- Europe = $(T1) \cdot (R1) \cdot (M1)$;
- France = $(T1) \cdot (R1) \cdot (M1) \cdot (L1)$;
- UnitedKingdom = $(T1) \cdot (R1) \cdot (M1) \cdot (T2)$.

Within the context of each `<node>` element, there is a well-defined coordinate system in which we can instantiate (create instances of) geometry and other objects. A family of elements is designed to instantiate a specific type of object, as follows:

- `<instance_camera>` element creates an instance of a `<camera>`;
- `<instance_controller>` element creates an instance of a `<controller>`;
- `<instance_geometry>` element creates an instance of a `<geometry>`;
- `<instance_light>` element creates an instance of a `<light>`;
- `<instance_node>` element creates an instance of a `<node>`.

All of these instancing elements perform a similar operation. They take an object defined in a corresponding library element and create a copy of it in the coordinate system of the node. In this manner, objects are placed into a spatially organized tree of information that describes the visual scene.

Visual Scene

The `<visual_scene>` element contains all the information that describes the visual aspects of the scene and often some related data that is tightly coupled to it by authoring tools (see Figure 4.6). The main example is animation data that is tightly coupled to the visual geometry of an articulated character.

In the original design of COLLADA, the visual scene was the only type of scene. Later when another domain was introduced into COLLADA (namely, physics), the concept of multiple domains was formalized. The name of the element was changed, to `<visual_scene>`, with the expectation that more

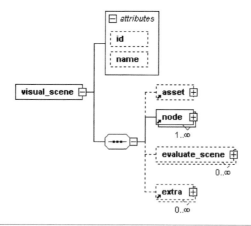

Figure 4.6. The `<visual_scene>` element.

types of scenes would be introduced as COLLADA expands to cover more domains of interest [48].

The visual scene is an asset and has an optional `id` attribute so it can be referenced. It can also have a `name` attribute and can be extended directly using `<extra>` elements.

Each `<visual_scene>` element must contain at least one `<node>` element. The nodes contain the geometry, lights, and cameras that make up the scene. The `<visual_scene>` element acts as the root of the node hierarchy (scene graph).

Next comes an optional `<evaluate_scene>` element (see Figure 4.7). There can be more than one per visual scene.

The `<evaluate_scene>` element acts as a simple form of command scripting [49] as represented by a sequence of `<render>` child elements. It contains the information needed to process the scene contents for each rendering pass. This information includes layer designations, effects instantiation, and the choice of camera to be used as the observer. The details of effects are discussed in the next chapter. The layer names are matched against the `layer` attribute values of the `<node>` elements to select only the matching nodes during the current evaluation pass. One camera is needed during the evaluation, so the `camera_node` attribute is required.

Scene

Each COLLADA document can contain one scene. This scene represents the instantiation of visual objects and physical simulations that comprise the

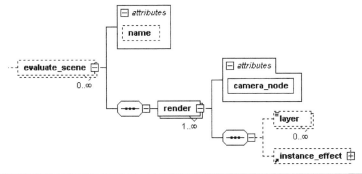

Attribute	Type	Default
name	xs:NCName	—
camera_node	xs:anyURI	required

Figure 4.7. The `<evaluate_scene>` element.

content created by the artist. The `<scene>` element may embody a single character, an inanimate rock, or a detailed cityscape used as a level in a video game.

It may seem like a good idea to be able to store more then one scene per document, but there are several reasons why the document and the scene have a one-to-one relationship. The document is the unit of storage and transmission of XML-encoded content, just as the game level is for video games. Loading in a game level is therefore a simple matter of loading the document that represents it. The one-to-one relationship also makes it easy to discern what content within the document is actually in the scene. Documents can be complex, containing large amounts of information. By easily finding the `<scene>` element and parsing the information backward from it, software tools can efficiently load the content that is contained only in that scene.

The `<scene>` element can instantiate one visual scene and any number of physical simulations (see Figure 4.8). It can be extended with the `<extra>` element as well. The one-to-one relationship between the scene and its visual representation is designed to maintain some simplicity that might otherwise become an explosion of content if it were within a single document. It is possible that this constraint will be relaxed in a future revision of the COLLADA schema.

```
<scene>
 <instance_physical_scene url="#earthly_physics"/>
 <instance_visual_scene url="#earthly_visuals"/>
 <extra type="Weather"/>
</scene>
```

As with the `<node>` element described previously, the `<scene>` element has elements that can create instances of specific types, as follows:

* `<instance_physics_scene>` element creates an instance of a physics simulation;

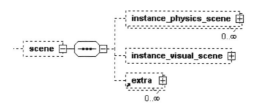

Figure 4.8. The `<scene>` element does not have any attributes.

- `<instance_visual_scene>` element creates an instance of a visual scene.

The actual content for these instantiations is defined in a library element of the corresponding type, for example:

```
<library_physics_scenes>
  <physics_scene id="earthly_physics">
  </physics_scene>
</library_physics_scenes>

<library_visual_scenes>
  <visual_scene id="earthly_visuals">
  </visual_scene>
</library_visual_scenes>
```

The `<physics_scene>` element is described in the section "Physics Scenes" in Chapter 7.

Example Scene

Bringing it all together into a comprehensive example that includes materials, geometry, lights, cameras, and action! (... I mean animation) will fill up several pages with XML. Instead, here are the salient points we have covered in this chapter in an outline-style example.

First, we have the libraries of information organized by type. The simple object declarations for this outline include a camera, geometry, an effect, and a light.

```
<library_cameras>
  <camera id="Eyes"/>
</library_cameras>

<library_geometries>
  <geometry id="Globe">
    <mesh>
      <source/>
      <vertices/>
      <polygons count="365" material="Blue"/>
    </mesh>
  </geometry>
</library_geometries>

<library_effects>
  <effect id="Shiny"/>
</library_effects>

<library_lights>
  <light id="Sun_Light"/>
</library_lights>
```

The material is a little bit more complicated since it references the effect.

```
<library_materials>
  <material id="Shiny_Blue">
  <instance_effect url="#Shiny"/>
  </material>
</library_materials>
```

The node binds several things together including the geometry, material, and the light.

```
<library_nodes>
  <node id="Earth">
    <instance_geometry url="#Globe">
      <bind_material>
        <technique_common>
          <instance_material symbol="Blue" target="#Shiny_Blue"/>
        </technique_common>
      </bind_material>
    </instance_geometry>
  </node>
  <node id="Sun">
    <instance_light url="#Sun_Light"/>
  </node>
</library_nodes>
```

Next, the visual scene creates the scene graph from the available nodes. A camera can be created here or be part of the incoming node hierarchy already. In this example, we'll create the camera here.

```
<library_visual_scenes>
  <visual_scene id="World">
    <node id="Root">
      <instance_node url="#Earth"/>
      <node>
        <matrix sid="Roving"/>
        <instance_camera url="#Eyes"/>
      </node>
    </node>
  </visual_scene>
</library_visual_scenes>
```

Finally, the visual scene is instantiated in the document.

```
<scene>
  <instance_visual_scene url="#World"/>
</scene>
```

5 COLLADA Effects

Overview

The content for this chapter was provided by Daniel Horowitz, NVIDIA Corporation, and chairman of COLLADA FX Sub-Working Group at the time the book was created. His work concentrates on improving content creation for PCs, consoles, and handheld devices. Prior to NVIDIA, he worked with Microsoft's Direct3D Solutions team. Daniel has also worked on game engine animation systems and content pipelines for *Halo 2* at Bungie, engaged in game development at Electronic Arts, and procedurally generated stylizations of animation at Intel.

This chapter covers key elements of COLLADA effects (COLLADA FX) technology. Effects are used within COLLADA 1.4 as visual appearance definitions to describe the coloring of geometries combining style, material, and reaction to scene placement. Additionally, effects are used to describe the use of processes such as blurs and blooms during the compositing (creating complex images or moving images by combining images from different sources) of multiple layers of visual scenes into a final image. Within this chapter, these applications of effects are described in further detail. The visual material and visual scene are each referred to as material and scene, respectively, since we are only discussing the visual domain.

Materials

To understand what effects are and how they are used, it is helpful to first understand how an artist works. When an artist produces an image, he or she considers the visual domain of a scene very carefully. In an artist's scene, each object is colored slightly differently by considering combinations of substance, placement, and style. Each object in a scene is composed of one or more substances, such as wood, leather, fur, or metal, and subtle variants, such as youthful or aged skin (see Figure 5.1).

Each object may also appear to be unique because its *placement* within an environment changes how it might fall into shadows or which lights may

(a) (b)

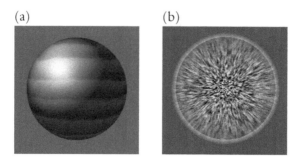

Figure 5.1. Visual materials: (a) wood; (b) fur.

shine down upon it at different locations, intensities, distances, and colors (see Figure 5.2). The *substance* of the object may dictate how light is absorbed or reflected, based on the intensity or angle of the light. For instance, unpolished wood is not as shiny as plastic or metal. The *style* of the object also affects its representation. Styles consist of techniques such as realistic, cell-shaded cartoons, newspaper printing, pencil sketching, or abstract, like a Picasso. A cartoon style may require that shadows be very hard-edged as opposed to a soft, realistic look. Wood, stylized as a cartoon, would have only one color between each ring rather than the realistic look of naturally rich tones and transitions between each ring. The combination of placement, substance, and style is called a *material*.

An artist must also consider the sections (a.k.a. layers) of a scene. Each section has a concept of its order in relation to other sections of a scene. When discussing the ordering of a section, *layer* is more commonly used. Two common layers are the foreground and background. Each section also has a technique used to combine it into the final image (see Figure 5.3). Common compositing techniques are in focus, out of focus, over-exposed, or under-exposed, among many other possibilities and combinations. Each describes a process of ordering, adjusting, filtering, and combining sections of a scene to produce a final image (see Figure 5.4).

Effect Overview

At a high level, an *effect* is the definition of how colors are calculated and combined based on geometries. Much like a mathematical equation that can only be solved when its variables are substituted for values, an instance of an effect provides the required substitutions for an effect's parameters. To draw a parallel, when an artist creates a Phong material in a favorite 3D art software package, the Phong lighting equation is the definition, but the colors chosen

(a)　　　　　　　(b)　　　　　　　(c)

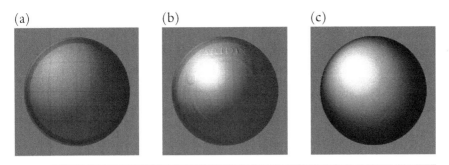

Figure 5.2. Illumination techniques: (a) flat; (b) Phong reflection model [50]; (c) Cook/Torrance reflection model [51].

Composition　　=　　background　　+ image1 +　　image2

Figure 5.3. Composition of materials.

Figure 5.4. Distortion filter (see also Plate X). (Image courtesy of NVIDIA © 2005, 2006)

for the ambient and albedo (diffuse) parameters are part of the instance of a material.

Unlike many other technologies, COLLADA FX does not attempt to produce a universal superset of all features in all application programming interfaces (APIs) in order to attempt consistent visual styles. Instead, it enables an effect developer to customize the visual styles to best utilize the target API and platform that it will be running on. If a developer can target multiple APIs and platforms with one effect, a more efficient, effective production pipeline can create a lowest-common-denominator development, where the least feature-rich platform is set as the highest bar for complexity. COLLADA FX calls these customizations *profiles*.

At a low level, an effect framework is a declarative syntax to manage, group, parameterize, and organize the hardware graphics processing unit (GPU) state and code to prepare for 3D rendering. The parameterization is what makes an effect like a mathematical equation. An effect that is instantiated (substituting values for parameters) and bound to geometry completes the equation to produce a solution, for example, the description of an object's material or an image post-processing operation (see Figure 5.5).

Placing all of this into an asset such as a file allows for external authoring, sharing, and management under a source control system. This enables greater flexibility and portability in both the art and software development process. Some developers choose not to use existing effect API frameworks, because they have produced their own. Unfortunately, they also lose the ability to use

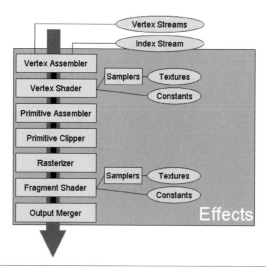

Figure 5.5. Effects data-driven model.

their files with third-party software to increase the efficiency of their art pro-duction. Additionally, not using existing effect framework APIs requires more time, increasing the likelihood of engineering errors and results that may not be as good. Effect frameworks also help insulate an application from many of the underlying platform specifics by providing a much cleaner and simpler interface to the developer.

Shaders

Older GPUs performed a fixed set of operations to render geometry with flat, Gouraud [52] or Blinn [53] calculations. GPUs today have removed these sections of the fixed rendering pipeline in favor of flexibility. They have been replaced with highly programmable units. Before rendering, assembly code can be uploaded into these programmable units to replicate the older calcu-lations or produce new and novel calculations. The calculations performed during rendering are often referred to as *shading* because they traditionally performed illumination calculation on geometry. Also, the code uploaded to a programmable unit is called a *shader*, and higher-level programming languages designed to program these units efficiently are called *shading languages.*

Some popular languages today are NVIDIA's Cg, OpenGL's GLSL, and Microsoft's HLSL. The shaders supported in today's OpenGL 2.0 and DirectX 9 APIs are vertex and fragment (or pixel) shaders. In the future, more fixed-function pipeline states will be consolidated and replaced by pro-grammable units. Currently, profiles in COLLADA FX manage the combina-tion of fixed-function state, shader assignment, and resource assignment.

Following is a fragment of Cg shader code that performs simple Phong-like shading. For more information on how to write shader code, please refer to the many excellent books on this subject [54].

```
float4 fragmentShader(
  float3 worldSpaceNormal: NORMAL0,
  uniform float3 worldSpaceLightDirection,
  uniform float3 worldSpaceViewDirection,
  uniform float3 materialColor,
  uniform float3 lightColor,
  uniform float lightPower,
  ) : COLOR0
{
  float diffuseTerm = dot(
      worldSpaceNormal,-worldSpaceLightDirection);
  float3 reflectionVector = reflect(
      -worldSpaceViewDirection,worldSpaceNormal);
  float specularTerm = pow( dot(reflectionVector,
      -worldSpaceLightDirection), lightPower);
```

```
float3 finalColor = lightColor * materialColor *
    (diffuseTerm + specularTerm);
return float4( finalColor, 1.0f );
}
```

COLLADA FX

COLLADA FX guards external COLLADA assets from the more complicated, API-specific nature of effects by creating a clear and simple interface
from which to communicate. The building blocks of an effect form a shal-
low hierarchy (see Figure 5.6). The first two levels of the hierarchy inside
an effect, profile and technique, enable multiple similar representations of a
given visual appearance that the developer is trying to achieve. The deeper
elements represent the specific implementations.

An <effect> element has a friendly name attribute and a globally unique
name. Effect assets also contain parameters (see Figure 5.7). At this level,
parameters are shareable between all profiles. Parameters will be discussed
in more detail in a later section. Additionally, effects may also have images.
Developers may place images within the <effect> element for surface
parameters that are only internal and resources used frequently such as noise
maps or lookup tables.

Profiles Overview

The first level of hierarchy is called a profile. Each profile is designed for a
specific platform, usage scenario, or mixture of APIs. All profiles share a common interface and structure. An effect must contain one or more profiles.
There are a variety of different profile types. A particular profile type uses its
own unique schema, but all profiles share the concept of techniques, which
are described in later sections. All API-centric profiles share the concept of
passes, which reside in techniques.

COLLADA 1.4 includes four different standard profiles:

* profile_COMMON for basic interchange between digital content creation
  (DCC) tools;
* profile_CG for OpenGL plus NVIDIA's Cg Shading Language;
* profile_GLSL for OpenGL plus the OpenGL Shading Language;
* profile_GLES for OpenGL ES 1.0 and 1.1.

Additional profiles such as HLSL and OpenGL ES 2.0 are in the works and
will be added in future releases of COLLADA. Experimental implementations for HLSL are already available in FX Composer 2.0 and 3ds Max.

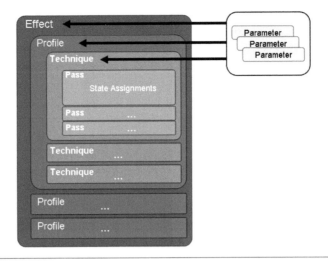

Figure 5.6. Effect overview.

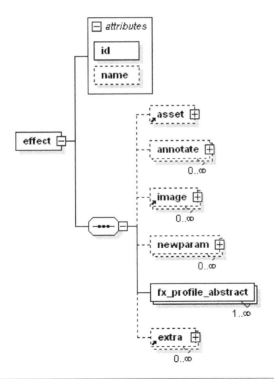

Figure 5.7. The <effect> element.

All of these profiles can coexist within a single effect. Some applications may understand multiple profiles such as NVIDIA's FX Composer 2.0 [55] (see Plates XIII and XIV). All applications are expected to understand profile_COMMON, which is API-agnostic. Many applications prioritize profiles based on the API that best matches its platform environment. If the application cannot find the desired profile, it uses profile_COMMON as a fall back.

Some profiles have a platform attribute designed to enable keywords for describing a class of hardware. In profiles such as OpenGL ES, platform may be used to indicate the family of cellphones for which this profile is designed or to distinguish between OpenGL ES 1.0 and 1.1 support. If an effect is designed for OpenGL ES or other multiplatform profiles, the profile type will probably appear multiple times, each with a different platform identifier. A <profile> can define parameters at its level and share them between the <technique> elements. In addition, an <effect> can define at its level parameters and images that will be shared between the <profile> elements.

Some specific profiles are discussed in more detail later in this chapter.

Technique

A <technique> element describes one of several methods for achieving a similar effect. There are many different axes on which to permute effects, which we call levels of detail (LODs). LODs often include hardware constraints, runtime resource constraints, distance from camera to model, pixel coverage, velocity, scene over-draw. Although LODs, such as those listed above, are considered the most common use for techniques, they are not limited to only these. For instance, an effect to mimic the appearance of leather may have techniques for representing cow, alligator, and snake skins.

The current usage scenarios for techniques are not their original intent. Traditionally, techniques were designed to enable developers to write versions of the effect for different generations of GPU hardware. At runtime, the engine would request validation from the effect API validation on whether the contents of a particular technique could operate on currently running hardware. In this scenario, techniques were ordered from highest hardware requirements to lowest so that the best technique could be found for that particular hardware. However, the original effect APIs did not enforce this policy, but instead allowed developers to manually iterate over the technique to validate and choose whichever one they deemed appropriate. The lack of policy enforcement enabled the usage scenario seen today to evolve. Due to this legacy, technique validation is still considered a best practice and a subset of LOD.

Even though a technique resides inside an API-specific profile, a technique is not an API-specific construct. It is a generalized container for holding passes. It is the role of the passes to set up the API for rendering. Why would one or more techniques exist inside a profile? The reason is that not every technique may make sense for every API. Hardware may vary greatly between the different platforms that use a given API. Additionally, the levels of detail for one API or platform may not be understood by another. For instance, if one profile were designed for the movies and took days to render an image, it may only need one technique. However, a profile designed for a video-game platform that must render 30 times per second on a plethora of different hardware configurations would probably require many LODs and many techniques. Older versions of COLLADA FX were designed so that a profile was inside techniques. This was eventually reversed for the reasons just described.

Techniques can be named globally (id attribute) and relative to a parent (sid attribute). They can also declare new parameters (<newparam> element) that are unique to that technique and use the <setparam> element to change the value of a parameter within this technique or higher up in the profile or effect (see Figure 5.8).

More details and descriptions of some amazing features that have been supported through annotation in applications such as NVIDIA's FX Composer are discussed below.

Pass

When an artist draws an object, the work may not be complete after only one application of paint. The first application may only be the base color, a second may add a glow around an object, and a third may add shadows. In effects, each of these applications of paint is called a <pass>.

In effects, passes are used the same way that an artist uses multiple applications of paint. There are many reasons to use multiple passes.

- The hardware may not be able to support such a complicated procedure in one pass because of resource constraints.
- A simple task is often a reusable task.
- One procedure may need to be repeated multiple times.
- It is easier to identify bugs if each step in the process can be visualized.
- It is necessary to create a blend of colors from neighboring areas.

For optimal performance, passes should be minimized, so one should try to identify which passes can be combined. Some passes, such as blending

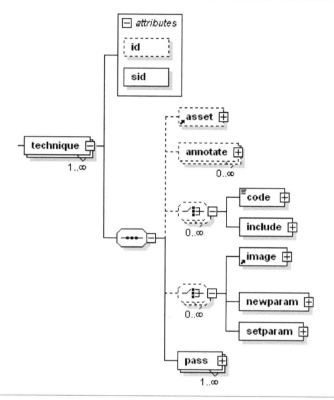

Figure 5.8. The `<technique>` element.

colors from neighboring areas, must be independent because they require reading from or blending into the previous image.

A pass is where most of the low-level details of an effect takes place. It is buried deep within an API-specific profile. The profile, in turn, provides the schema for the pass to describe which target APIs are necessary to bridge the two worlds. Passes utilize this schema to set up the GPU hardware and prepare it for rendering. Later sections will cover specific profiles.

Each `<pass>` has a `sid` attribute providing it with a unique name relative to a parenting `sid` or `id` attribute.

There are seven common states optional inside of all passes designed for APIs supporting these constructs (see Figure 5.9):

- `<color_target>`
- `<depth_target>`;
- `<stencil_target>`;

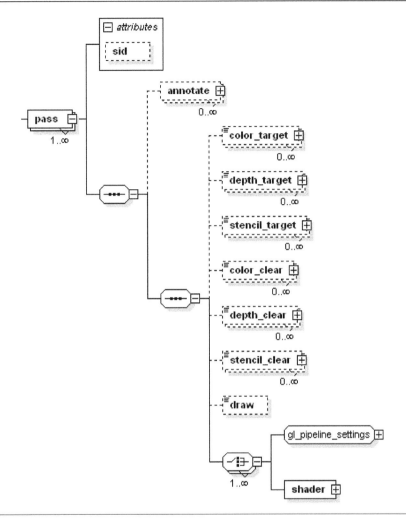

Figure 5.9. The <pass> element.

- <color_clear>;
- <depth_clear>;
- <stencil_clear>;
- <draw>.

The <color_target> and <color_clear> elements are designed for APIs that support multiple render targets (MRT). MRT is a technology designed to enable 3D hardware to draw images into one or more surfaces or subsurfaces rather than directly to the frame buffer. The `<color_target>` element enables a render target to be set by index from a subsection of a surface, identified by `slice`, `face`, and `mip`. The `<depth_clear>` element enables the render target to be reinitialized with a given color. The elements prefixed with depth and stencil act the same way as the color elements, although the depth elements are designed to work with z-buffers, and stencil elements are designed to work with stencil-components. In some hardware, stencils may be tied to the same surface as the depth; on more flexible hardware, they may be separate.

The `<draw>` element enables the developer to use a string to indicate the geometry that should be drawn after setting up the pass. At first glance, this may not seem necessary since most effects are bound to a specific piece of geometry, but more advanced effects may require additional geometry to be rendered, for example, a full screen quad (FSQ) to composite multiple surfaces together. Developers should be wary of these features, though, because they could cause side effects if the surface being modified is not a temporary surface internal to the effect. A common list of strings to use for the `<draw>` element to select which geometry to draw will be added to the COLLADA 1.4.1. specification (which will be published before this book is). In addition, any user-specific parameter can be used in this element. The `<shader>` element is the container for shader programs, if the profile supports programmable shaders. This element describes the selection and binding of a specific shader. Multiple API-specific states are also enumerated.

Parameter

The words *parameter* and *variable* are often used interchangeably. A parameter is one of a set of independent variables. It defines a factor that restricts what is possible or what results. In effects, parameters are used as variables to enable customization of a GPU hardware state. A common variable is the color of an object. An effect rendering a particular lighting equation can provide a reusable color parameter so that different geometries can use the same lighting equation with different colors when instantiating the effect.

Parameters may exist at three levels of the effect hierarchy: effect level, profile level, and technique level. COLLADA FX defines a common set of parameter types, and individual profiles may declare additional parameter types. The common parameter types are grouped into scalars, vectors, matrices, surfaces, samplers, strings, and enumerations. Scalars, vectors, and matrices are built from integers, floats, or Booleans, but not a combination of them. Vectors and matrices have no more than four dimensions. Most rendering calculations

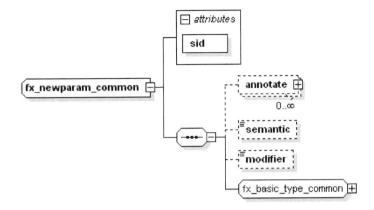

Figure 5.10. Anatomy of a common parameter.

do not exceed four-wide vectors so graphics hardware has been customized to accelerate calculations on variables of this type through operations known as single instruction multiple data (SIMD).

Figure 5.10 shows the anatomy of a common parameter. Specializations may exist with each profile.

When parameters are declared, they are given a name via the `sid` attribute. Conveniently, the parameter is typed and initialized at the same time by adding an element from within the group `<fx_basic_type_common>`.

Parameters also contain three optional elements: `<modifier>`, `<annotate>`, and `<semantic>`. The `<modifier>` element provides additional information about the usage characteristics of a parameter.

- `VARYING`—The value bound to this parameter is intended to change for each vertex during vertex shading.

- `UNIFORM`—This value will not change during the execution of any vertex or pixel shader on a given piece of geometry.

- `CONST`—This value will never change. Do not allow it to be overridden.

- `SHARED`—In all effects, parameters with the same name and type should all share the same value.

`STATIC`, `VOLATILE`, and `EXTERN` are also allowed but are not useful for any of the COLLADA FX profiles.

One or more `<annotate>` elements and one `<semantic>` element may occur. Semantics and annotations are both metadata mechanisms for usage external to an effect. Semantics play a crucial part in linking geometry and scene data to an effect. These are discussed in more detail later in this chapter.

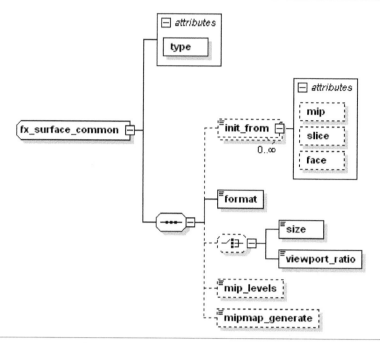

Figure 5.11. A surface parameter.

Surface

A surface is a type of parameter. It is a hierarchical storage mechanism for accessing multiple images in an effect. Surfaces are designed to enable special GPU hardware access patterns to image data. The schema for a surface is shown in Figure 5.11.

There are several different types of surfaces designated by the `type` attribute:

- "1D"—one-dimensional image represented by a 2D image with one dimension's size equaling 1;
- "2D"—two-dimensional rectangular image;
- "3D"—three-dimensional rectangular image constructed of multiple 2D slices;
- "RECT"—two-dimensional rectangular image that may be mipmapped;
- "CUBE"—six two-dimensional square images that represent the sides of a cube;
- "DEPTH"—two-dimensional rectangular image designed to store depth information.

Some hardware may require that images have dimensions that are powers of 2. If they are not, the application may rescale the images for the user and should emit a diagnostic warning.

Surfaces have additional levels of detail known as *mipmaps* (MIPs). Mipmapping is intended to increase rendering speed and reduce aliasing artifacts. MIP is an acronym of the Latin phrase "multum in parvo," which means "much in a small space." Each MIP level of an image is a parenting image reduced in size. When 3D hardware reads from a surface, it reads the MIP images whose texels that are closest in size to the screen pixel, or fragment of the geometry, it will be placed on. If the fragment's area covers a 4 × 4 texel area, it can read from a small MIP image that has already averaged those texel colors together, rather than averaging 16 pixels. The `<mip_levels>` element indicates how many levels of "power of two" reductions are expected for each primary image in a surface. If not specified, it will be expected to go down to the dimensions 1 × 1. The `<mipmap_generate>` element indicates that the user will upload at least the primary images, and then all MIPs will be generated by the application using an undefined filtering technique.

Surface size may also be important to specify. If it is not specified, it is assumed to come from the primary surface that best matches these characteristics:

```
mip="0", slice="0", face="POSITIVE_X"
```

Either the `<size>` or `<viewport_ratio>` element can be used to specify the dimensions. The `<size>` element is for exact dimensions, whereas the `<viewport_ratio>` element is for a proportion related to the rendering surface's resolution in floating-point. A `<format>` element may also be provided if the effect requires more color channels, larger bit precision, or numerical range to enable advanced features such as high dynamic range imagery.

Finally, surfaces are initialized with one or more `<init_from>` elements. This element may address specific images inside a surface including a cube surface's face, a 3D surface's slices, and a surface's MIP images. Note that more will be added in the COLLADA 1.4.1 specification. There are a few file formats that are abnormal. The most popular abnormality is Microsoft's Direct Draw Surface (DDS) file that may contain a complete surface description. If the `<init_from>` refers to a DDS, it must match in type and will load all primary surfaces and MIPs.

There is an additional special version of a surface called "UNTYPED". An untyped surface should only occur inside an effect. It is intended to act as a variable for any surface type that may be assigned into it. Indirectly, a type is enforced at runtime or compile-time by the type of sampler that reads from the surface parameter. A parameter with an untyped surface becomes usable only when a <setparam> assigns a properly typed and initialized surface into it.

Sampler

A sampler is another type of parameter. A sampler describes how to read from a surface. When a shader asks to read from a surface, it requests the color at a particular coordinate. The coordinate may not be at an exact texel location but instead could be in between texels. Samplers select filtering methods and texel read patterns when coordinates exceed the zero to one range. When coordinates are outside of the zero to one range, the sampler considers whether to wrap around back to the beginning, mirror, or read from the border color. The schema for a sampler that reads from a surface of type 2D is shown in Figure 5.12.

The <source> element identifies the surface that the sampler will be reading from. The <wrap_s>, <wrap_t>, and <border_color> elements instruct the sampler how to deal with out-of-bounds coordinates. The <minfilter>, <magfilter>, <mipmap_maxlevel>, and <mipmap_bias> elements instruct the sampler how it should select and filter texels when the fragment size falls between MIP levels. Refer to the "Surface" section earlier in this chapter for more details about mipmapping

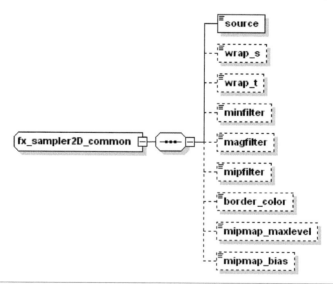

Figure 5.12. Schema for a sampler parameter.

and MIPs. There are several other types of samplers: 1D, 2D, RECT, 3D, and CUBE. Each is customized for a specific surface type.

Annotation

An annotation is defined as a critical or explanatory note, or a commentary. Effects, parameters, techniques, and passes may contain one or more <annotate> child elements. Annotations are a metadata mechanism for an external application to store and retrieve additional information that may be engine-specific. Common annotations may include a parameter's user-interface descriptions or a technique's engine-specific LOD characteristics. As metadata, annotations are declared, but their values are not used inside an effect.

One common use of annotations is the Microsoft DirectX Standard Annotations and Semantics (DXSAS). The prefinal version 0.8x had a simple scripting language that was accessed via annotations. The script described how to operate the passes within the techniques, describing in what order to execute the passes and whether looping was required, among many other features. DXSAS 0.8x is supported in NVIDIA's FX Composer version 1.5 and greater. With the inclusion of this feature, FX Composer has become one of the most flexible FX authoring platforms, enabling it to describe complicated effects such as fur shading, post-processing blooms, blurs, trails, etc. Without DXSAS 0.8x scripts, these effects could not be described in a way that was portable between applications. The scripts were designed to be extremely easy for an engine to parse and operate. Unfortunately, they are somewhat difficult for users to read because of the unusual syntax, but they can be learned with a little patience and plenty of examples in the NVIDIA SDK. Microsoft did not include the scripting system in DXSAS 1.0 in favor of concentrating on a solid scene and user-interface binding layer description, which was also expressed primarily in annotation. There was not enough consensus at the time about the host application complexity versus language and feature richness to release the scripting system for DXSAS 1.0.

Semantic

Semantics describe the intention or purpose of a parameter or function argument. Much like annotations, semantics are also metadata except they are reserved for a special purpose. Their intent is to provide secondary names for parameters and arguments that are more meaningful outside the effect. Other areas of COLLADA use semantic names to bind objects and values together. Semantics are often used to bind geometry information to an effect

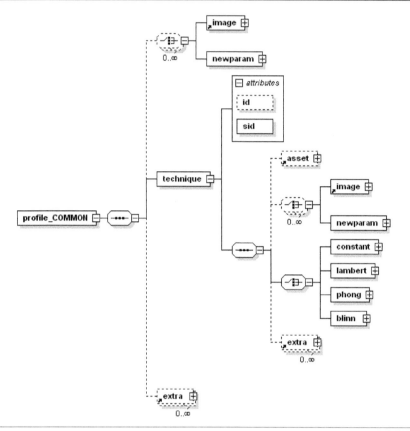

Figure 5.13. The `<profile_COMMON>` element.

and properties of scene objects, such as cameras and lights, into parameters. The COLLADA specification provides a list of common semantics but does not limit the system to this list. There is no formal standard for semantics in COLLADA at this time, except a small list of common semantics.

Developers must be careful not to abuse semantics for other purposes. Semantics are for linking inside of COLLADA documents. There is only one semantic on a parameter so developers are advised to consider its usage carefully. They are encouraged to simulate semantics via annotations to produce application-specific linking. Annotations of type `string` can use a common name such as "myApp_semantic" and provide the application-specific semantic as its value. This prevents multiple applications from colliding unless they want to share a common annotation name for retrieval. DXSAS 1.0 heavily utilizes annotation and prefixes each name with "Sas" to avoid collisions.

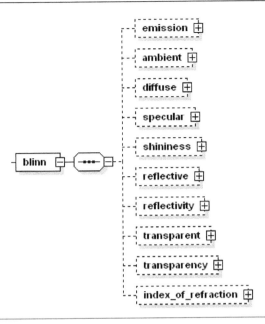

Figure 5.14. The <blinn> element.

Additionally, DXSAS uses only one semantic to avoid collisions with other applications, which is a sharp departure from the pre-release version 0.8x.

Profile for Common Exchange

The common profile <profile_COMMON> should be understood by every application. If an application does not understand any of the platform- and API-specific profiles, <profile_COMMON> is the fall back. Its schema is shown in Figure 5.13.

Inside each technique is one of several common shading algorithms: <constant>, <lambert>, <phong>, and <blinn>. These shading methods are well known and implemented in all DCC applications that have not fully adopted a shader language.

Blinn is the most common shading algorithm (see Figure 5.14). It is very similar to Phong except that with Phong, the specular term is computed with the reflection vector, and with Blinn, it is computed with the half-angle between a vector to the light and a vector to the camera.

Each of Blinn's properties include choices for encoding a color value, referencing a parameter so that materials may modify the color, or requesting a potentially unique color per pixel by using a texture (see Figure 5.15).

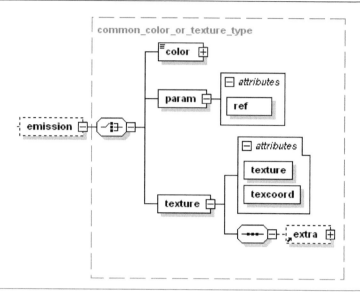

Figure 5.15. The `<emission>` element.

The `<color>` element encodes the value directly. A `<param>` element uses its `ref` attribute to identify by name the parameter that will provide the color. The `<texture>` element is a bit more complicated. Its `texture` attribute references a sampler that identifies the two-dimensional surface where the per-pixel data is stored. The `texcoord` attribute provides a semantic name describing the two-dimensional texture coordinate per vertex that will be interpolated per pixel to access a texel from the texture's surface via the sampler.

Profile for NVIDIA's Cg Shading Language

The `<profile_CG>` should be understood by applications that use OpenGL and NVIDIA's Cg shading language. Since COLLADA FX is designed to provide an effect framework to APIs and shader languages, this profile looks almost identical to NVIDIA's CgFX file format (see Figure 5.16).

There is slightly more flexibility in COLLADA FX. Some of the features previously accomplished through standard annotations and semantics have become a core part of the COLLADA FX schema. Since there are many hardware platforms that may use `<profile_CG>`, there is an attribute to specify the platform as a string.

Within the `<profile_CG>`, code may be included directly via the `<code>` element or referenced via an external Cg file with the `<include>` element. Each has a `sid` attribute so that it may be referenced later. The content of a

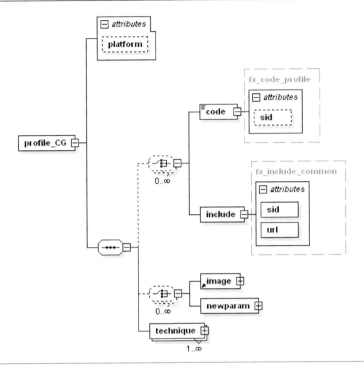

Figure 5.16. The `<profile_CG>` element. Techniques and passes with `<profile_CG>` can define `<code>` and `<include>` elements.

`<code>` element is the same as would be placed in the Cg file referenced by the `url` attribute of the `include` element.

Within `<profile_CG>`, techniques and passes work generally as described previously. They each carry the ability to define a `<code>` and `<include>` element in addition to any parameters or states previously described. In the previous paragraphs about `<pass>`, the schema shows how a `gl_pipeline_settings` group type exists in a pass. The `gl_pipeline_settings` group represents all of the GL state. This group type is also shared by `<profile_GLSL>`.

The `<code>` and `<include>` are finally put to use inside a `<shader>` element, which describes how a particular GPU hardware shader stage will be initialized.

The `stage` attribute can be either "VERTEX" or "FRAGMENT" to identify that the shader will be loaded into either the vertex shader or fragment shader stage of the GPU hardware. Typically, both vertex and fragment shaders are loaded, so there may be two `<shader>` elements inside a pass.

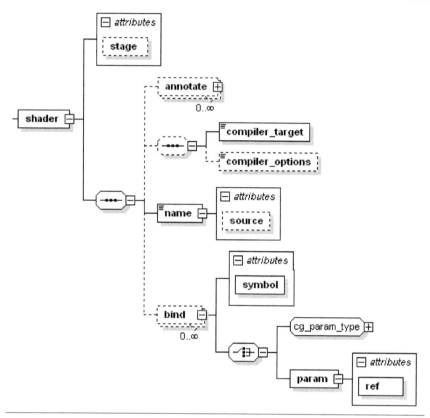

Figure 5.17. The `<shader>` element.

The `<compiler_target>` element (see Figure 5.17) enables the developer to identify a hardware generation to which it will compile. This token is usually `vs_2_0`, `vs_3_0`, `ps_2_0`, or `ps_3_0`. Similarly, the `<compiler_options>` element also dictates options for how assembly code may be generated.

Shaders, like all applications, need an entry point. In C programming, this is usually `main` or `winmain`. In `<profile_CG>`, the entry point can be specified with the `<name>` element. The `<name>` element also has a `source` attribute with an `id/sid` address to a `<code>` or `<include>` element that will contain the Cg and entry point to compile. Finally, a shader has one or more `<bind>` elements. Each `<bind>` element binds a uniform parameter or entry point argument in the Cg code (the `symbol` attribute) to a constant value or parameter (`<param>` element) by reference (`ref` attribute).

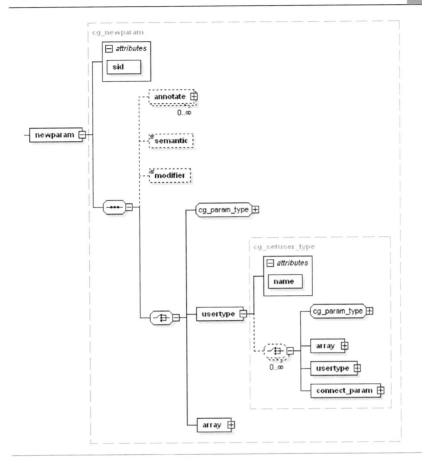

Figure 5.18. The `<newparam>` element.

The Cg profile has a few additional advanced features. Arrays have been standard in Cg for some time, and the newer language specification also allows for unsized arrays. Within `<profile_CG>` it is possible to use the `<array>` element inside of `<newparam>` (see Figure 5.18) and `<setparam>` elements to utilize sized and unsized arrays. In COLLADA FX, everything is treated as unsized and the `length` attribute is used to identify the intended number of elements in the array.

A new addition to the Cg 1.4 language specification is the interface feature. In `<profile_CG>`, the `<usertype>` element reflects this feature. Within Cg, a C/C++-style virtual interface can declare structs that implement the interfaces in one or more ways. For instance, a "Light" interface can be created and have four different struct types that implement it: Ambient-

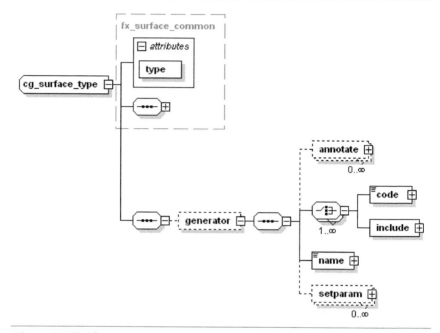

Figure 5.19. The `<cg_surface_type>` element.

Light, PointLight, DirectionalLight, and SpotLight. The `name` attribute on a `<usertype>` is the name of the struct that implements the desired interface or, in a `<newparam>`, the name of the interface if you intend to change it later with a struct type. The contents of the `<usertype>` element are the members of the struct initialized in their proper sequence.

Another powerful feature is the procedural initialization of textures (known as *surfaces* in COLLADA). This feature first appeared in CgFX via an annotation convention. This entails running a shader program over each texel of the surface. Inside a `<profile_CG>`, a `<surface>` element is re-typed to be a `<cg_surface_type>` instead of `<fx_surface_common>`.

The `<cg_surface_type>` has added one new element called `<generator>`. This element is used to trigger the procedural surface initialization.It looks almost identical to the `<shader>` element described above and is operated the same way (see Figure 5.19).

Profile for OpenGL ES Version 1.0 and 1.1

The OpenGL ES profile for v1.0 and v1.1 `<profile_GLES>` is commonly understood by embedded systems such as mobile phones, PDAs, and other set-top or consumer electronic (CE) devices.

In general, `<profile_GLES>` follows the same technique and pass model as `<profile_CG>`. It even uses a subset of the GL states that are assigned in the pass blocks, just like `<profile_CG>`. The GLES profile is for the OpenGL ES 1.x fixed function API that does not support shaders, so all states and XML elements related to shaders are missing. Besides being simplified by removing unsupported features, the differences between the profiles mostly revolve around the texturing systems.

The GLES profile reverses the relationship between texturing operation and hardware texturing units that is expressed by the OpenGL ES 1.x API. You may be asking, "Why did COLLADA FX not match the OpenGL ES 1.x API directly?" The design provided by `<profile_GLES>` allows authors to concentrate on the logic required to achieve the look and feel rather than worry about the details of the hardware texture unit order and association of textures to hardware texture units. For the remainder of this section, the text will be referring to the OpenGL ES texture units as hardware units and COLLADA FX texture units as texture units or virtualized texture units. In OpenGL ES 1.x, textures include 2D data, sampling state, and combiner operations; then they are assigned to texture units. But in the GLES profile, these components have been separated out to allow the authoring of combinations in a more pragmatic way. A "texture pipeline" contains a series of texturing operations, ordered the way the author intends for them to be executed. The texturing operations reference texturing units, which bring together the 2D data and its sampling state. By creating the texture pipeline and texturing operations, many of the cluttered pass states that would exist in the equivalent GLSL profile have been factored out into convenient reusable objects and have been replaced with only two states called `<texture_pipeline>` to assign a pipeline and `<texture_pipeline_enable>` to enable the pipeline. An engine can easily make the associations necessary to map operations and texture data to the API's index hardware units, as described later. The system is also designed in a way that is simple enough for tools to validate during the authoring of the effect, rather than just leaving it up to the engine.

Samplers are a concept that we see in most shading languages. The representation of a hardware texture unit is broken into two objects. The first object is a sampler, which contains the sampling state. The second object is a texture or surface referencing variable, which is referenced by the sampler (see Figure 5.20).

The `<profile_GLES>` texture units were designed to act very much like samplers, but they were modified to map to the fixed function nature of the OpenGL ES 1.x APIs. In this profile, the hardware texture unit is virtualized just like samplers are in shading languages. Once virtualized, they can

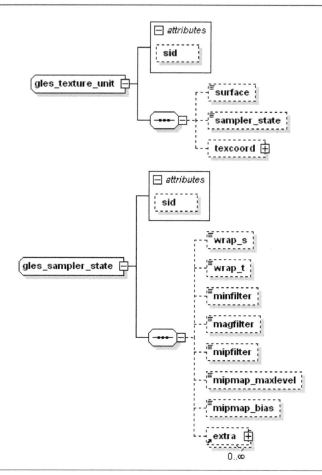

Figure 5.20. Hardware texture unit.

be referenced by name rather than index. The GLES profile also separated the sampler state into its own object so that it can be shared among multiple virtual texture units since there is so much repetition. Sampling state is, more often than not, the same across most texture-units. Texture-units also reference a surface ("texture" in GL terms, "surface" in COLLADA FX) just like a sampler. Finally, a texture-unit provides a semantic name for the texture coordinate data stream from which it will be reading. This is the same as the texture mechanism found in `<profile_COMMON>` already described in a previous paragraph.

The texturing pipeline is the key object in our texturing system (see Figure 5.21). It coalesces an entire multitexturing pipeline into one object. Each

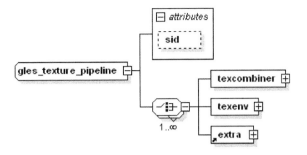

Figure 5.21. The `<gles_texture_pipeline>` element.

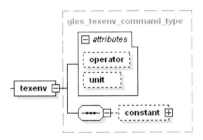

Figure 5.22. The `<gles_texenv>` element.

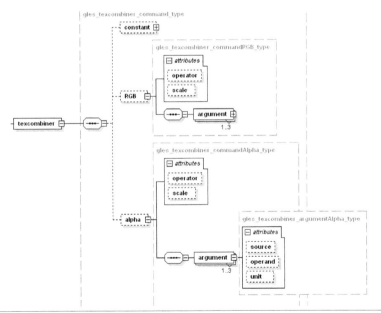

Figure 5.23. The `<gles_texcombine>` element.

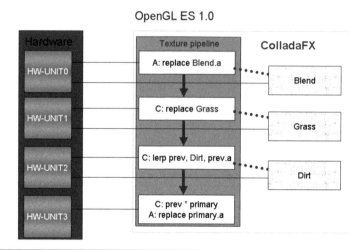

Figure 5.24. OpenGL ES 1.0 version of the API.

multitexturing stage is represented by one command in the pipeline. It can also be reused across multiple techniques and passes because it is a parameter type. This is the root of abstraction of the texenv-related state from the hardware units.

There are two types of commands: texture environment and texture combiner (see Figures 5.22 and 5.23). These commands map to the setup of multiple calls to glTexEnv per hardware unit. Many setups require a texture (surface) as a source. The `<unit>` element refers to a virtual texture unit by name. The specifics of these command can be found in OpenGL 1.4 and greater or OpenGL ES 1.x references.

Eventually, the `<texture_pipeline>` must be mapped to hardware-units. Commands are assigned in their existing order because the logic must happen in the same order to reproduce the effect. Gaps are fine as long as the data is passed through. There are slightly different rules for crossbar support. There is no crossbar support in OpenGL ES 1.0 so the virtual texture unit must be assignable to the same hardware-unit as the command that is referencing it. As a result, one command cannot reference two or more texture units as sources and be OpenGL ES 1.0 compliant. Multiple commands can reference the same virtual texture unit, and in this case, the texture unit is duplicated into each hardware unit. If a crossbar is available, virtual texture units can be copied into any hardware unit. A crossbar is available in OpenGL ES 1.1.

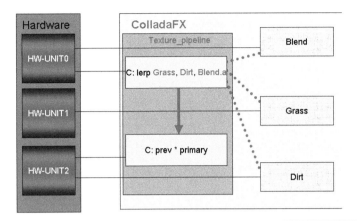

Figure 5.25. OpenGL ES 1.1 version of the API.

Figures 5.24 and 5.25 represent virtual texture unit to OpenGL ES hardware unit assignments for both 1.0 and 1.1 versions of the API. The effect that it represents is a textured per-pixel transition on terrain from dirt to grass so that artists can paint tufts of grass, jetties, and fading or speckling.

6 COLLADA Animations

Overview

This chapter discusses COLLADA animation techniques, including animation curves, parameter animation, and more advanced techniques such as morphing and skinning.

Animations

Animations are used to describe the evolution of a parameter (see Figure 6.1). An `<animation>` is composed of three elements:

- one or more `<source>` arrays of values;
- a `<sampler>` element creating animated values computed from these `<source>` arrays;
- a `<channel>` element binding the animated values to the parameter to be animated.

One simple form of animation is the key-frame animation, in which a list of (values, key) samples is used. In other words, one or more values are sampled for a given key. The key is used as the index into the input data.

For example, an animation can represent a value evolving over time. The goal is to be able to calculate the value for any given time. If the time matches exactly one of the keys, the value returned is the value associated with this key. If the time is between two samples, several techniques can be used to calculate the output value. One technique is linear interpolation. Each sample can define a different interpolation method, which is very useful in defining the behavior before the first key and after the last key.

An `<animation>` does not affect its target outside of its available time range. COLLADA does not define cycle-based behaviors, but some DCC vendors provide this type of information in their particular profile extensions; see Appendix B, "COLLADA Plug-In for Maya."

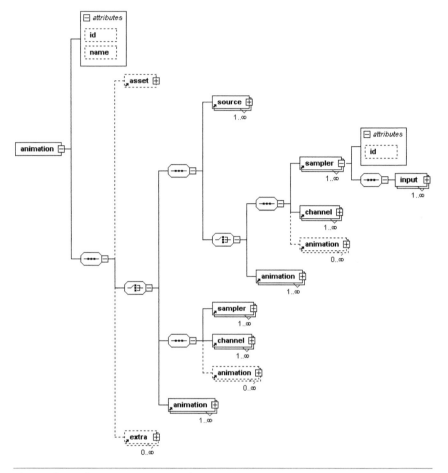

Figure 6.1. The `<animation>` element.

It is not necessary to use time as the sampling element. It is possible to represent a complex mechanism in which the position of an element is computed from the position of another.

The `id` and `name` attributes are optional and enable external referencing. Animations can have an `<asset>` element and can be extended using the `<extra>` element.

Animations can also contain other animations, which is very useful for representing the movement of several parts of a more complex mechanism. For example, a walk animation can be composed of the animations of all the body parts.

The schema is a bit convoluted because of that, but a simple rule makes it easier to understand. In an `<animation>`, you can have either a child `<animation>` and/or a `<sampler>` and a `<channel>`.

It is also possible to group different possible animations for the same object, such as different gestures that will be selected at runtime. Here's an example of one of the possible constructs:

```
<animation>
  <source/>

  <animation>
    <source/>
    <sampler/>
    <channel/>
  </animation>

  <animation>
    <source/>
    <sampler/>
    <channel/>
  </animation>

</animation>
```

Source

The `<source>` element is identical to the one described in Chapter 3, "COLLADA Geometry." It is a reference to a one-dimensional array of values. In the previous example, the first source is used as the reference value for all the animations, such as the time, and the sources defined in the child `<animation>` elements contain the output values.

Let's take an example of a propeller that makes a complete revolution, from 0 to 360 degrees, in 0.5 seconds.

One of the sources has the semantic `"TIME"` expressed in seconds. It is used as the key for all the samples:

```
<source id="inputANGLE">
  <float_array count="2" id="inputANGLE-array">
    0 0.5
  </float_array>
  <technique_common>
    <accessor count="2" source="#inputANGLE-array">
      <param name="TIME" type="float"/>
    </accessor>
  </technique_common>
  <technique profile="MAYA">
```

```
<pre_infinity>CYCLE</pre_infinity>
<post_infinity>CYCLE</post_infinity>
</technique>
</source>
```

Another source is used to give the corresponding angles, using the "ANGLE" semantic:

```
<source id="outputANGLE">
<float_array count="2" id="outputANGLE-array">
 0 360.000000
</float_array>
<technique_common>
  <accessor count="2" source="#outputANGLE-array">
   <param name="ANGLE" type="float"/>
  </accessor>
</technique_common>
</source>
```

Sampler

The `<sampler>` element is used to create the set of parameters that contain the *N*-dimensional array, using one of these arrays as the index in order to calculate the output animated values. The `<sampler>` element is composed of `<input>` child elements (see Figure 6.2).

The `<sampler>` has an `id` so it can be referenced by the `<channel>`, although this could have been a local `sid` since it does not need to be referenced outside a given `<animation>`.

The semantics possible for the `<input>` element are described below. The formulas are given for the index key and $(k1, V1)$, $(k2, V2)$, such that $k1 \le key \le k2$. The interpolation method used is the one associated with the leftmost key: $k1$.

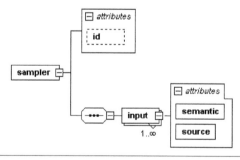

Figure 6.2. The `<sampler>` element.

"INPUT"—One, and only one of the inputs can be marked as input. That one will be used as the key.

"OUTPUT"—Most of the time, a single value will be the output of a sampler. However, it is possible to have several outputs. For example, three values are necessary to animate a 3D position; 16 for a matrix.

"IN_TANGENT", "OUT_TANGENT"—These sources contain the tangent at origin and endpoint, used for the Bézier or Hermite interpolation methods. Here are examples from the propeller example:

```
<source id="intanANGLE">
  <float_array count="2" id="intanANGLE-array">
    687.5 6875.5
  </float_array>
  <technique_common>
    <accessor count="2" source="#intanANGLE-array">
      <param name="ANGLE" type="float"/>
    </accessor>
  </technique_common>
</source>

<source id="outtanANGLE">
  <float_array count="2" id="outtanANGLE-array">
    6875.5 687.5
  </float_array>
  <technique_common>
    <accessor count="2" source="#outtanANGLE-array">
      <param name="ANGLE" type="float"/>
    </accessor>
  </technique_common>
</source>
```

The tangents are not expressed directly as a 2D vectors, but rather by one float value which is used to calculate the control points. Following is an example with IN_TANGENT and OUT_TANGENT given for the key $k1$:

$$C(0) = (k1, V1)$$

$$C(1) = \left(\frac{2k1 + k2}{3}, V1 + \text{out\_Tangent} \right)$$

$$C(2) = \left(\frac{k1 + 2k2}{3}, V1 - \text{in\_Tangent} \right)$$

$$C(3) = (k2, V2)$$

"INTERPOLATION"— <sampler> element must contain an <input> element with a semantic attribute of "INTERPOLATION" since COLLADA does not specify a default interpolation type. There is one interpolation technique per sample, so it is possible to change the interpolation method anywhere on the curve. Here is the source for "INTERPOLATION" used in the propeller example:

```
<source id="interpANGLE">
  <Name_array count="2" id="interpANGLE-array">
   BEZIER BEZIER
  </Name_array>
  <technique_common>
   <accessor count="2" source="#interpANGLE-array">
    <param name="ANGLE" type="Name"/>
   </accessor>
  </technique_common>
</source>
```

The following are descriptions of the interpolation modes that are recognized.

- STEP—In this mode, the value returned is the one from the smaller index:

$$V_{out} = V1 .$$

- LINEAR—A linear interpolation is used:

$$V_{out} = V1 + \frac{(V2 - V1) \times (key - k1)}{(k2 - k1)} .$$

- BEZIER—The Bézier interpolation needs the two additional tangential values given by the "IN_TANGENT" and "OUT_TANGENT" at $k1$. Here is the matrix form of the Bézier interpolation:

$$s = \frac{(key - k1)}{(k2 - k1)} \quad S = \begin{pmatrix} s^3 & s^2 & s & 1 \end{pmatrix}$$

$$M = \begin{pmatrix} -1 & 3 & -3 & 1 \\ 3 & -6 & 3 & 0 \\ -3 & 0 & 3 & 0 \\ 1 & 4 & 1 & 0 \end{pmatrix} \quad C = \begin{pmatrix} V1 \\ V2 \\ T1 \\ T2 \end{pmatrix}$$

$$V_{out} = S \times M \times C .$$

- HERMITE—The Hermite interpolation can be computed in the same manner as the Bézier except with a different interpolation matrix:

$$M = \begin{pmatrix} 2 & -2 & 1 & 1 \\ -3 & 3 & -2 & -1 \\ 0 & 0 & 1 & 0 \\ 1 & 0 & 0 & 0 \end{pmatrix}.$$

- CARDINAL—Cardinal splines are just a subset of the Hermite curves. Instead of using provided tangents, the tangents are calculated from four input values: $T_I = a \times (V_{i+1} - V_{i-1})$, where a is a constant that affects the tightness of the curve. This constant is not specified in COLLADA 1.4 but is decided by the runtime.

- BSPLINE—COLLADA uses a uniform cubic B-spline. It uses four input values instead of tangents, as in the CARDINAL case:

$$M = \begin{pmatrix} -1 & 3 & -3 & 1 \\ 3 & -6 & 3 & 0 \\ -3 & 0 & 3 & 0 \\ 1 & 4 & 1 & 0 \end{pmatrix} \quad C = \begin{pmatrix} V0 \\ V1 \\ V2 \\ V3 \end{pmatrix}$$

$$V_{out} = S \times M \times C.$$

Following is the sampler for the propeller example. The "INPUT" uses the "TIME" source. The "OUTPUT", "IN_TANGENT", and "OUT_TANGENT" reference the values necessary for the "INTERPOLATION", which references the Bézier source.

```
<sampler id="samplerANGLE">
  <input semantic="INPUT" source="#inputANGLE"/>
  <input semantic="OUTPUT" source="#outputANGLE"/>
  <input semantic="IN_TANGENT" source="#intanANGLE"/>
  <input semantic="OUT_TANGENT" source="#outtanANGLE"/>
  <input semantic="INTERPOLATION" source="#interpANGLE"/>
</sampler>
```

Channel

The <channel> element is used to connect the output values to the parameter that will be animated (see Figure 6.3). It is an empty element (it does not have content) and has two mandatory attributes: source and target.

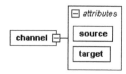

Attribute	Type	Default
source	URIFragmentType	required
target	xs:token	required

Figure 6.3. The `<channel>` element.

The source is a `URIFragmentType`, which is a type specific to COLLADA, that limits the URI to the document. It is a # sign followed by an `xs:ID`.

Here is the `<channel>` for the propeller example. It animates the *Z* rotation angle of the prop `<node>`. The prop references an ID of any element in the same document.

```
<channel source="#samplerANGLE"
    target="prop/rotateZ.ANGLE"/>
```

If the sampler were creating three values, the channel would be able to map those values directly to a vector. For example, a translation could be targeted as `prop/translate`, instead of `prop/translate.X`.

The `<animation>` elements are stored in `<library_animations>` in the COLLADA document. The schema does not specify which animation is to be used at runtime.

Animation Clip

Animation clips provide a start and end time, in seconds, that specify which subset of the instantiated animation it defines. For example, an `<animation>` may include both a walk and a run animation in the same curve, and two `<animation_clip>` elements can be used to separate the two types of animations in order to play them separately (see Figure 6.4).

An `<animation_clip>` also allows the aggregation of multiple animations into one element. For example, separate animations can be created for different body parts of a character, such as arms, legs, and head. The `<animation_clip>` can be used to create a run-and-shoot-looking-right instance.

Animation clips are assets stored into `<library_animation_clips>`. It is up to the runtime to decide whether they should be used.

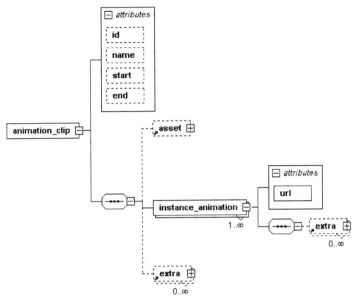

Attribute	Type	Default
id	xs:ID	
name	xs:anyURI	
start	xs:double	"0.0"
end	xs:double	

Figure 6.4. The `<animation_clip>` element.

The `id` and `name` attributes are optional and enable external referencing. Animations can have an `<asset>` element and can be extended using the `<extra>` element.

The start and end values only affect animations that use the "TIME" input semantic; the others are not affected, because they are not driven by time.

The `start` attribute is the time in seconds at the beginning of the clip; it is specified within the range of the instantiated animations. The `end` attribute specifies the end of the clip. If not specified, the value is set to the length of the longest instantiated animation.

Figure 6.5 shows the definition of an animation clip providing the output curves of three animations. In this example, all the animations start at a different time, based on their minimum value in their "TIME" source. The animation clip is specified with a start time that corresponds to the beginning of the second animation. It does not specify the end, so the end of the longest

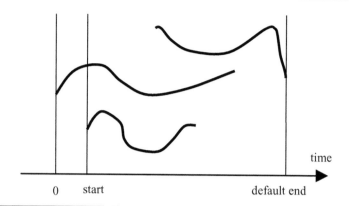

time

0   start   default end

Figure 6.5. Example animation clip with three instanced animations.

animation is used. Unless extended, the default behavior for sampling animations outside of their time range is not to animate the parameter, so it keeps its original value.

Here are some examples of an `<animation_clip>`:

```
<animation_clip id="walk" start="0" end="1.25">
  <instance_animation url="#someAnimation"/>
  <instance_animation url="#someOtherAnimation"/>
</animation_clip>

<animation_clip id="run">
  <instance_animation
    url="file:///animations.dae#someAnimation"/>
</animation_clip>
```

Please note that COLLADA does not specify the behavior when two or more instantiated animations in a clip target the same parameter.

Skinning and Morphing

COLLADA supports skinned animations.

- One skeleton can animate many meshes.
- Meshes are bound to a default pose by an arbitrary array of weights and an array of inverse bind matrices.

COLLADA also supports morphing animations.

- Multiple mesh targets and weights are defined. All meshes must have the same number of vertices.
- The blend of those meshes creates the final shape.

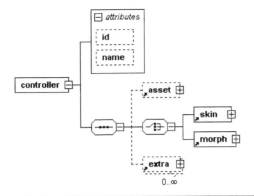

Figure 6.6. The `<controller>` element.

These two advanced animation techniques are provided in COLLADA as two types of the `<controller>` element.

Controller

The controller is an asset and has an optional id, a name, and an `<extra>` element (see Figure 6.6). The ID is used to instantiate the controller in the `<visual_scene>`. Controllers are stored in `<library_controllers>` within the COLLADA document.

Two types of controllers can be defined depending on whether the child element is a `<skin>` or a `<morph>`.

The controller is not a different type of animation as defined above; it is a technique that allows for the deformation of meshes based on animation.

Controllers are instanced in nodes at the same level of geometries, using the `<instance_controller>` element. When instantiated, controllers are equivalent to geometry; they have all the children that `<instance_geometry>` has, plus the `<skeleton>` list that is explained next in the section "Skinning."

The `<instance_controller>` has one mandatory attribute, url (xs: anyURI), which points to the `<controller>` being instantiated (see Figure 6.7).

Skinning

Skinning is a mesh deformation that is the result of the animation of a skeleton that has a skin attached to it. The resulting animated mesh is the skin itself; the skeleton is used as a tool and usually not displayed. The skeleton is described by a hierarchical set of joints (see Figure 6.8).

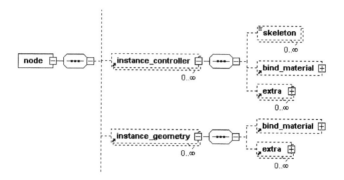

Figure 6.7. The `<instance_controller>` element is similar to the `<instance_geometry>` element.

The `<skin>` has a source parameter that is an `xs:anyURI` referencing the mesh on which the skinning deformation will be applied.

It also contains a `<source>` child element that contains all the data that is necessary to calculate the skinning. Three sources are required for skinning: an array of joints, an array of inverse bind matrices, and an array of weights. The joints are given as `sid` that will be mapped to the skeleton nodes when instantiated. An inverse bind matrix is the transformation that is applied to a vertex to express it in the joint coordinate system.

The `<bind_shape_matrix>` is the transformation that moves the skin in the skeleton coordinate system. This element is optional; if it is not specified, its default value is the identity matrix.

The `<joints>` element is used to associate an inverse bind matrix to each joint. It contains two `<input>` elements of equal length. One semantic `"INV_BIND_MATRIX"` references inverse bind matrices, and one semantic `"JOINT"` references the joints.

For each vertex, the `<vertex_weights>` element contains the list of joints that have an influence and the weight of this influence. It contains two `<input>` elements: one semantic `"JOINT"` that references an array of joints and one semantic `"WEIGHT"` that references an array of weight values. The first child is the `<vcount>` integer array, which indicates how many joints are influencing each vertex.

The second child is `<v>`, a list of indexes for each joint that gives the index of the joint and the index of its weight in the input arrays. Therefore, there are two indexes per entry in the `<v>` table. The weights should be normalized so that the sum of the weights is equal to one.

A special index of value `"-1"` can be used for each vertex. It is used when the vertex is attached to the bind-pose skeleton, prior to its animation.

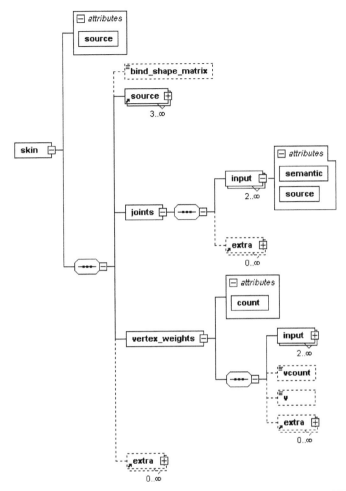

Attribute	Type	Default
source	xs:anyURI	required

Figure 6.8. The `<skin>` element.

Here is an example of an animated character. First, the controller is declared:

```
<controller id="skinCluster5">
  <skin source="#boyShape-lib">
```

The controller `<skin>` element indicates the id of the `<geometry>` that contains the skin `<mesh>`.

The joint name array is then declared. In this example, 19 independent joints are utilized.

```
<source id="Joints">
  <Name_array count="19" id="Joints-array">
    root l_hip l_knee l_ankle l_null_toe pelvis spine
    l_humerus l_ulna l_wrist r_humerus r_ulna r_wrist
    neck null_head r_hip r_knee r_ankle r_null_toe
  </Name_array>
  <technique_common>
    <accessor count="19" source="#Joints-array">
      <param type="Name"/>
    </accessor>
  </technique_common>
</source>
```

The inverse bind matrix array is then declared, followed by the array of weights.

```
<source id="Matrices">
  <float_array count="304" id="Matrices-array">
    1.0 0 0 -0.0 ... -1.0 0.95 0 0 0 1.0
  </float_array>
  <technique_common>
    <accessor count="19" stride="16"
        source="#Matrices-array">
      <param type="float4x4"/>
    </accessor>
  </technique_common>
</source>

<source id="skinCluster5-Weights">
  <float_array count="3257" id="Weights-array">
    1.000 0.078 0.9218 ... 0.015 0.984
  </float_array>
  <technique_common>
    <accessor count="3257" source="#Weights-array">
      <param type="float"/>
    </accessor>
  </technique_common>
</source>
```

The <joints> element is then used to associate the joints with their inverse bind matrices:

```
<joints>
  <input semantic="JOINT" source="#Joints"/>
  <input semantic="INV_BIND_MATRIX" source="#Matrices"/>
```

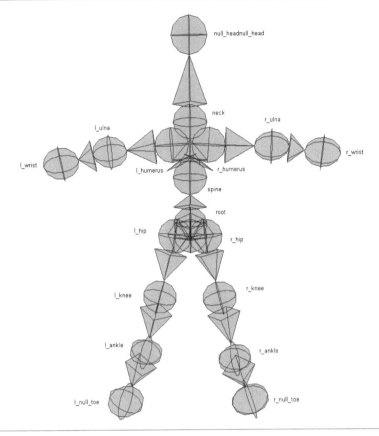

Figure 6.8. Skeleton of Boy sample.

```
</joints>
  <vertex_weights count="2619">
    <input semantic="JOINT" offset="0" source="#Joints"/>
    <input semantic="WEIGHT" offset="1" source="#Weights"/>
    <vcount>2 2 1 1 1 1 1 ... 1 1 1 2 1 1</vcount>
    <v>1 1 5 ... 9 3256 9 0 9 0</v>
  </vertex_weights>
  </skin>
</controller>
```

The instantiation of the controller is done within a <node> in the <visual_scene>.

```
<visual_scene ...
  ...
  <node id="boy" name="boy" sid="boy">
```

```
<instance_controller url="#skinCluster5">
  <skeleton>#root</skeleton>
  <bind_material>
    <technique_common>
    ...
    </technique_common>
  </bind_material>
</instance_controller>
</node>
...
```

The `<skeleton>` element is a URI that points to the root of a hierarchy where the `<joints>` sid can be found. It is possible to reference several hierarchies by adding as many `<skeleton>` elements as necessary. Using this mapping, it is possible to create different instances of a controller that can use different skeletons, which contain the same set of sid.

Morphing

The morphing controller creates a mesh by a similar, but simpler, technique. Several meshes are created to represent different poses, and the result of the morphing is a weighted combination of those different meshes.

The `<morph>` element contains two sources. One is an `<IDREF_array>` containing an array of target meshes; the other is a `<float_array>` containing an array of weights. The targets are referenced using `xs:ID` and are mapped to the `<node>` when the controller is instantiated (see Figure 6.10).

It also contains a `<targets>` child element that has two `<input>` children: the first semantic "MORPH_TARGET" indexes the targets, the second semantic "MORPH_WEIGHT" indexes the weights in the source arrays. The targets are referenced using sid and will be mapped to the `<node>` when the controller is instantiated.

The `source` attribute is an `xs:anyURI` referencing the mesh on which the morphing deformation is applied.

The `method` attribute indicates which of the two possible morphing equations will be applied.

NORMALIZED—The result of morphing is given by the formula:

$$base \times \left(1 - \sum weights\right) + \sum weights \times target$$

This means that when the weights are normalized $\sum(weights = 1)$, the equation is simplified to $\sum weights \times target$.

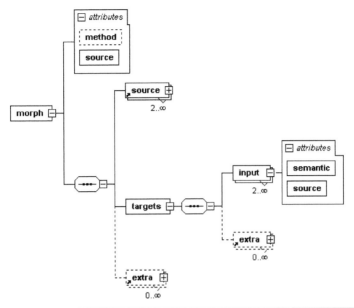

Attribute	Type	Default
method	MorphMethodType	"NORMALIZED"
source	xs:anyURI	required

Figure 6.10. The `<morph>` element.

RELATIVE—The morphing equation is not an absolute value but a modulation of the original mesh; the result is given by the formula: $base + \sum weights \times target$.

Here is an example of a `<morph>` controller.

```
<morph method="NORMALIZED" source="#base-mesh">
  <source id="morph-targets">
    <IDREF_array id="morph-targets-array" count="...">
    Target1 Target2 Target3 ...
    </IDREF_array>
    ...
  </source>
  <source id="morph-weights">
    <float_array id="morph-targets-array" count="..."/>
  </source>
  <targets>
    <input source="#morph-targets" semantic="MORPH_TARGET"/>
    <input source="#morph-weights" semantic="MORPH_WEIGHT"/>
  </targets>
</morph>
```

It is theoretically possible to combine skinning and morphing by using a morph controller with a base mesh that is a skin controller. The skin controller could be any of the targets. (This feature is not supported by the exporters at the time this book was written.) The preferred way to get a morphed and skinned character is the reverse order: skin the final morph mesh.

7 COLLADA Physics

Overview

This chapter explains COLLADA Physics technology, including analytical shapes, convex meshes, rigid bodies, and their composition into articulated rigid bodies with constrained joints. The physics model is a container for those entities with their physical parameters, ready to be instantiated into the physics scene. Finally, a top-down description is provided, as well as a discussion about the possible evolution for this technology.

Physical Simulation

The previous chapters have dealt with the visual representation of the scene, including animation. COLLADA Physics is the first addition to the schema that expresses the physical properties rather than the visualization properties. It provides an API-independent description of rigid body and jointed models.

The first real-time computers were analog machines designed to do physical simulations. These analog computers were great at solving differential equations, although they were not very accurate because of the very nature of analog circuitry. Real-time visualization came much later, with the first real-time digital computer in 1951: the Whirlwind [56]. The Whirlwind was designed to track airspace traffic and was able to draw 2D vectors on a circular video display. With the invention of Sketchpad by Ivan Sutherland in 1963, real-time visualization took a step forward with the first graphical user interface [57].

Although real-time computers were created to solve physical simulation problems, game developers have rarely used it. The main reason is that to be entertaining and tell a story, the application cannot simply set up a scene and hope the laws of physics will do the rest. Instead, to keep the entertainment quotient high, games currently use scripted animation and state-machine logic.

Although the number of objects and characters that are driven by the game is growing exponentially, the animations are becoming more complex, and the cost of creating all the possible animations and interactions is becoming prohibitive. In addition, there is an increasing demand for character-based games, with even more realistic behavior and better interaction with the environment.

Recently, physical simulation has been successfully used in the game *Half-Life® 2* [58], in which physics was used in a controlled way as part of the game design. This early success has increased the demand for correctly handling physics in the game pipeline. It represents an additional requirement on the CPU power of the new-generation game console.

Graphics capability has historically been a high priority for interactive applications, and graphics hardware accelerators have been developed to provide more power. Recently, AGEIA [59] applied the same idea to physics processing, introducing the first hardware accelerator for physics. Whether or not AGEIA's accelerator proves successful, games will continue to make increasingly advanced use of physics.

Hardware vendors generally support standards that do not handicap their hardware, because a given standard often ensures that more content will be available for their platform. At first, hardware vendors were interested in API standards. However, with increasing frequency they are now supportive of higher-level standards such as COLLADA.

AGEIA decided to preempt the lack of content issue from which all hardware accelerator companies suffer and focus on tools that will enable game developers to incorporate proper physical properties in their production pipelines. The issue for AGEIA was deciding what format to use. Since the need for AGEIA was to foster the creation of content, they decided to join the COLLADA effort and were a major contributor to the COLLADA Physics specification. Their motive is completely in sync with the other COLLADA contributing members—that is, making sure that all content is readily available for developers to create the best possible titles.

Prior to COLLADA Physics, there had been no effort to create a standard open format for physics. DCC tools' support for physics is far behind what is required by today's developers. Using DCC tools, developers had to create ad-hoc tools and exporters or rely on proprietary middleware solutions. The introduction of COLLADA Physics is having a significant impact on the integration of physics features and DCC tools and should enable more realistic content in the near future.

Before its release, all the major technology providers in the computer-game industry reviewed the COLLADA Physics specification. The purpose of this in-depth review was to make sure it could be used directly in physics engines such as ODE [61], Havok® [62], PhysX [63], Bullet [65], or proprietary solutions [64].

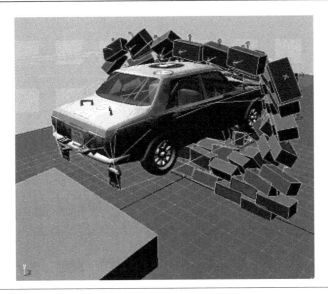

Figure 7.0. Car crash. This is a screen shot from the Nima plug-in, illustrating collisions between convex and non-convex rigid bodies. A non-convex rigid body car slides along a ground plane and ramp. In front of it, a wall of bricks is "bouncing" in expectation. The car goes through the brick wall (see also Plate VII). (Image courtesy of Feeling Software © 2005-2006)

How COLLADA Physics Works

COLLADA Physics enables the definition of independent physical simulations, currently limited to rigid body dynamics. The goal of the simulation is to calculate the position and orientation of all the rigid bodies at a given time. COLLADA Physics provides all the elements necessary for this. Ultimately, rigid bodies in the physical simulation are linked back to nodes in the visual scene so the visual representation is updated by the physical simulation.

Most of the time, the transforms of rigid bodies are directly specified in the world coordinate system, which is what the simulation calculates. This is very different from how transforms are usually handled in the visual scene, taking advantage of the hierarchical definition of scene graphs, where each object's transforms are provided relative to the object to which it is attached in the hierarchy. Some special attention is required by application writers to make sure the transforms are applied correctly.

Physics engines do not require the data to be specified in any particular unit system. Like any mathematical description of a physics system, the units of the result will be the same as the units used for the input. For example, if length is described using kilometers and the time in hours, the speed will be in kilometers per hour.

The unit of length of COLLADA 3D data is defined (the default is meters, but it can be changed for each document or for each `<asset>`), and the unit of time for animations is the second. It is recommended that the same units be used in the physics and rendering sections for the collision shapes to match with visible objects, to match regular and physically based animations, and to enable the merging of two different COLLADA Physics documents. In addition, it is necessary to specify in which unit the data is expressed to merge COLLADA Physics files from various sources. COLLADA 1.4.0 only allows for specifying the length unit, so it is recommended that the `<asset>` element be used to add information for other units until future versions support the inclusion of such information in the `<unit>` element.

Collision Detection

Although realistic physical simulation is not required by all games, a subset of physics is used by most: the detection of collision between moving objects. The need for fast and stable collision detection created the business opportunity for physics middleware companies.

Collision detection algorithms perform much faster with simple analytic convex shapes than with a mesh. Therefore, the detailed triangle-based representation used for visualization is often replaced by a simplified geometry that is created as a combination of simple shapes.

Visibility algorithms that eliminate hidden objects as early as possible can also take advantage of simplified shapes. Commonly, scene-graph representations contain a bounding-box or bounding-sphere that is used to determine quickly if an object, or a collection of objects, is intersecting with the view frustum. COLLADA Physics shapes can also be used for that purpose.

A common problem with collision detection is that object speed is too fast compared to object size. For instance, a bullet, replaced by a sphere for the collision, can go through a wall undetected. To solve this problem, physics engines are often run at a higher frequency than graphics engines that only need to create a new result at the same frequency as the display system [66].

Raising the sampling rate high enough to detect the impact of a bullet on a thin wall would be prohibitive. A possible solution could be to change the bounding volume in real time, including all the locations where the object will be between two samples. Therefore, the sphere used in the previous example is transformed into a capsule, which will successfully detect collision with the wall (see Figure 7.1).

| Collision undetected | Time capsule |

Figure 7.1. Time capsule.

The bounding shape can be complex for objects when their motion cannot be approximated by a simple translation. Fortunately, current physics engine developers are implementing continuous collision detection systems [67] that calculate, either algebraically [60] or iteratively, the collision of two objects in motion. This calculation can be very expensive, but there are many methods to accelerate the detection. One method widely used is to maintain a distance graph between the closest points of objects. The first calculation is to compare the traveled distance with the previously stored distance, so that no further calculation is needed to detect objects that are too far apart. If needed, the collision computation is done with the bounding volume first. If the result shows that a collision is possible, more calculation is done with the exact mesh.

In short, physics engines are quite sophisticated and optimized. Therefore, it is often adequate to use the geometry mesh rather than an analytical approximation. Note that the collision done by the physics engines work better and faster when limiting the number of concave objects.

Analytical Shapes

Spheres, boxes, planes, cylinders, tapered cylinders, capsules, and tapered capsules are defined as simple shapes in COLLADA. It is possible to extend any shape using the optional <extra> element.

Shapes are defined in the COLLADA default "Y_UP" (see <asset>, page 68) coordinate system. All the shapes are subject to the transforms, like any other geometry. Therefore, it is possible to position and rotate any shape as necessary. It is important to note that many collision algorithms are optimized for the special case of axis-aligned shapes, such as boxes. Therefore, a rotated box will perform slower in most cases or will be transformed in a larger bounding volume.

COLLADA Physics defines a large set of shapes, listed below, from the simplest to the more complex. Most COLLADA Physics implementations support the sphere, box, convex mesh, symmetric capsule, and plane. At the moment, very few recognize all of the other more complex shapes. An appli-

```
<sphere>
  <radius> 1.0 </radius>
</sphere>
```

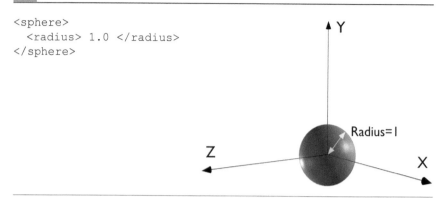

Figure 7.2. <sphere> element.

cation is free to approximate shapes that its physics engine does not support by simpler sets of shapes or meshes containing the original shape.

<sphere>

A centered sphere whose size is given by its <radius> (see Figure 7.2).

<box>

The <box> element is an axis-aligned, centered box primitive, defined by <half_extents>, a vector of three values representing the size of the box on each axis (see Figure 7.3).

This convention is consistent with using the radius for the sphere, but it is necessary to pay attention since most physics engines APIs use the total size of the box, rather than its half size.

```
<box>
  <half_extents>
  3.0 1.0 2.0
  </half_extents>
</box>
```

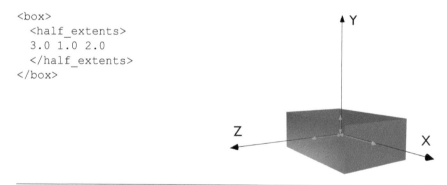

Figure 7.3. The <box> element.

```
<plane>
  <equation>
  0 0.707 0.707 2.0
  </equation>
</plane>
```

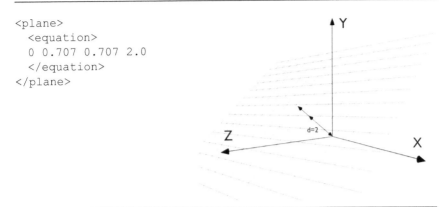

Figure 7.4. The `<plane>` element.

`<plane>`

An infinite plane defined by its equation $a \cdot x + b \cdot y + c \cdot z + d = 0$, meaning a point (x, y, z) is on the plane if the equation is true (see Figure 7.4).

The vector $\overrightarrow{(a, b, c)}$ is perpendicular to the plane and should be normalized so that $\sqrt{a^2 + b^2 + c^2} = 1$. The vector is therefore the normal of the plane, and d is the distance from the origin to the plane.

The plane separates the space in two half-spaces; the positive and the negative. The positive half-space is defined by $a \cdot x + b \cdot y + c \cdot z + d > 0$ and the negative half-space by $a \cdot x + b \cdot y + c \cdot z + d < 0$.

`<cylinder>`

The cylinder in Figure 7.5 has an elliptical section centered about the Y-axis. The elliptical section is defined by two numbers: the radius along the X-axis and the radius on the Z-axis.

```
<cylinder>
  <height> 4.0 </height>
  <radius> 2.0 1.0 </radius>
</cylinder>
```

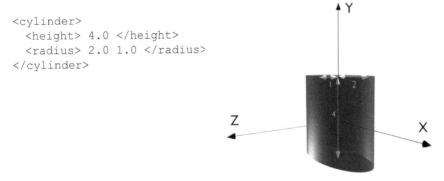

Figure 7.5. The `<cylinder>` element.

```
<tapered_cylinder>
  <height> 4.0 </height>
  <radius1> 2.0 1.0 </radius1>
  <radius2> 4.0 2.0 </radius2>
</tapered_cylinder>
```

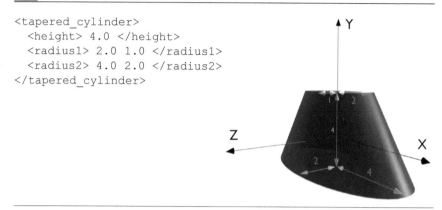

Figure 7.6. The `<tapered_cylinder>` element.

`<tapered_cylinder>`

The tapered cylinder has four radii: two for the top ellipse and two for the bottom one, enabling them to have independent dimensions. It can also be referred to as a truncated cone (see Figure 7.6).

`<capsule>`

A capsule is a cylinder with an elliptical section, centered around the *Y*-axis, capped by hemispheres at both ends (see Figure 7.7).

`<tapered_capsule>`

A tapered capsule is a capsule that has four radii: two radii for the top ellipse and two radii for the bottom ellipse, enabling them to have independent dimensions (see Figure 7.8).

```
<capsule>
  <height> 2.0 </height>
  <radius> 2.0 1.0 </radius>
</capsule>
```

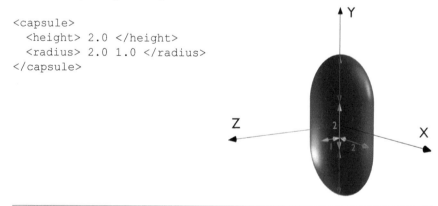

Figure 7.7. The `<capsule>` element.

```
<tapered_capsule>
  <height> 2.0 </height>
  <radius1> 1.0 2.0 </radius1>
  <radius2> 2.0 1.0 </radius2>
<tapered_capsule>
```

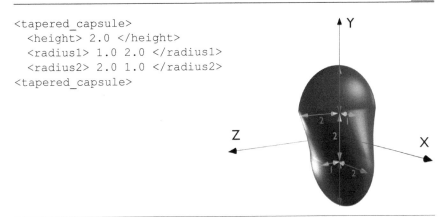

Figure 7.8. The `<tapered_capsule>` element.

`<convex_mesh>`

If none of the analytic shapes defined in COLLADA Physics can be used to approximate enough of a given geometry, it is possible to use the mesh of the `<geometry>`. Since collision detection works much faster or sometimes only with convex shapes, a special type of mesh has been added: `<convex_mesh>` (see Figure 7.9).

A `<convex_mesh>` element is almost identical to the `<mesh>` element already defined (see page 68), except it may simply point to any `<mesh>` element using the `convex_hull_of` attribute. If that is the case, this means that the physics engine has to compute the convex hull from the referenced geometry.

A `<convex_mesh>` can also be specified only by its vertices, from which the convex hull must be computed. Otherwise, if the convex mesh has geometry, it already contains the complete mesh information to be used by the physics engine directly.

Unlike all the other analytical shapes that are not designed to be visible, the `convex_mesh` can be used for display. In other words, the same `<convex_mesh>` description can be used for both display and physics if the object is already convex. Therefore, the `<convex_mesh>` is a child of `<geometry>` (see Figure 7.10).

`<shape>`

The `<shape>` element is a container for the following child elements (see Figure 7.11):

- one of the analytical shapes or mesh(es) elements;

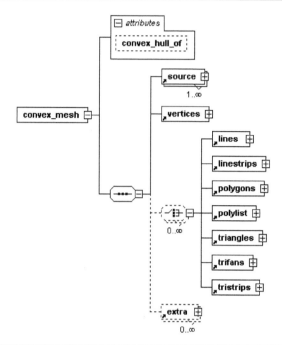

Attribute	Type	Default
convex_hull_of	xs:anyURI	

Figure 7.9. The <convex_mesh> element.

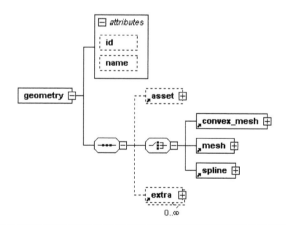

Figure 7.10. The <geometry> element.

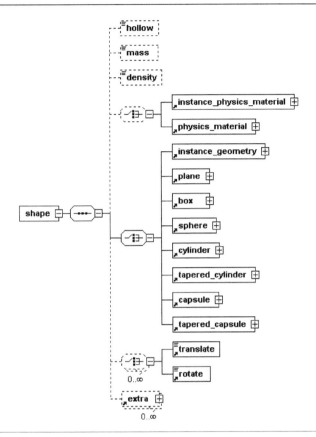

Figure 7.11. The `<shape>` element.

- an optional transformation built with `<translate>` and `<rotate>` elements (to move the shape around the object it is bounding, in its local coordinate system);

- additional physical properties contained in `<extra>` elements.

The mass information can be provided using the three optional child elements:

- `<mass>`—This is the mass of the shape, in kilograms if the length is in meters;

- `<density>`—Density can be provided instead of the mass (*mass* = *density* × *volume*). If the mass is defined, the density will be ignored. If neither the mass nor the density are specified, the default value for density is 1 (pure water at 4°C), and the mass is calculated from the volume of the shape.

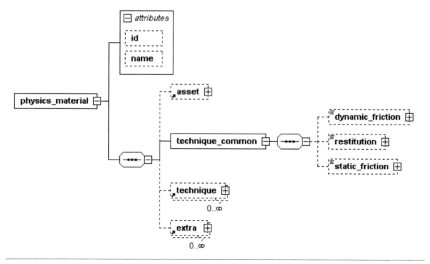

Figure 7.12. The `<physics_material>` element.

- `<hollow>`—If set to TRUE, the shape is a shell; therefore, the mass is distributed on the surface.

Meshes, convex or regular, cannot be directly embedded in the `<shape>` but need to be instantiated using the `url` parameter inside the `<instance_geometry>` element.

Optional physical properties can be embedded directly in the `<shape>` using `<physics_material>` (see Figure 7.12) or can be instantiated from the `<library_physics_materials>`, using `<instance_physics_material>`.

COLLADA defines `<physics_material>` with three parameters:

- `<restitution>`—Default value 0. This coefficient is the proportion of the kinetic energy preserved in an impact. It can also be called *bounciness* or *elasticity* by physics engines. In general, a rigid body absorbs energy when bouncing off a collision, so this coefficient is usually between 0 (all energy absorbed) and 1 (no energy loss). A coefficient larger than 1 can be used for objects that have their own energy source and overreact to collisions.

- `<static_friction>`—Default value 0. Static friction (informally known as *stiction*) occurs when objects are not moving relative to each other. The initial force to get an object moving is often dominated by static friction. The coefficient is the ratio between the force that keeps the contact and the force that must be applied to make it move. Static friction depends on the size of the contact surface.

- `<dynamic_friction>`—Default value 0. Dynamic friction (also known as *kinetic friction*) occurs when objects are moving relative to each other and rub together. Dynamic friction is usually less than static friction. As opposed to static friction, dynamic friction does not depend on the size of the contact surface.

Each physics engine can add its own technique, with its own parameters in the `<technique>` element. For even more flexibility, the `<extra>` element can be used to add additional parameters to the common technique. Physics materials have the `<asset>` element so they can be managed correctly as individual assets, since they have a `name` and `id` attribute to be referenced.

Rigid Body

In physics, a rigid body is a solid that does not deform, regardless of the external forces exerted on it. The distance between any two given points of a rigid body remains constant. Rigid body volume is also a constant.

The `sid` is a required attribute. It must be unique among its sibling elements. It is used to associate each rigid body with a visual `<node>` when a `<physics_model>` is instantiated. The `name` is an optional text string containing the name of the `<rigid_body>` element.

COLLADA defines a `<rigid_body>` as a collection of `<shape>` elements that creates a nondeformable body (see Figure 7.13). By definition, each part of an articulated object must be represented with several `<rigid_body>` elements. Objects that are composed of parts that have different physical properties must have a separate `<shape>` for each property. A hammer is the example given in the COLLADA specification. It is a rigid body composed of two shapes: a metal head and a wooden handle. The transform element inside the `<shape>` is used to move the analytical volumes at the right place to compose the rigid body.

Figure 7.14 is an example of a rigid body composed of two metallic spheres and a wooden box that could be used to represent a weight.

```
<rigid_body sid="complexRigidBody-RB">
  <technique_common>
    <mass>5</mass>
    <shape>
      <instance_physics_material url="#metal_phx"/>
      <sphere>
        <radius>1.</radius>
      </sphere>
      <translate sid="translate">3.5 0 1.8</translate>
    </shape>
```

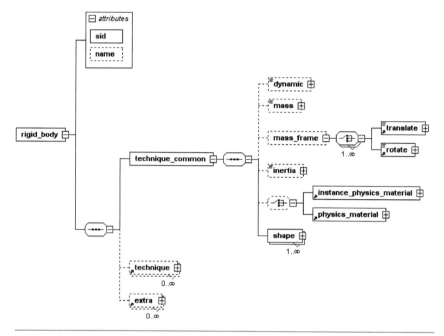

Figure 7.13. The `<rigid_body>` element.

```
<shape>
  <instance_physics_material url="#wood_phx"/>
  <box>
    <half_extents>0.5 0.5 1 </half_extents>
  </box>
  <translate sid="translate">3.5 0 0 </translate>
</shape>
<shape>
  <instance_physics_material url="#metal_phx"/>
  <sphere>
    <radius>1.000000</radius>
  </sphere>
  <translate sid="translate">3.5 0 -1.8</translate>
</shape>
</technique_common>
</rigid_body>
```

The `<rigid_body>` contains several optional physical properties:

- `<mass>`—COLLADA defines the volume and mass of a rigid body as the sum of the volumes and masses of the shapes included. This is true, as a measure of simplification, even if the shapes intersect. If all the shapes have a mass associated with them and add up correctly, there is no need to

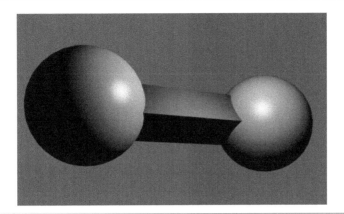

Figure 7.14. Example of a rigid body.

specify a mass at the rigid body level. Otherwise, it is possible to override this calculation and directly provide the mass of the rigid body using this element. In that case, the mass of the shapes will be scaled so that their sum is equal to the rigid body mass.

- `<dynamic>`—Default is "TRUE". If this flag is set to "FALSE", the object cannot be moved, regardless of the forces applied to it. In other words, the object is static. It is necessary to use this flag for the ground and other static objects in the scene.

- `<mass_frame>`—By default, the center of mass is at the local origin, and the mass reference frame axes are the local axes. This alignment is important to reduce the inertia matrix to a diagonal matrix (all values are 0 except on the diagonal).

- `<inertia>`—This is a vector of three floats composing the moments of inertia in the mass reference frame.

Articulated Rigid Bodies

The `<rigid_constraint>` element is used to connect several rigid bodies into articulated objects, using constrained joints (see Figure 7.15).

Articulated rigid bodies can define complex objects, such as rag dolls. Operations, such as inverse kinematics, can be applied at runtime by the physics engine.

COLLADA supports constraints that link two rigid bodies or a rigid body and a coordinate frame in the `<scene>` hierarchy.

Most physics engines implement a set of joints, such as pivot, hinge, and slider. Instead of defining a large combination of constrained `<joints>` ele-

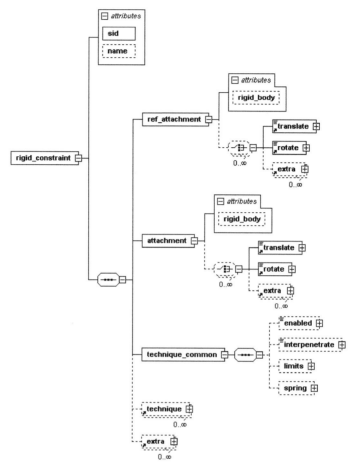

Attribute	Type	Default
sid	xs:NCName	required
name	xs:NCName	

Figure 7.15. The `<rigid_constraint>` element.

ments, COLLADA provides only one in its common technique: the general six degrees of freedom (DOF). All other joints can be created as a specialization. It is possible to use the `<technique>` and `<extra>` elements to extend the joints.

To define a constrained joint, two pieces of information are necessary:

- the attachment between two rigid bodies;
- the DOF that are authorized.

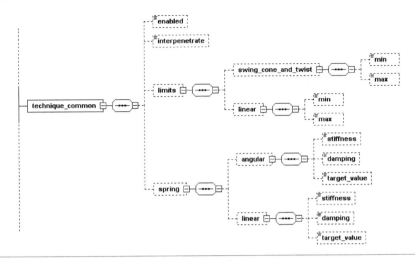

Figure 7.16. The <technique_common> element.

Attachment

The reference attachment <ref_attachment> and the second attachment <attachment> both have a rigid_body parameter that is used to link to a rigid body within the same <physics_model> (which is defined below).

The reference attachment can also be a link to a frame of reference in the <scene> instead of the rigid body. In this case, the first attachment is static. The attachments are defined relative to the rigid body's local space by a transformation using the usual <translate> and <rotate> elements.

Constraint

A DOF specifies the possible movement along a given axis of translation or axis of rotation. For example:

- a hinge has one degree of freedom, a *rotation*;
- a slider joint has one degree of freedom, a *translation*.

DOF and limits are specified by the very flexible set of elements in the common technique (see Figure 7.16).

- <enabled>—Default is "TRUE". This optional flag can be used to disable the constrained join. If set to "FALSE", the two attachments are simply disconnected.
- <interpenetrate>—Default is "TRUE". This optional flag indicates if the physics engine should consider the interpretation of the rigid bodies as an additional constraint on the joint.

- `<limits>`—The `<limits>` element provides a flexible way to specify the constraint limit, expressed in the reference attachment coordinate system. It may contain one or both of the following elements:

  ○ `<linear>`—This element describes translation limits along each axis. `<min>` and `<max>` are vectors of three floats indicating the limits on each axis.

  ○ `<swing_cone_and_twist>`—This element describes rotation limits along each axis. `<min>` and `<max>` are vectors of three floats indicating the limits. The first two floats describe a "swing cone," and the third describes the "twist angle" range. Values of `"INF"` and `"-INF"` indicate that there is no limit along that axis.

- `<spring>`—By default, the constraints are infinitely rigid. The rigid body can move freely, without effort, until the constraint is reached, and all movement is abruptly stopped. The `<spring>` element enables more softness in the constraints and provides parameters stored in three float vectors to indicate the value along each axis.

  ○ The `<target_value>` is the spring rest position.

  ○ The `<stiffness>` factor is used to compute a force proportional to the distance from the `<target_value>`, so that the spring will want to bring itself back to its rest position.

  ○ The `<damping>` factor is used to create a resistance to any movement. It is used to reduce the amplitude of oscillations.

`<limits>`, `<linear>`, and `<angular>` springs can be used simultaneously on the different DOF of the same constrained joint. Currently, COLLADA Physics does not allow these combinations on the same axis, but this may be added in future releases of COLLADA because some game engines and tools support it.

The following example illustrates a linear slider constraint. The *Flap* on the *Floppy* can translate on the *X*-axis from its position to a maximum of 2.5 units.

```
<rigid_constraint sid="SliderJoint">
  <ref_attachment rigid_body="rigidFloppy">
    <translate sid="translate"> 0 0 300 </translate>
  </ref_attachment>
  <attachment rigid_body="rigidFlap">
    <translate sid="translate"> 1 0 300 </translate>
  </attachment>
  <technique_common>
    <interpenetrate>true</interpenetrate>
    <limits>
      <linear>
        <min> 0 0 0 </min>
```

```
        <max> 2.5 0 0 </min>
      </linear>
    </limits>
  </technique_common>
</rigid_constraint>
```

The next example illustrates a point-to-point constraint, without angle limitations, indicated by INF and -INF.

```
<rigid_constraint sid="BallJoint">
  <ref_attachment rigid_body="Sphere1">
    <translate sid="translate"> 0 -7 0 </translate>
  </ref_attachment>
  <attachment rigid_body="Sphere2">
    <translate sid="translate"> 0.5 -3 -6 </translate>
  </attachment>
  <technique_common>
    <limits>
      <swing_cone_and_twist>
        <min> -INF -INF -INF </min>
        <max> INF INF INF </max>
      </swing_cone_and_twist>
    </limits>
  </technique_common>
</rigid_constraint>
```

Force Fields

The <force_field> element is a container for the external forces to be applied to the physics simulation (see Figure 7.17). In this first release of COLLADA Physics, no common technique has been defined. The <force_field> element is defined with the <technique> element, so it is possible to add any valid XML into this element and include this extension in the profile parameter.

Force fields are stored in the <library_force_fields> in the COLLADA document. Gravity is considered a special-case representation of a force field. It is defined in the common technique of the <physics_ scene> element as a global parameter for the physical scene (see "Physics Scenes" in this chapter.)

Physics Model

The <physics_model> element is the container node for rigid bodies and rigid constraints elements (see Figure 7.18). It allows for building complex combinations of rigid bodies and constraints that can then be instantiated multiple

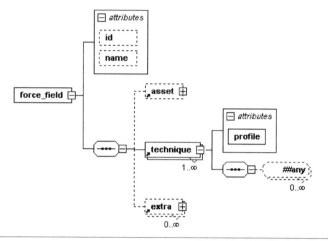

Figure 7.17. The `<force_field>` element.

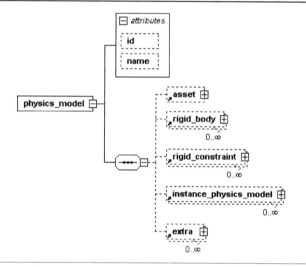

Figure 7.18. The `<physics_model>` element.

times. Physics models are stored in the `<library_physics_model>` in the COLLADA document.

A regular physics model will contain one or more rigid bodies, with their optional constraint joints. Each child element defined inside a physics model has a `sid`. The `sid` is used to access and override components of a physics model at the point of instantiation or to be targeted by an animation.

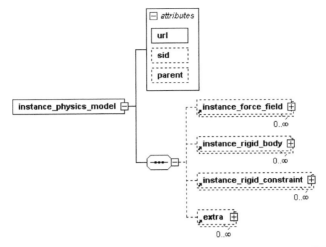

Attribute	Type	Default
url	xs:anyURI	required
sid	xs:NCName	
parent	xs:NCName	

Figure 7.19. The `<instance_physics_model>` element.

The `id` and `name` attributes and `<asset>` elements are the usual information to reference and manage the physics model's assets. In addition, `<physics_model>` makes it possible to create a more complex hierarchical combination of physics models, using the `<instance_physics_model>` element that will instantiate another predefined physics model (see Figure 7.19).

The `<instance_physics_model>` element has three attributes: `url`, `sid`, and `parent`.

The `url` is the mandatory link to the `<physics_model>` element to be instantiated. The `sid` is optional. The `parent` is a reference to a `<node>` in the `<visual_scene>`, using its `id`. This allows a physics model to be instantiated under a specific transform node, which will dictate its initial position and orientation and can be targeted by an animation controller, allowing a combination of key-frame animation with physical simulation.

Physics Scenes

The `<physics_scene>` element is where all the parts come together through instantiation (see Figure 7.20); it is the sibling of the `<visual_scene>`.

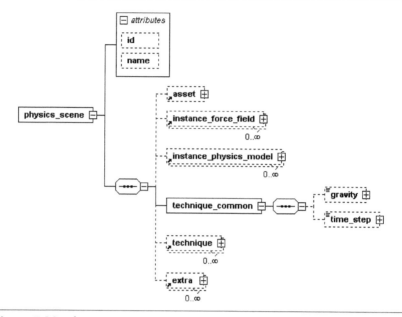

Figure 7.20. The `<physics_scene>` element.

Several physical simulations can run independently of each other and are all represented by different `<physics_scene>` elements, so no interaction exists between the two different simulations. Physics scenes are stored in the `<library_physics_scenes>` in the COLLADA document.

It is also possible to create several levels of complexity of simulation for the same group of rigid bodies, so that the application can decide which level of simulation detail to use at a given time to optimize for performance.

The physics scene contains one or more instances of physics models and may contain one or more force fields. The common technique defines two additional optional parameters to be used in the real-time simulation:

- `<gravity>`. The Earth's gravity is often used. In the default "Y_UP" orientation, it is best approximated by $(0, -9.8, 0)$ in N/kg (or m/s^2).

- `<time_step>`—The time step, in seconds, is the interval at which the simulation needs to be calculated. A small time step will give more accuracy at the cost of more computation. A time step too large will result in incorrect results and unstable simulations. It is important to find the right time step for a given physics scene.

When instantiating a physics model inside a physics scene, the list of rigid bodies included in the simulation must be instantiated, as well as the list of constrained

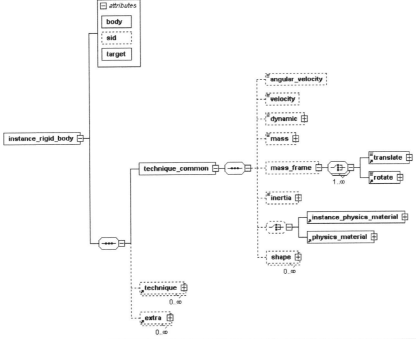

Attribute	Type	Default
body	xs:NCName	required
sid	xs:NCName	
target	xs:anyURI	required

Figure 7.21. `<instance_rigid_body>` element.

joints using the child elements of the `<instance_physics_model>` element.

The rigid bodies that are included in the physics model should each be linked with the associated visual transform node they will influence. This link is provided as a parameter to the `<instance_rigid_body>` element (see Figure 7.21).

Two parameters are required: `body` indicates which rigid body is to be instantiated, and `target` indicates which `<node>` in the `<visual_scene>` is influenced by this instance.

The `sid` is optional. It specifies an identifier that is unique within the parent element. This allows for targeting elements of the instance for animation.

In addition, the following optional child elements allow for specialization of the rigid body instance:

- `<angular_velocity>`—Default is (0, 0, 0). Specifies the initial angular velocity of the rigid body instance around each axis as a Euler rotation;

- `<velocity>`—Default is (0, 0, 0). Specifies the initial linear velocity of the rigid body instance;

- `<dynamic>`—Indicates if the rigid body is dynamic—overrides the value in the instanced rigid body;

- `<mass>`—Mass of the rigid body—overrides the value in the instanced rigid body;

- `<mass_frame>`—Frame of reference for the moments of inertia—overrides the value in the instanced rigid body.

Top-Down Description

This chapter has described COLLADA Physics from its basic shape elements to the physics scene. This section gives a different perspective to help explain the relationship among the elements (see Figure 7.23).

The COLLADA document contains one `<scene>` element that instantiates one `<visual_scene>` and one or more `<physics_scene>`.

The instantiated `<physics_scene>` can be found inside the `<library_physics_scenes>`. It instantiates a `<force_field>`, a `<physics_model>`, one or several `<rigid_body>`, and all the `<rigid_constraint>` that need to be applied. A `target` parameter is given with each `<rigid_body>` instantiated that indicates which `<node>` of the `<visual_scene>` has its transform linked to the `<rigid_body>`.

The referenced `<force_field>` can be found inside the `<library_force_fields>`.

The referenced `<physics_model>` can be found inside the `<library_physics_model>`. It includes the `<rigid_body>` instanced in the `<physics_scene>` as well as the instanced `<rigid_constraint>`.

The `<rigid_body>` contains a `<shape>` and an instance to a `<physics_material>`. The `<shape>` contains an analytical shape and its transformation (`<translate>` and/or `<rotate>`), or it can contain a `<convex_mesh>` referencing a `<geometry>`, found in the `<library_geometries>`.

The instantiated `<physics_material>` can be found in the `<library_physics_material>`.

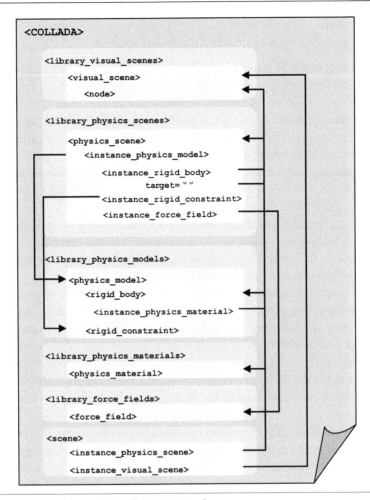

Figure 7.22. Relationship of COLLADA elements.

Future Evolution

COLLADA 1.4 introduced physics properties into a standard format for the first time. It is currently limited to rigid-body physics. Future evolution will depend on user feedback to the contributors and may include:

- definition of a common technique for force fields;
- deformable bodies, also known as *soft bodies*, with or without constant volume constraint;

- fluids and particle dynamics;
- cloth simulations, with or without ripping capability.

Although very few games currently use such advanced features, some technology demonstrations have already shown the capability of the latest game consoles to manage such content (see PS3 Duck Demo, Plate XV).

The main problem is that DCC tools are far behind in real-time physics asset creation, and they are currently the bottleneck, even with the current limitations of COLLADA Physics.

The main reason for this is that it is difficult to add real-time physics information to DCC tools that are designed principally for rendering attributes. It is also quite difficult to create the necessary exporting tool. This technology is a competitive advantage for the companies that master it; therefore, the short-term market considerations are not in favor of creating a standard. Nevertheless, this technology is evolving quite rapidly in regards to developments such as Nima [68].

Game developers are already taking advantage of physics engines to calculate some of the animations in real time. This is less work for artists who do not have to create each possible key-frame animation. In theory, it also produces a more entertaining result because the animation will never be the same. However, it is actually a challenge to find the right technology for controlling the result. After the first few games using rag dolls, the reaction is not as positive now, because all the games using this technology have similar animations.

Therefore, there is a big challenge ahead in creating technology that will give control to the game designer over what the physics can do. Harnessing the laws of physics is necessary for creating good entertaining content [69].

Another evolution in game physics acceleration is that both GPU (graphics processor unit) and PPU (physics processor unit) vendors are competing in almost the same market segment: the add-on card for the PC market. GPU vendors want to show that it is possible to accelerate physics simulation on the GPU, while PPU vendors need to prove that players prefer games that take advantage of their hardware, therefore generating a demand for the new hardware.

8 COLLADA Content Pipeline

Overview

This chapter describes how to build a content creation pipeline using COLLADA and introduces several utility libraries that are being developed for this purpose. One of these is the COLLADA DOM [78], a library that provides a document object model (DOM) and application programming interface (API) for creating COLLADA processing tools. These tools are called *conditioners* because each one transforms the content for a specific reason as a single step in the overall pipeline. A simple pipeline configuration tool called the *refinery* provides a graphical user interface (GUI) that enables the user to assemble and configure content pipelines easily. The chapter ends with a discussion of possible evolutions of COLLADA for content pipeline and build process improvements.

Content Creation Pipelines

The process by which all the different tools are organized and configured to create the final content from all the assets is the content creation pipeline. In fact, several content creation pipelines are often involved at different stages of the production. Usually, there are at least two pipelines.

- The full production pipeline (full pipeline). This is the process by which all the data is optimized and packaged into the final product. This pipeline is often a very long, complicated process that can take several hours.

- The fast-path (fast pipeline). This is the fastest pipeline to get the data into the game for preview purposes. This path is necessary to maximize productivity during the production phase.

Several pipelines are in use during the course of a production. Usually, a prototype application is developed first, using a fast pipeline that will evolve into the full pipeline during full production. Historically, the prototype application has been used to secure a publishing deal, but more recently, this is not enough. Now, publishers evaluate the proposed application and the content creation pipelines and tools that the developer has written in order to create the prototype application. The publisher, being aware of the spiraling cost of content creation, wants to see that the developer also understands the importance of a robust content creation pipeline and tool chain.

One of the main differences between the fast pipeline and the full pipeline is the formatting of the data. In the full pipeline, the data is optimized for loading time and size. It is often binary encoded and embedded in monolithic files that are application-specific. On the other hand, the fast pipeline retains the assets in the intermediate format that is exported from the DCC tools.

Loading the data coming out of the fast path is slower than loading the data from the full pipeline, since the full pipeline can process the data into a form that is ready to use. Also, since the data itself does not go through a lot of optimization, such as polygon reduction or level-of-detail (LOD) calculation, it is slower to display.

During the development phase, it is recommended that the application be designed to load both the data coming out of the fast pipeline and the full pipeline. The idea is to enable content creators to have most of the content running at full speed and to be able to interact quickly with some of the assets.

Some applications and platforms use XML to encode and distribute their content, so that a format directly derived from COLLADA can be used directly in the final product. This is a very special case because COLLADA has not been designed as a distribution format and lacks features such as data encryption and copy protection schemes.

The fast pipeline uses COLLADA as an intermediate format as designed. Therefore, it is necessary to enable direct import of a COLLADA document into the final application on the target hardware. One possible design approach to achieve this is to create an API that offers a consistent interface to the COLLADA document yet can be flexible in how the document is stored. This is one objective of the COLLADA DOM that is described in subsequent sections.

Content pipelines are effectively composed of many data transformation processes that must be executed in sequence. Interactive tools enable the user to monitor the processing pipeline and visualize the final result. An interactive tool created for this purpose will preferably include the same rendering engine as that used in the final application. If the tools cannot work on the target platform, a remote viewing capability can be created for this purpose instead.

Once the data has been processed and the configuration is known, it is necessary to be able to store the pipeline configuration itself. With the con-

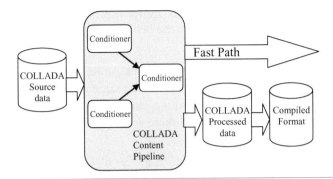

Figure 8.1. COLLADA conditioning pipeline.

figuration information available, the process can be reapplied automatically when the source data is modified. To be able to do this, all the tools in the pipeline must have a scripting interface, including the DCC tools that export the data. For this reason, the COLLADA specification mandates that the export/import implementations be called from a script.

Figure 8.1 shows a COLLADA content pipeline, composed of a collection of tools that inputs COLLADA documents or assets and outputs transformed COLLADA documents or assets. Ideally, the final conversion process of the full pipeline is one of the last steps in the overall processing pipeline. A combination of several tools can even be stored and used directly as content pipelines.

A prototype implementation of this concept, using the name *conditioner* for the pipeline tools, is presented in subsequent sections of this chapter. A further development of this methodology would enable a collection of conditioners to be created and made available, commercially or not, to developers for direct inclusion into their own content creation pipelines. An example of a tool that enables the combination of conditioners, called *refinery*, is described in a subsequent section.

COLLADA DOM

A specification can be documented in several ways. Three different ways are commonly used.

- The written specification or reference manual. A good reference manual defines the product in human language.

- The formal definition. A specification that defines the product using a formal language, often readable by machines, that is more precise than human languages.

- A reference implementation. It is always possible to answer a question about the specification by testing the behavior of the reference implementation.

These forms of specification are very useful. Although additional work, it is very useful to have all of them available at the same time. This enables cross-checking and makes it easier to find inconsistencies between any two of the three definitions. Also, by having all three definitions, it is less likely there will be gaps in the specification.

It is necessary to select one of these forms of specification as the master document, so any inconsistency can be resolved. In the case of COLLADA, the choice was made to use the formal definition, written in XML Schema language, as the master document. A second document, called the COLLADA specification, is the human readable form of the COLLADA schema. The schema document authoritatively specifies most of COLLADA. Some important information regarding the implementation policies of COLLADA that cannot be stored in the XML schema is only available in the COLLADA specification. For example, the policy on how valid implementations should extend COLLADA for their own needs using the <extra> element is best explained in the COLLADA specification.

There are many commercial and noncommercial (some open-source) tools that can load an XML schema and process it to create an implementation, or at least an interface, in a number of programming languages. While exploring this approach to rapid development, various problems were discovered with several of the leading XML packages available that prevented users from automatically generating an implementation. Those problems were reported to the respective vendors and, hopefully, have been fixed by the time this book is published.

Having several implementations of COLLADA is actually very valuable because this is one of the best ways to have a robust specification. When some parts of the specification are not defined precisely enough, there is a chance that two independent implementations will behave differently, introducing interoperability problems. Once discovered, these problems require fixes in the specification, thereby improving its quality. Several implementations have been developed using different methodologies. Some implementations were written during the design process and used as verification tools while writing the COLLADA specification. Some of these implementations were developed by DCC vendors to create their import/export plug-in.

Many early adopters of COLLADA decided to wait for the release of a reference implementation before developing support for COLLADA in their application. This stance prompted the development of the COLLADA Document Object Model (DOM) software [79]. When COLLADA 1.0 was released, developers tried to use the source code of the sample viewer application that Sony Computer Entertainment provided. Because this sample code was incomplete, it frustrated the efforts of those developers trying to implement the complete specification. It is unfortunate that most software in the game development world is created without a formal specification. Game developers consider their implementations to be the authoritative reference document. If an actual reference manual or formal specification exists, they feel that it was created later by unhappy programmers forced to write documentation. As a result, most developers in the game industry do not read the documentation. The development culture has reached a point where developers brag that they were able to complete their project without reading any documentation and by reverse engineering the reference implementation. This behavior is so ingrained in the game development culture that the industry has learned to include reverse engineering practices into their software strategy.

Although a COLLADA implementation cannot be considered to be "the specification," because a formal specification exists, it was clear from the demand that a good reference implementation for importing and exporting COLLADA documents was necessary. Sony Computer Entertainment (SCE) therefore decided to create such a reference implementation: the COLLADA DOM.

Having decided to create a reference implementation, a development approach was needed. Even though developers were demanding a reference implementation for COLLADA, the COLLADA schema document was still to be the formal definition of COLLADA. The approach chosen for COLLADA DOM development reinforces the importance of the COLLADA schema. The COLLADA DOM is a C++ API that is, in part, automatically generated from the COLLADA schema.

Code generation is a powerful programming methodology associated with computer aided software engineering (CASE) and fourth-generation programing environments. The importance of this approach as applied to COLLADA DOM development cannot be underestimated. An entirely handwritten API would represent a duplicate formal definition of COLLADA, and this redundancy would create confusion if the DOM implementation deviated from the schema definition. Developers who ignored the schema, and they do exist, in favor of the reference implementation might not create conforming software tools if there were any such deviation. Eventually, the interoperability of COLLADA tools could erode and defeat the promise of

COLLADA to make content creation easier. Additionally, more effort would be required to provide the quality assurance that a handwritten COLLADA DOM conformed to the COLLADA schema. To alleviate all these concerns, the decision was made to generate as much of the COLLADA DOM code from the schema as possible.

Starting with the XML Schema language definition of COLLADA, a C++ code generator was written in the PHP script language. The COLLADA DOM code generator is a general purpose XML to C++ source code generator that is limited to the subset of the XML Schema language actually used in the COLLADA schema. Whenever the schema document changes, a matching implementation of the COLLADA DOM is generated in minutes. The documentation for most of the COLLADA DOM is also embedded inside the schema document using the `<xs:annotation>` element. This helps to synchronize the formal definition of COLLADA with this reference implementation's programming documentation. The COLLADA DOM online reference manual is itself generated from the COLLADA schema annotations using the Doxygen [80] documentation system. As long as the schema document is maintained and correct, the reference implementation and its documentation will also be correct with a high degree of assurance.

The COLLADA DOM is an *intermediate* DOM with respect to the W3C Document Object Model standard specifications at this stage of its development. The software has been difficult to create because it can be difficult to balance the right level of features with the need to integrate it easily with any application. This software was in beta testing for several months while different developers built applications on top of it. Two primary adopters were FX Composer 2.0 from NVIDIA Corp. and the COLLADA importer for OpenSceneGraph [81] from 3Dlabs Inc. and UMEA University Sweden. The COLLADA DOM has since been released as open source and can be used freely in commercial or noncommercial applications.

Structure of the COLLADA DOM

The COLLADA DOM framework includes four basic components (see Figure 8.2).

- Object Model—This includes the COLLADA Document Object Model (DOM) created automatically from the COLLADA schema and the internal reflective object model, called the *DAE object model*.
- Runtime Database—This acts as a searchable cache for COLLADA documents. When the API is asked to load a document, it is stored in the

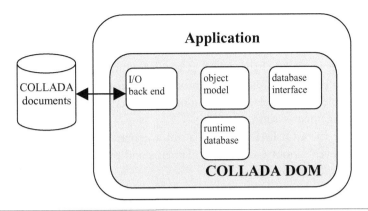

Figure 8.2. COLLADA DOM structure.

runtime database. This part is implemented using the Standard Template Library (STL) and can be replaced if needed.

- Database Interface—This allows users to interact with COLLADA documents and elements through a database query style interface.

- I/O Back End—This input/output plug-in consists of the component responsible for transferring and translating COLLADA documents to and from the runtime database.

Integration Classes

This set of classes provides the developer with integration hooks into the DAE object model in order to marshal COLLADA data directly in and out of their application's native data structures during load and save operations.

The database interface is the main interface from the application to the COLLADA DOM. Objects returned from queries can be directly accessed by the application. Alternatively, it is possible for the application to directly interface with the object models or the I/O back end if necessary.

The I/O back end is designed as a plug-in so it is possible to interface the DOM with any type of repository. The DOM currently includes a libxml2-based plug-in that supports http- and file-based document retrieval. The libxml2 library is an open source XML parser available from the World Wide Web (xmlsoft.org) that also provides document validation against the COLLADA schema.

The intent is to be able to replace this I/O module with others, depending on where the COLLADA DOM is to be used. For example, if the COLLADA DOM is to be used directly in a game application, as opposed to in the tool chain, it may be desirable to replace the XML formatting with a platform-specific binary format that is integrated with the game engine.

Ultimately, the goal for COLLADA is to be a communication layer between applications in a tool chain as well as a standard intermediate file format. In this case, a production data server model may be more appropriate, and the I/O module can be replaced with an interface to a proper database system or asset management system.

Because the COLLADA DOM is not a generic XML DOM interface, it can be "clever" about COLLADA elements and provide additional processing such as the following:

- automatic resolution of URIs on loading a COLLADA instance document—a quite complex task to implement a URI resolver correctly;
- aggressive conversion of text strings within the COLLADA instance document into their appropriate binary forms, such as IEEE floating-point numbers;
- data access functions specifically designed to integrate with the `<asset>` element to enable an incremental database update and better integration with asset management systems.

While designing COLLADA 1.4.0, it became obvious that there are advantages to using a strongly typed schema in which elements in the schema are fully described types with associated constraints. This enables generic XML validation tools to do a better test for conformity. It allows the COLLADA DOM code generator to produce code that directly serializes and marshals binary values, rather than its text encoding. This also makes it much easier to replace the I/O module with direct binary interfaces or to interface with various connection APIs.

Using the COLLADA DOM 1.4.0

Following are instructions for using COLLADA DOM 1.4.0. First, open an XML document into a fresh database.

```
DAE* input = new DAE;
errval = input->load("input_url_name.xml");
```

After loading, one can query for particular elements that may exist in the instance document using the database query interface. For example, query for the number of `<image>` elements that also have the name "mossyRock":

```
unsigned int imageCount = input->getDatabase()->
  getElementCount("mossyRock", "image", 0);
```

Next, loop over all of those <image> elements in the database, processing them.

```
daeElement* mossyRockImage;
for (unsigned int i=0; i<imageCount; ++i) {
  error = input->getDatabase()->getElement(
  (daeElement**)&mossyRockImage, i,
  "mossyRock","image",0);
// process mossyRockImage
}
```

After processing the elements, write the altered database to a new document.

```
error = input->save(output_url.c_str());
```

Database Interface

The COLLADA database interface is the main interface to the application. It is implemented as a C++ class, called daeInterface, that provides functions for loading, storing, translating, and querying COLLADA documents and elements.

The DAE class provides a simple, general-purpose interface to the I/O back end and runtime database. This class serves as a wrapper for the entire COLLADA DOM implementation, ensuring a consistent interface regardless of extensions to, or replacements for, the various underlying components.

Creating a new DAE interface object automatically creates and initializes default versions of the I/O back end and runtime database.

The following is a subset of the daeInterface class interface.

```
virtual daeInt load(daeString name);
virtual daeInt saveAs(daeString fileName,
                    daeString collectionName);
virtual daeDatabase* getDatabase();
virtual daeInt unload(daeString name);
```

The COLLADA DOM implementation introduces the daeCollection class that is a representation of an instance document. From the user's perspective, the collection is approximately equivalent to a COLLADA document, even though the collection in the 1.4.0 release does not support several W3C DOM core level 1 features such as comments, CDATA sections, and processing instructions.

A collection represents a set of COLLADA elements that are grouped based on a URL. The COLLADA DOM is designed to allow the runtime database to contain any number of collections, although this feature is not fully functional in version 1.4.0.

The COLLADA DOM can be used to create a new document. To do this, create a new database and add a collection to it. Each collection requires a document root element of the type domCOLLADA. The method insertCollection() takes care of creating the collection. It also creates and inserts a domCOLLADA object as the root of the collection.

The following example shows the steps required to create a DOM from the beginning and save it to an XML instance document.

```
// create a DAE object:
DAE* daeObject = new DAE;
// Create a new database
daeObject->setDatabase(0);
// Define the daeCollection variable
daeCollection* collection;
// insert a new collection into the database.
int res = daeObject->getDatabase()->insertCollection(
    "file:///myDoc.xml",&collection);
if (collection) {
  // getDomRoot returns the domCOLLADA object
  domCOLLADA* domRoot =
    (domCollada*)collection->getDomRoot();
  if (domRoot) {
    // Then add subsequent objects underneath
    // domRoot using createAndPlace().
    // For example add a library of images
    domLibrary* newLib =
      (domLibrary*)domRoot->createAndPlace(
        COLLADA_ELEMENT_LIBRARY_IMAGES);
...
    //Write out the new collection, no arguments are
    //required because save defaults to saving
    //collection 0 (the only one loaded) and
    //saves it to the URI already specified
    int res = daeObject->save();
  }
}
```

All other objects are added underneath the root node, by using the createAndPlace() or placeElement() methods. The method createAndPlace() creates a new element as a child of the current element and places the new element in the appropriate field of its parent element, based on the className parameter provided in the method invocation.

The method `daeElement::removeChildElement()` or the static method `daeElement::removeFromParent()` can be used to remove a child element from its parent element. The following example demonstrates how to add a new light element to an existing library of lights.

```
daeDatabase* db = daeObject->getDatabase();
// Find the light library, in this example,
// it has the name "lightLib".
error = db->getElement((daeElement**)&myLib, 0, "lightLib",
    COLLADA_ELEMENT_LIBRARY_LIGHTS);
// Add a new light to the library
domLight* newLight =
  (domLight*)myLib->createAndPlace(
    COLLADA_ELEMENT_LIGHT);
// Now you can add data to the new light.
```

The following example demonstrates how to remove a light element from a library of lights.

```
DaeDatabase* db = daeObject->getDatabase();
// Find the light we want to remove,
// the one with name "frontLight"
error = db->getElement((daeElement**)&myLight, 0,
  "frontLight", COLLADA_ELEMENT_LIGHT);
// Get its parent
daeElement* lightParent = myLight->getXMLParentElement();
// Remove the light
daeBool removed = lightParent->removeChildElement(myLight);
```

Unfortunately, the COLLADA DOM was first designed and implemented as a reference importer/exporter. All the internal bookkeeping that is necessary to enable manual modifications of the DOM were not included in the first releases of this API. Since then, several tools have used the COLLADA DOM and required the ability to edit, copy, and otherwise manipulate elements. Therefore, much effort has been devoted to enabling these features and achieve conformance with the W3C DOM level 1 specifications [80]. The patch 3 release of the DOM has all of these improvements built in and is already used successfully by applications such as FX Composer 2.0.

Querying the Database

Two methods are provided by the `daeInterface` class to query the database and get information about specific elements: `getElementCount()` and `getElement()`.

`getElementCount()` returns the number of elements of a particular type. For example, the following code asks how many `<image>` elements are in the database:

```
imageCount =
  daeObject->getDatabase()->getElementCount(0,
      COLLADA_ELEMENT_IMAGE, 0);
```

The additional parameters to `getElementCount()` make the request more specific. The first parameter represents the ID or name of the element. The third parameter represents the name of the collection, in case multiple instance documents have been loaded. The method `getElement()` requests that the database return a specific element.

For example, the following code returns an image element with a specific index.

```
error = daeObject->getDatabase()->getElement(
      (daeElement**)&thisImage, index, 0,
      COLLADA_ELEMENT_IMAGE, 0);
```

The element is returned in the first parameter. The third parameter restricts the query to a specific element by ID or name, and the fifth parameter restricts the search to a specific collection.

Typically, `getElementCount()` and `getElement()` are used as a pair, first getting the number of elements that match a particular name, type, or collection query and then iterating through those by using the `getElement()` method. Here is an example showing how to process all of the images in the runtime database:

```
unsigned int imageCount =
  daeObject->getDatabase()->getElementCount(NULL,
      COLLADA_ELEMENT_IMAGE, 0);
for (unsigned int i=0; i<imageCount; ++i){
  error = daeObject->getDatabase()->getElement(
  (daeElement**)&thisImage, i, 0,
  COLLADA_ELEMENT_IMAGE, 0);
  // process this image
}
```

Here is another example that processes only the image(s) whose ID or name is "grass":

```
imageCount = daeObject->getDatabase()->getElementCount(
  "grass", COLLADA_ELEMENT_IMAGE, 0);
for (unsigned int i=0; i<imageCount; ++i){
  error = daeObject->getDatabase()->getElement(
```

```
       (daeElement**)&thisImage, i, "grass",
    COLLADA_ELEMENT_IMAGE, NULL);
    // process this image
}
```

The index (i) passed to getElement() is not directly associated with the element within the database; it relates to the query itself.

COLLADA RT and CFX

The COLLADA RunTime (RT) and the COLLADA FX (CFX) libraries have been recently added to the COLLADA DOM open-source repository as sample code. RT demonstrates how to use the DOM to load a COLLADA document and display its <scene> using the OpenGL API. The CFX library uses the new Cg 1.5 library from NVIDIA to load COLLADA FX files with the Cg profile, making it very easy to integrate effects in various applications. These libraries have been tested with content from all the exporters, and in particular with COLLADA FX documents exported from tools such as FX Composer 2.0. The COLLADA DOM, RT, and CFX source code are available to PS3 developers in the SDK, almost identical to the open-source version (see Plate XVI).

Conditioners

A conditioner is a program, written using the COLLADA DOM, that has the following basic algorithm:

- load a COLLADA instance document;
- process a subset of the assets;
- save a COLLADA instance document.

Conditioners are modular pieces of the production pipeline for 3D content creation. Here are some examples of what conditioners can do:

- create triangle strips;
- preprocess a model for global illumination, writing the result back as a new version of the model;
- generate multiple levels ofsdetail (LODs), visibility structures, or collision bounds, and embed the result directly into the document;
- calculate tangent and binormal data for textured models;
- batch rename URL within a set of documents;
- triangulate *N*-sided polygon models, writing the result back as a new version of the model;

- resample animation curves at constant time-steps;
- de-index skinned meshes;
- generate continuous LODs of models.

Fundamentally, a conditioner is just a small application that reads COLLADA data, processes it in some way, and then writes COLLADA data back again. Of course, conditioners should accept any valid data and must output valid data according to the COLLADA schema.

Conditioners are executed on the entire COLLADA instance document. They can be pipelined because all the output of a conditioner can be used directly as the input of the next conditioner. Because they are implemented using the COLLADA DOM API, the intermediate results are not going to an external storage, but instead stay in the runtime database cache.

Some simple conditioners are provided as sample code in the COLLADA 1.4.0 release, and many more will become available:

Copyrighter

This conditioner performs a very basic operation. It allows the user to set, add, or replace a copyright within a COLLADA file. This conditioner's behavior is simply to access the `<asset>` element of the document and search for a `<copyright>` element within that.

- If a copyright is not found, the one specified in arguments to the conditioner is added.

- If a copyright is found, it is replaced if the option to overwrite is set. Otherwise, the new copyright is appended to the existing ones.

This is very basic tool, but it has been very useful for confirming that all files contain the correct copyright before they are distributed.

Triangulation

This conditioner converts the geometric primitives in a COLLADA document from polygons to triangles using a simple fanning algorithm and outputs a COLLADA document in which all `<polygons>` elements have been replaced with `<triangles>` elements.

This demonstrates the creation of a new `<triangles>` element that uses the same parameters and inputs as an existing `<polygons>` element. It also demonstrates how to insert and delete elements using the DOM.

This simplistic triangulation conditioner is not sophisticated enough to handle all COLLADA documents because the `<polygons>` element can contain complex topology. A full triangulation is a nontrivial algorithm that must accept concave polygons, potentially with holes or intersections, and convert them into triangles.

Alternatively, a different conditioner could be written to analyze the polygons and alert the user when they are not within the COLLADA specification (nonplanar, for example). It is also possible for a developer to mandate that artists create only convex polygons, without holes, and create a conditioner that then tests for this condition automatically.

There are numerous examples of such processing that require much effort and complex algorithms to work well. Having a library of such conditioners would be a very valuable tool for application developers.

Triangle Strip Generation

This conditioner performs another sophisticated operation because it creates triangle strips from polygonal meshes. Since there is already a triangulation conditioner, this triangle strip conditioner can be simplified to process only `<triangles>` elements. The content pipeline will have to connect the triangle strip conditioner to the output of the triangulation conditioner.

There are several triangle-stripping algorithms, and there are specific parameters, such as optimal strip length and restart primitive, that must be tuned specifically for different target platforms.

Animation Resampling

This conditioner processes key-frame animation channels and uses a linear key-frame interpolation to sample scalar function curves at regular intervals.

De-indexer

This conditioner processes `<geometry>` elements and optimizes their indexes to prepare them for rendering with vertex array primitives. This demonstrates how to reorganize the contents of `<triangles>` and `<controller>` elements and how to resolve references to `<source>` elements.

Filename

Another simple conditioner that is very useful finds all the `<image>` elements and modifies their URI `source` attributes so that they are relative URI references. This is useful because some tools export absolute system-dependent URIs that must be changed to more portable relative URIs.

Cache Optimizer

This conditioner revises the order of triangles to optimize vertex cache efficiency on the rendering hardware. The code that simulates the operation of the cache is replaceable, so the conditioner can be extended to handle different cache configurations. This demonstrates how to reorganize the `<p>` elements within a `<triangles>` element.

Current Limitations

The current design of the sample conditioners involves processing entire COLLADA documents. However, this may not be practical when only conditional processing is needed as part of the operation. For example, if a given process is to be executed only on objects whose name contains a specific string, this constraint must be tested within the conditioner and passed as an additional parameter.

A possible solution to this use case is to create special conditioners that can filter the document using some specific predicate or set of predicates (a complex query). Ideally, the COLLADA DOM would be able to support this type of filtering without creating a copy of the data, but that is not currently possible.

Another enhancement would be to make conditioners more finely grained in their operations so that they do not take whole documents as input. This would require a more complex runtime environment for conditioners, but this enhancement would probably be more efficient. It would enable conditioners that would accept specific assets of a given type. It could then process the individual assets, which would be much more efficient because it would enable better incremental build systems (see the section "Creating a Build Tool for COLLADA").

Refinery

Joining conditioners should be simple. Designing a data pipeline out of modular conditioners leaves room for experimentation and optimization techniques. Refinery is a graphical user interface to create pipelines of conditioners, execute them, automate various tasks, reuse components wherever possible, and visualize the results. Pipelines can be exported and imported by refinery as macros. Those macros can be executed later in batch scripts when used in the automatic build process.

Tri-Sample Pipeline Files

There is a whole range of applications where COLLADA can be used. For each kind of application, some processing may be required. Some optimizations may make a huge difference in performance on certain target platforms. Some target platforms may support only a subset of the features contained in the COLLADA document, and the content can be optimized for that platform.

Therefore, for some target platforms, the user wants to output different results, reflecting the same algorithms with different parameters to match several targets. The user may want to split, merge, duplicate, or otherwise filter the data. A conditioning pipeline is not just a single input with a single link from the beginning to the end going through a set of conditioners. It can be much more complex, having several inputs, several outputs, and many connections. Each processing box may require several inputs and have its output used by more than one other processing box.

Editing

A refinery's user interface enables interactive editing of the conditioning pipeline as follows:

- uses several conditioners in the same pipeline, or several instances of the same conditioner but with different parameters to match several targets;
- easily links the inputs and outputs of conditioners together into a pipeline;
- provides a graphical representation of the pipeline, the conditioners inside it, and the links between them;
- performs typical document editor functions: load/save and undo/redo;
- allows several document inputs and outputs in the pipeline;
- enables the reuse of blocks of the pipeline (macros);
- displays a list of available conditioners.

Execution

Execution can be done in two ways: from the GUI or from the command line. A screen shot of refinery executing a pipeline composed of a triangulation and a triangle stripper is shown in Figure 8.3.

Creating a Build Tool for COLLADA

The process of creating all the final data from the source COLLADA documents is called the *build process*. A *build tool* is the tool that will be used for this process. The goal for a build tool is to make sure that all intermediate and final results are correct. Each result must be systematically reproducible from the source data. With the exponentially growing number of assets, a manual build process can be error prone and time consuming, which has a direct impact on the productivity of the developer.

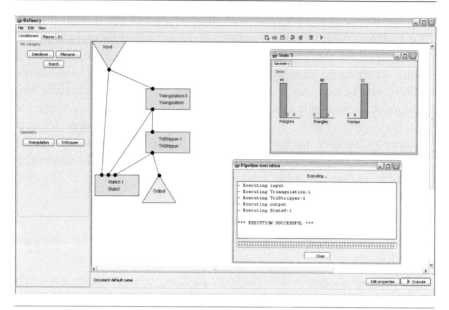

Figure 8.3. Refinery execution of a content pipeline. This is a screen shot of Refinery executing a sample content pipeline, transforming all geometries to triangles, and then all triangles to triangle strips. The stats box produces the windows with three drawings, the number of `<polygons>`, `<triangles>`, and `<tristrips>`. Each drawing has three values plotted, one for each input. The lower-right window is the text output from the execution of the pipeline (see also Plate I). (Image courtesy of Sony Computer Entertainment © 2005-2006)

Standardized build tools, such as the *make* command [70] have been used for many years in software development. This tool takes the project information from a configuration file, or *makefile*.

All build tools for software development work on the same principle: the configuration file contains a hierarchical list of files that need to be built, the dependencies of each file, the tool, and tool parameters needed to create the output from the input. Parameters can be given to the build tools that are then used to conditionally build the targets. File extension rules are used to simplify the creation of the makefile:

```
.o.c:
        cc -c $<
lib.a: x.o y.o z.o
        ar rvu lib.a x.o y.o z.o
        ranlib lib.a
```

In this example, the library `lib.a` depends on the the object files `x.o`, `y.o`, and `z.o`. A two-step process using `ar` and `ranlib` is indicated that produces `lib.a`. If one of the object files does not exist or is out of date, it can be built using the `.o.c` rule. For example, if `x.o` needs to be built, the build system will look for the `x.c` file and call the `cc` tool as specified in the `.o.c` rule.

The difficulty is knowing whether the object file needs to be built. Obviously, if the file does not exist, it needs to be built. What should be done if both the source and object files exist? Systematically rebuilding the object from the source produces the correct answer, but it would be much faster if it were possible to establish whether the object file was valid without rebuilding it.

The build tool uses the time stamps on the files to decide whether the object needs to be rebuilt. If the source file is older than the object file, there is no need to execute the compiler. In a project that contains hundreds of files, calling the build process after modifying a single file may result in a significant speed improvement when that file is largely independent.

The problem is that this simplified rule does not work in all cases because additional dependencies can exist. For instance, the `x.c` file may include an `x.h` file. Therefore, the `x.o` file must be rebuilt if the `x.c` or the `x.h` file is newer than the `x.o` file. It is very important that the dependency graph is accurate; otherwise, the result of the build will be wrong, which creates numerous time-consuming problems for developers. It is important that the dependency tree be built automatically from the source files to avoid such mistakes. Each source language needs a specialized dependency builder that can be called by the build tool and create information in a format that the build tool recognizes.

A "clean" target is often added to the makefile that deletes all the objects that can be built from source, therefore forcing the next build to rebuild everything. A clean build is recommended under certain circumstances. For example, it is mandatory to do a clean build when the makefile has been modified. When the makefile has been changed, so that the tools or options have changed, it is often impossible for the build tool to detect if the steps to build the object file have invalidated any preexisting object file.

It should be possible to take advantage of existing build tools with the COLLADA conditioning pipeline. The major missing part is the tool that creates a list of dependencies from a COLLADA document. This can be easily created using a conditioner that extracts the external references embedded in the COLLADA document and tracks the asset metadata.

COLLADA-Specific Build Tool

Using standard build tools as described before would be a big improvement over manually updating scripts, which unfortunately is the common practice in most projects. Having a build tool that is specifically adapted to COLLADA would have many advantages.

With a better understanding of the type of references and the build process, tool chains could eliminate much of the unnecessary processing. For instance, changing the bit map of a given texture often does not need to trigger any rebuild of the objects referencing this image.

The major problem of all the existing build tools is that they are file-based. If anything in a file has changed, the entire file is considered "dirty" and must be reprocessed. This situation encourages the developer to split the content in several files. The ideal situation would be to store each individual asset in a separate file, but this is quite impractical and will definitely scare content developers.

A COLLADA build tool would use the `<asset>` element to determine which subset of the document has changed and which partial updates are necessary. This workflow would be a significant improvement over many current processes. The modification time stamp is a required piece of information in the `<asset>` element. Therefore, it is possible for a COLLADA build tool to determine the need to rebuild a given asset in a document as opposed to relying on the time stamp of the file that contains the document itself.

In addition, since COLLADA documents can contain several representations of the same asset, it is possible to have both the source and the processed asset in the same instance document, greatly simplifying the management of assets.

Recently, more portable build tools have been introduced, such as ant [71], using XML-based configuration files and Java as its runtime environment. Microsoft is also using the XML technology in their latest MSBuild [72] tool integrated in Visual Studio 2005, which is a great improvement from the previous versions using opaque binary formats. A possible extension for COLLADA is to include the build configuration as part of the standard itself. This build information, a common description for all the tools, is very valuable.

Having this extension of COLLADA would make it possible to create a data-driven tool chain that would allow the COLLADA documents to instantiate the build process. The documents would contain the additional information in the `<asset>` element that indicates the specific parameters that must be applied for the type of asset. For example, the process that must be applied to a piece of terrain geometry is different from that needed for an indoor environment or a character. The terrain may be processed to create dynamic levels of detail, the indoor scene may be processed to obtain visibility tree information, and the character may go through a completely different process.

Asset Management

A good asset management policy is absolutely necessary to manage the vast quantity of data and the growing number of artists involved in its creation. In the software development world, several source control systems have been developed and are in use today, such as Concurrent Versions System (CVS) [73], subversion (SVN) [74], and Perforce [75].

The problem with these tools is that they are designed to handle software development and provide tools that help manage text file changes, such as `merge` and `diff`, which are absolutely not adapted to the management of 3D graphical content. These tools consider such content to be opaque files, for which they only have the information that the file system is providing and cannot even display the content of the files to the user.

Alienbrain [76], a commercial tool from Avid, Inc., is one of the few tools that has been developed to handle 3D graphical content. It provides a database with a large amount of additional information and enables visualization of the content.

Although all of these tools still suffer from the same issue, they work on files and are blind to the inner content. Enabling asset management tools to take advantage of the `<asset>` element in the COLLADA document would have a significant impact since those tools would effectively become asset management tools, rather than file management tools. As a start, it would be possible to manage asset versions on a finer granularity without having to fragment the assets into an unmanageable number of individual files.

Good asset management tools must be able to incorporate company policies, such as access control and departmental approvals. For example, it is necessary to know who created the asset and be able to collect all the notes and comments that have led to the existing modifications, as well as indicate that such an asset is frozen after it has been accepted by the artistic director. Those parameters could be added to the `<asset>` element, providing a standard way of exchanging such information and making sure this valuable information was synchronized with the asset.

Future Improvements

Asset management is an active area of research for the Khronos COLLADA working group. Only by testing design concepts in real production cases will it be possible to formulate a good design for asset metadata. A tighter connection between the asset management and build processes, through proper integration of COLLADA, should lead to valuable improvements for content developers.

Another necessary evolution is to move from the concept of interchanging files between applications as the only method to communicate. Rather, we can abstract away the medium and enable finer-grained communication between applications. Just as applications need an interface to the same file systems in order to exchange files, it will be necessary to have a standard COLLADA exchange protocol.

The Khronos Group welcomes additional contributors who want to be involved in the exciting future development for COLLADA [77].

Appendix: COLLADA Plug-In for 3ds Max

Overview

This appendix was provided with permission to reprint by Feeling Software, Inc. It provides information on the installation and usage of the COLLADA plug-in for 3ds Max at the time the book was written. This information is reproduced in this book for reference. First download an up-to-date plug-in and refer to its documentation if you are interested in using it.

ColladaMax is a COLLADA importer and exporter plug-in for 3ds Max. It supports all COLLADA 1.4 core features (e.g., animation and skinning) and a subset of COLLADA FX. There is no support for physics at the moment. Backward compatibility is also considered important: COLLADA 1.3 documents can generally be imported without problem, and in the future we plan to continue supporting older versions.

Installation and General Usage

Installation

To install ColladaMax, you will need 3ds Max 8 or 3ds Max 7 SP1 (Service Pack 1). Service packs for 3ds Max can be downloaded from the Autodesk support website. Make sure to install the right service pack for your system language. Note that service packs are not compatible with the debug builds of 3ds Max.

ColladaMax relies on the 3DXI (formerly IGame) library. This library is provided by Autodesk to Sparks members. Feeling Software keeps fairly up to date with the add-on, which can be downloaded freely from the Sparks download website. The basic Sparks membership is free and gives you the rights necessary to download the 3DXI library. On the Sparks download page, scroll down to "Game Export Interface builds" and download the latest version of 3DXI. At the time of this writing, the latest version is 2.0, which came out on January 31, 2006.

To install ColladaMax, first download from Feeling Software's COLLADA downloads page the zip file that corresponds to your version of 3ds Max.

Extract the zip file in your 3ds Max folder. Answer "Yes" if the system asks whether to overwrite any files.

General Usage: Export

To export a scene from the UI, click on the menu: File ➠ Export..., then select the "COLLADA (*.DAE)" file type. You can then select which export options to use. Please see the "Export Options" section in this appendix for more information. You can also use the menu: File ➠ Export Selected... to export only the selected objects. Note that the current exporter may not export all dependent objects automatically, especially in the case of interrelated objects such as skins and morphers.

To export a scene from within MaxScript, use: `exportFile <filename>.DAE #noprompt`. Please consult the 3ds Max documentation for more information on automating 3ds Max.

General Usage: Import

To import a COLLADA document from the UI, click on the menu: File ➠ Import..., then select the "COLLADA (*.DAE)" file type. There are no import options. If there is an error in the COLLADA document, no data will be imported, and an error message will be displayed. Otherwise, your COLLADA document should be imported silently after a short moment.

To import a scene from within MaxScript, use: `importFile <filename>.DAE #noprompt`.

3ds Max Extension

The COLLADA specification allows for custom parameter export through custom profiles. The ColladaMax plug-in adds a 3ds Max specific profile, through the `<extra><technique profile="MAX3D">` extension. This section lists the parameters, along with a short description.

Domain	Name	Type	Default
`<node>`	`<user_properties>`	IDref	—

User-defined properties of an object. Within the UI: menu: Edit ➠ Object Properties... ➠ User Defined ➠ User Defined Properties textbox, with a given object selected.

Domain	Name	Type	Default
`<camera>` `<light>`	`<target>`	string	—

Target node for a light or camera. The presence of this element indicates that the camera/light is targeted. The string contained by the element indicates the `id` of the COLLADA scene node that is targeted.

Domain	Name	Type	Default
`<light>`	`<intensity>`	`float`	`"1.0"`

Intensity for the color of a light. Within the Modify tab for a selected light: Intensity/Color/Attenuation ➥ Multiplier. Can be animated.

Domain	Name	Type	Default
`<light>`	`<aspect_ratio>`	`float`	`"1.0"`

Aspect ratio for rectangular directional/spot lights. Within the Modify tab for a selected light: Spotlight Parameters (or Directional Parameters) ➥ Aspect.

Domain	Name	Type	Default
`<light>`	`<outer_cone>`	`float`	`"hotspot - 2.0"`

Falloff for directional/spotlights. Within the Modify tab for a selected light: Spotlight Parameters (or Directional Parameters) ➥ Falloff/Field. Can be animated.

Domain	Name	Type	Default
`<phong>`	`<spec_level>`	`float`	`"100"`

Specular level of a Phong or Blinn material. In the COLLADA document, this value is in percent. Within the Material window for a standard material: Blinn Basic Parameters ➥ Specular Highlights ➥ Specular Level. Can be animated.

Domain	Name	Type	Default
`<phong>`	`<emission_level>`	`float`	`"100"`

Self-illumination level of a Phong or Blinn material. In the COLLADA document, this value is in percent. Within the Material window for a standard material: Blinn Basic Parameters ➥ Self-Illumination text field, when the "Color" checkbox is off. Can be animated.

Domain	Name	Type	Default
`<phong>`	`<displacement>`	`float`	—
`<phong>`	`<filter_color>`	`float`	—
`<phong>`	`<shininess>`	`float`	—
`<phong>`	`<index_of_refraction>`	`float`	—
`<phong>`	`<bump>`	`float`	—

Extra map channels of a standard material. These extra map channels are available for export, within the MAX3D extension. Within the Material window for a standard material: Maps ➥ Displacement, Maps ➥ Filter Color ...

Domain	Name	Type	Default
<phong>	<wireframe>	bool	"false"
<phong>	<double_sided>	bool	"false"
<phong>	<face_map>	bool	"false"
<phong>	<faceted>	bool	"false"

Material flags for standard materials. Within the Material window for a standard material: Shader Basic Parameters ➡ Wire, Shader Basic Parameters ➡ 2-Sided ...

Domain	Name	Type	Default
<phong>	<texture><amount>	float	100

Amount multiplier for a map channel for standard materials. This parameter is exported for all the textured map channels, represented as a percentage in the COLLADA document. Within the Material window for a standard material: Maps ➡ Amount column (for all the map channels). Can be animated.

Export Options

The ColladaMax exporter provides a number of options, which are detailed in this section. The options can be modified from the export UI or by editing the ColladaExporter.ini file located in the "3dsmax[7,8]\plugcfg\" folder. This configuration file is loaded in before every export and saved to when the user clicks "Ok" in the export options dialog. The configuration file is particularly useful when automating, to set per-scene options.

Standard Options

Bake Matrices—The transforms of scene nodes and their animations will be exported as matrices. This is used mostly for interoperability, e.g., with another DCC tool. Note that bipeds automatically have their matrices baked. Default: off.

Relative Paths—Whether the absolute or relative file path will be written to the COLLADA document. Mostly impacts textures and shader filenames. Default: on.

Geometry

Normals—Whether to export the normals of meshes. Default: on.

Triangles—Whether to export the tessellation of a mesh as triangles or N-sided polygons. In the COLLADA document, this will generate either the <triangles> or the <polylist> element. Since 3ds Max does not support holes, the 3ds Max exporter will never write the <polygons> element.

It is recommended to keep this option on, as *N*-sided polygon export is still experimental. Default: this option is disabled and always on.

XRefs—Whether externally referenced meshes will be exported as external references. If this option is checked off, they will simply be dropped. Default: on.

Object Space—Whether the normals and vertex positions of geometries are exported in object-space or in world-space. It is recommended to keep this option on, as COLLADA does not allow for world-space normals and vertex positions, so this should be kept for debugging purposes or very specific uses. Default: on.

Animation

Sample animation—Enables time-sampling the animated parameters, within the Start and End time interval. One sample is always taken per time unit. If this option is disabled, ColladaMax will attempt to export the animated parameters as key-frames. Animated bipeds and other objects involving IK are automatically sampled, since COLLADA doesn't have direct support for these features yet. Default: off.

Single <animation>—Whether the <animation> elements within the exported COLLADA document will be placed under a single root <animation> element, named after the scene. This is especially useful when exporting animation clips for 3ds Max 7. Default: on.

Experimental

These options are experimental and should be left unchecked until they are deemed stable and useful enough. They are exposed so that users can see their progress and preview their usage. The behavior explained below is the desired target behavior and is very likely not completed yet. The "Tangent/Binormals" export option is almost complete and is definitely worth trying.

Y Up—Exports all positions and vectors with the *Y* and *Z* components inverted, in order to emulate the basis used in OpenGL and other applications (e.g., Maya) where the *Y*-axis is considered the up axis.

Tangents/Binormals—Exports the texture tangents and binormals for all given map channels of meshes, as well as their indices within the mesh tessellation.

Mixed FX—If enabled, all the COLLADA FX parameters parsed from the HLSL files are exported as COLLADA FX parameters. Since HLSL is at the same abstraction level as COLLADA FX, by default and when this option is turned off, NVIDIA's <import> mechanism is used at the effect level, and the modified parameters are exported at the material level.

History

Autodesk Media and Entertainment developed the first versions of the COLLADA translators for 3ds Max. Feeling Software was contracted in 2005 to redesign and rewrite it to make it conform with COLLADA 1.3 and 1.4. The final result was called the COLLADA tools for 3ds Max and was copyright Autodesk Media and Entertainment, Feeling Software and distributed under the MIT license.

Feeling Software is now the official developer of ColladaMax.

We would like to thank Autodesk Media and Entertainment (especially Jean-Luc Corenthin and his team) for starting this plug-in, Igor Kravtchenko for his patch on materials, and Kevin Thacker for his work on sampling/baking matrices and his many generous fixes.

More Information

- About COLLADA:
  https://collada.org/public_forum/welcome.php
- About this plug-in:
  https://collada.org/public_forum/viewforum.php?f=6
- About Autodesk:
  http://www.autodesk.com/

Appendix: COLLADA Plug-In for Maya

Overview

This appendix was provided with permission to reprint by Feeling Software, Inc. It provides information on the installation and usage of the COLLADA plug-in for Maya at the time the book was written. This information is reproduced in this book for reference. First download an up-to-date plug-in and refer to its documentation if you are interested in using it.

ColladaMaya is a plug-in for Maya supporting importing/exporting scenes according to the COLLADA specifications. Feeling Software officially maintains this plug-in and was originally contracted by Alias to improve and extend an early version. The plug-in is available in two versions: COLLADA 1.3 and 1.4.

Plug-In Installation

Windows Binaries

ColladaMaya is available precompiled for Maya 7.0 on Windows. Other versions (Linux, Mac OSX) can be built from the source code.

ColladaMaya supports environment variables if Maya is not installed in its default path. These environment variables are per-version of Maya: `MAYA_PATH50`, `MAYA_PATH601`, `MAYA_PATH65`, and `MAYA_PATH70`.

If you did not install Maya in its default path, the first thing you must do is set the appropriate environment variable. To do this, on Windows XP:

1. Open Control Panel ➡ System ➡ Advanced.
2. Click on the "Environment Variables" button.
3. In the "System Variable" section, click the "New" button.
4. In the "Variable Name" text box, enter the name of Maya environment variable for your version.

   Example: `MAYA_PATH70`
5. In the "Variable Value" text box, enter your full Maya path in the text box.

   Example: `C:\Program Files\Alias\Maya7.0`

6. Click on the "Ok" button for the "New System Variable" dialog box.

7. Click on the "Ok" button for the "Environment Variables" dialog box.

Your settings are now changed. If you have a command prompt or MSVC. NET opened, they must be restarted for the changes to take effect.

Windows Binaries Installation

Extract the zip file in a folder of your choice:

Example: `C:\ColladaMaya\`

Copy the appropriate plug-in binary files and MEL scripts in the Maya folders. If you set the correct environment variable(s) or if you installed Maya in its default path, you can run the batch file.

For example, if you use Maya 6.5 and extracted the zip file in the folder mentioned above, open the `C:\ColladaMaya\Maya6.5\` directory and run the `copyIntoMaya.bat` batch script.

If Step 2 fails, you can always copy the plug-in and the scripts manually. To do this, copy the scripts from `C:\ColladaMaya\scripts` and the .mll file for your version of Maya into Maya's `scripts/others` and `bin/plug-ins` folders, respectively.

Plug-in Compilation

If you are a developer and want to make changes to the plug-in, please follow the detailed instructions on how to set your build environment from the Maya online documentation: Developer Resources ➥ API guide ➥ Setting up your plug-in build environment.

Building for Windows

Please see the above section about environment variables if you did not install Maya in its default path.

To compile Maya plug-ins on Windows, you need the Microsoft Visual Studio .NET 2003 compiler. Open the following solution: `C:\ColladaMaya\DaeTranslator.sln`. Choose the desired configuration, for example, `Maya6.5Debug`. A post-build step is provided so that, after a successful build, the .mll file is automatically copied into the Maya plug-in folder.

Building for Linux

Set up your default Maya plug-in development environment following the instructions from the Maya on-line documentation. Run `make` to compile the binary. Don't forget to copy the `collada.so` and `scripts/*.mel` in the right paths. Look at your `maya.env` file to find the default paths.

Building for Mac OSX

The following has been tested with Maya 6.5.

Open the project in XCode 2.1:

```
$COLLADAMAYA_SRC_DIR/COLLADA.xcodeproj
```

Ensure that you have installed the 10.3.9 development package that came with XCode 2.1.

Under XCode 2.1 running on OS X Tiger (which was the main porting platform), you need to cross develop for Panther in order for Maya to pick up the plug-in.

Depending on what build configuration was selected, you can find the compiled plug-in in one of the following directories:

```
build/Development/COLLADA_m65.lib
build/Debug/COLLADA_m65.lib
build/Release/COLLADA_m65.lib
```

Copy the plug-in to your home's custom plug-in directory, along with the scripts:

```
mkdir $HOME/Library/Preferences/Alias/maya/6.5/plug-ins
cp build/Development/COLLADA_m65.lib
      $HOME/Library/Preferences/Alias/maya/6.5/plug-ins
cp $COLLADAMAYA_SRC_DIR/scripts/*.mel
      $HOME/Library/Preferences/Alias/maya/6.5/scripts
```

Enabling the Plug-In

1. Open the plug-in manager: Windows ➡ Settings ➡ Preferences ➡ Plug-in Manager.
2. Verify that the folder you copied the `.mll` into is listed in the plug-in manager. If not, it is likely that you have a `Maya.env` file that overrides the default plug-in path. Add the standard plug-in path to your `Maya.env`. Alternatively, click the "Browse" button and manually browse to locate the `.mll` file.
3. Make sure the `COLLADA.mll` file (or `.so` on Unix) is in the list and that it is set to "loaded" and "auto load." If it refuses to load, check the script editor for error messages: Windows ➡ General editor ➡ Script editor.
4. Save your preferences: File ➡ Save preferences.

Using the Plug-In

Maya supports various types of plug-ins. This plug-in is an importer/exporter, so you use it to load COLLADA files in Maya and to save COLLADA files from a Maya scene. Here are two examples of how you can use the plug-in interactively:

To save a scene as a COLLADA file, open the File Export dialog: File ➡ Export all.

To load a COLLADA file into the scene, open the File Import dialog: File ➡ Import.

If you use file references in Maya, you must reopen the exported scene using File ➡ Open rather than File ➡ Import for the references to stay external.

Note that this plug-in can also be run in command-line mode, using the file MEL command described in the "Advanced Features" section in this appendix. It can also be run in batch mode using a similar approach.

Maya Profile

The COLLADA specification allows for custom parameter export through custom profiles. ColladaMaya adds a Maya-specific profile to the plug-in. The following is a list of the added technique nodes, their contents, and their domain.

Domain	Name	Type	Default
<mesh>	DOUBLE_SIDED	bool	"true"

Determines whether the faces of a mesh are meant to be rendered when viewed from both sides.

Domain	Name	Type	Default
<geometry>	GEOMETRY	name	—

Used by blend shapes to identify the source of the ids of the target shapes. This source should be found under the <geometry> <mesh> node.

Domain	Name	Type	Default
<geometry>	WEIGHT	float	—

Used by blend shapes to identify the source of weights of the target shapes. These may be animated. This source should be found under the <geometry> <mesh> node.

Domain	Name	Type	Default
<scene>	START_TIME	float	—

Sets the animation start time in the range slider.

Domain	Name	Type	Default
`<scene>`	END_TIME	`float`	—

Sets the animation end time in the range slider.

Domain	Name	Type	Default
`<scene>`	`<layer_name>`	`layer`	—

Contains a list of `ids` belonging to the named layer.

Domain	Name	Type	Default
`<camera>`	HORIZONTAL_ APERTURE	`float`	"3.6"

Sets the size of the camera horizontal view (in cm).

Domain	Name	Type	Default
`<camera>`	VERTICAL_ APERTURE	`float`	"2.4"

Sets the animation end time in the range slider (in cm).

Domain	Name	Type	Default
`<camera>`	LENS_ SQUEEZE	`float`	"1.0"

The amount the camera's lens compresses the image horizontally.

Domain	Name	Type	Default
`<texture>`	BLEND_MODE	`blend`	"NONE"

Sets the texture blend mode, used only when multitexturing.

Following is a list of the valid values for the multitexturing blend mode:

- "NONE"
- "OVER"
- "IN"
- "OUT"
- "ADD"
- "SUBTRACT"
- "MULTIPLY"
- "DIFFERENCE"
- "LIGHTEN"
- "DARKEN"
- "SATURATE"
- "DESATURATE"
- "ILLUMINATE"

The default blend mode is NONE.

More information is available in the Maya documentation: "All About: layeredTexture node."

Domain	Name	Type	Default
`<texture>`	`<place2dtexture params>`	—	—

Includes all the parameters for the place2dTexture nodes that are not included in the common profile. Almost all of the parameters for the 2D texture placement nodes are exported in the COLLADA file.

The `wrapU`, `wrapV`, `mirrorU`, `mirrorV`, `coverageU`, `coverageV`, `translateFrameU`, `translateFrameV`, `rotateFrame`, `stagger`, `fast`, `repeatU`, `repeatV`, `offsetU`, `offsetV`, `rotateUV`, `noiseU`, and `noiseV` parameters are included in the Maya-specific profile.

The `wrapU`, `wrapV`, `mirrorU`, `mirrorV`, `stagger`, and `fast` parameters are Boolean; the rest are single-float parameters.

More information is available in the Maya documentation: "All About: place2dTexture node."

Domain	Name	Type	Default
`<texture>`	`<program url="PROJECTION">` `<params>`	`projection`	`"PLANAR"`

Used to add a "projection" node in front of the file texture node, to represent 3D projection texture nodes. A `<program url="PROJECTION">` node will be added to the Maya-specific technique of the texture description in COLLADA.

Following is a list of the projection types accepted:

- `"NONE"`
- `"PLANAR"`
- `"SPHERICAL"`
- `"CYLINDRICAL"`
- `"BALL"`
- `"CUBIC"`
- `"TRIPLANAR"`
- `"CONCENTRIC"`
- `"PERSPECTIVE"`

`"MATRIX"`, a `float4x4` value, represents the inverse projection matrix.

Domain	Name	Type	Default
`<animation>`	`PRE_INFINITY`	`infinity`	—
`<animation>`	`POST_INFINITY`	`infinity`	—

Sets the animation curve pre-infinity and post-infinity mode. Following is a list of the valid values for the animation curve infinity mode: "CONSTANT", "LINEAR", "CYCLE", "CYCLE_RELATIVE", and "OSCILLATE". The plug-in does not enforce a default infinity mode. Maya uses "CONSTANT" as its default infinity mode when creating an animation curve.

- "CONSTANT" means that the end values persist outside of the input range.

- "LINEAR" means that the value will continue to increase or decrease at a linear rate, given the instantaneous slope of the curve at the endpoint.

- "CYCLE" means that the animation restarts at the end, so the key is modulo the input range.

- "CYCLE_RELATIVE" means the animation restarts, but the values are considered relative increments, not absolute value. For example, a ramp of [0,1] defined for the time interval [0, 2] will give a value of 3 for a sample at time=6.

- "OSCILLATE" is identical to "CYCLE" except that the animation is played backward when an endpoint is reached.

More information on animation curve infinity modes is available in the Maya documentation: "All About: Graph Editor menu bar," under the "Pre and Post Infinity" sub-heading. Please note that "CYCLE_RELATIVE" is also called "Cycle with offset."

Domain	Name	Type	Default
<animation>	WEIGHT	float	—

Identifies the array containing the "IN_TANGENT" or "OUT_TANGENT" weights. Its presence indicates a weighted animation curve.

Blend Shapes

Blend shapes are implemented in the Maya-specific profile. The deformed mesh and all the targets are normally included in the geometry library. Two source arrays are then added to the deformed mesh that lists the ids of the target meshes and the weights. Finally, an <extra> node is added after the <mesh> node for the deformed mesh. This <extra> node contains a combiner with two <input> nodes that point toward the already mentioned source array for the target names and weights. The combiner then contains dummy value nodes, <v>, for each name/weight.

Blend shape animation is also supported. As with vertex position animation, the matrix notation for the target is used directly with the source id.

Bézier Curve and Weighted Bézier Curve

ColladaMaya exports the Bézier curves as follows:

1. Assumes the inner control points are at equidistant time values;

2. The "IN_TANGENT" and "OUT_TANGENT" values represent offsets relative to the current and next output values for the two inner control points:

$K2 = K2 + \text{in\_Tangent}, K3 = K4 - \text{out\_Tangent}$.

The weights are supported only in the Maya-specific profile. To use the weights, you will need to first convert the tangents back to angles:

$$Angle = \arctan\left(\frac{\text{Tangent}}{\text{TimeInterval}/3}\right)$$

You then get the relative (time, value) or (T, K) pairs for the inner control points as follows: $T = \pm Weight \times \cos(Angle)$, $K = Weight \times \sin(Angle)$.

Unsupported Features

Here is a short and incomplete list of features that are not currently supported.

- Modeling
  - SubDs and NURBS are not exported.
  - Tangent space export is not currently implemented.
- Geometry
  - Animated normals are not supported by Maya (they will never be imported/exported by the ColladaMaya plug-in).
  - Only per-vertex blind data is supported.
- Lighting
  - Many light attributes: intensity, ambient shade, etc. cannot be included in COLLADA 1.3.
  - Area lights are not exported.
- Shading
  - Only Lambert and Phong shaders and the constant Surface shader are currently supported (most other shading nodes are unsupported: shading switches, procedural texture nodes. A possible workaround is to manually bake textures prior to export).
- Animation
  - Joint clusters are exported and imported as skin cluster(s) (other types are ignored).

- Dynamics, including rigid and soft bodies, particles, and fluids, are not supported.
- Expressions and constraints are exported using animation sampling (they will be keyed in on re-import).

- Cameras
  - Camera position animations are supported only with the decomposed transforms.

Known Issues

Imported skinned normals are not responsive enough during animations. They don't follow the animation precisely.

Even when a material attribute is textured, a constant color is still written for that specific material channel. That constant color should ideally follow the OpenGL convention, but due to demand from some game developers, the Maya exporter follows this convention:

- diffuse and ambient are set to white, to allow modulation;
- other attributes are left to their Maya default, which is generally black.

Advanced Features

Maya Transform Export

By default, the bake transform matrices option is disabled. The plug-in therefore exports a series of primitive-decomposed COLLADA transformations. Here are two examples of exported joints and transform that show the different possibilities:

```
<node id="joint3" name="joint3" type="JOINT">
  <translate>2.000000 0.000000 0.000000</translate>
  <rotate>0 0 1 -90.0</rotate> <!-- joint orient -->
  <rotate>0 1 0 0.0</rotate>
  <rotate>1 0 0 0.0</rotate>
  <rotate>0 0 1 0.0</rotate> <!-- standard rot. -->
  <rotate>0 1 0 0.0</rotate>
  <rotate>1 0 0 0.0</rotate>
  <rotate>0 0 1 0.0</rotate> <!-- rotation axis -->
  <rotate>0 1 0 0.0</rotate>
  <rotate>1 0 0 0.0</rotate>
  <scale>1.0 1.0 1.0</scale>
</node>

<node id="pCube1" name="pCube1">
  <translate sid="translate">0.0 2.127 0.00</translate>
```

```
<translate sid="rotatePivot">0.0 -2.01 0.0</translate>
<rotate sid="rotateZ">0 0 1 0.0</rotate>
<rotate sid="rotateY">0 1 0 0.00</rotate>
<rotate sid="rotateX">1 0 0 0.0</rotate>
<rotate sid="rotateAxisZ">0 0 1 0.0</rotate>
<rotate sid="rotateAxisY">0 1 0 0.0</rotate>
<rotate sid="rotateAxisX">1 0 0 0.0</rotate>
<translate sid="rotatePivotInverse">0. 2. 0.</translate>
<translate sid="scalePivot">0. -2. 0.</translate>
<scale sid="scale">1.0 1.0 1.0</scale>
<skew sid="shearXY">45.0 0 1 0 1 0 0</skew>
<skew sid="shearXZ">35.0 0 0 1 1 0 0</skew>
<skew sid="shearYZ">30.0 0 0 1 0 1 0</skew>
<translate sid="scalePivotInverse">0. 2. 0.</translate>
<instance url="#pCubeShape1-lib"/>
</node>
```

To obtain the right transform matrix, concatenate all of these operations in their exact order. For more information on the transform equation used by Maya, refer to the Maya documentation for the MFnTransform and MFnIkJoint classes.

Note that the following `sid` are currently supported:

```
jointOrient[XYZ]
```

```
translate
```

```
rotate[XYZ]
```

```
rotateAxis[XYZ]
```

```
scale
```

```
rotatePivot
```

```
rotatePivotInverse
```

```
rotatePivotTranslation
```

```
scalePivot
```

```
scalePivotInverse
```

```
scalePivotTranslation
```

```
shear[XY/XZ/YZ]
```

The `sid` attribute should not be used to identify where to put the transform within the stack, because you will not be able to import files from other DCC tools. We do not guarantee that the `sid` names will keep their current values in future versions.

Nearly all transformations can be animated. The only exceptions are the pivots; their associated translation, inverses, and skews are currently assumed constant. For more information, refer to the source code:

```
DaeTransform::exportDecomposedTransform()
```

Export Options

Here is a list of the available export options in the UI and through the command line. The default value is given in parentheses.

```
cameraXFov ("false")
cameraYFov ("true")
bakeTransforms ("false")
bakeLighting ("false")
exportCameraAsLookat ("true")
exportTriangles ("false")
isSampling ("false")
curveConstrainSampling ("false")
samplingFunction ("")
enablePhysics ("false")
exportWeaklyTypedArrays ("false")
exportPolygonMeshes ("true")
exportLights ("true")
exportCameras ("true")
exportJointsAndSkin ("true")
exportAnimations ("true")
exportControllerTargets ("true")
exportInvisibleNodes ("false")
exportBoundingBoxes ("true")
exportNormals ("true")
exportTexCoords ("true")
exportVertexColors ("true")
exportTangents ("false")
```

Baked (Sampled) Transform Matrices

The plug-in has an option for exporting transforms using baked matrices, sampled in every frame.

Import/export of static baked transform is supported. Export of animated baked transforms is supported, but import is not yet supported. The code in `DaeAnimationLibrary::importAnimation()` would need to be extended to do so. Note that information loss occurs when baking these transforms then reimporting; for example, joint angles may not be preserved even if the final transform looks identical.

Baked Lighting

This option can be used to force the export of per-vertex color, with the lighting information baked in. The `convertLightmap` MEL function is used, so that your mesh will be changed as a result of the export. After the export, you must manually undo to remove the effect of the light baking.

Export Camera as Look-At

The COLLADA specification allows two ways to specify the transform associated with a perspective camera. One is to use the `<lookat>` element. The other is to use regular transform elements (for example, translate, rotate, etc.) The advantage of the former is that it is very easy to parse, and it directly specifies the object that is the center of the attention. This is useful for simple viewer applications in which the user is able to pivot around some important part of the scene. The disadvantage of this technique is that it cannot be animated. Therefore, if animations are desired, this option must be disabled, which forces the exporter to use regular Maya transforms.

The bake transforms option, described above, takes priority. If it is enabled, the camera transforms are exported as baked matrices regardless of the value of the `exportCameraAsLookat` option.

Filtering Export

Sometimes it is desirable to disable the output of some elements of the scene. For example, you may want to export only the geometry (along with materials and texture) and joints and skin. In this case, you may want to use these options to disable the export of lights and cameras.

Export invisible nodes will include the default cameras: `persp`, `top`, `side`, and `front`. The reference transform nodes that are marked invisible will not be exported, regardless of the value of the `exportInvisibleNodes` export option.

You can select which per-vertex attributes to export, as unwanted per-vertex attributes can quickly increase the size of your COLLADA files. These are the per-vertex export options: `exportNormals`, `exportTexCoords`, exportVertexColors and exportTangents. The exportTangents option includes both tangents and binormals.

Some combinations of these options may not make sense. In a production setting, it may be preferable to do an Export Selection instead.

Weakly Typed Array Export Option

COLLADA 1.3 adopted strongly typed arrays, to support an API that is code-generated automatically from the COLLADA schema. So basically, a pre-1.3, weakly typed array, looks like this:

```
<array type="float" id="blabla1" count="3"> 1.0 2.0 3.0
</array>
```

while a strongly typed array looks like this:

```
<float_array id="blabla1" count="3"> 1.0 2.0 3.0
</float_array>
```

Even though weakly typed arrays have been deprecated in COLLADA 1.3, the plug-in can import and export both types of arrays. By default, the export uses strongly typed arrays. To enable weakly typed array export (e.g., for backward-compatibility purposes), use the exportWeaklyTypedArrays.

Variable Animation Sampling

You can force the plug-in to sample all animations at a user-defined rate. This is useful when exporting nonkeyed animations, for instance, when using expressions that include the time variable. When reimported, keys will be placed at each of the sampled times/attribute pairs. You need to set the sampling function in order to get a variable sampling rate.

This is the sampling function syntax: Start with a string value that corresponds to a list of three floating-point values. The three numbers identify the sampling start time, end time, and the sampling period. A list of such numbers allows the user to choose different sampling rates at different times in the animation. Additionally, the user can enter just one number representing a constant sampling period or an empty string to disable sampling.

Unordered time intervals or time intervals smaller than the sampling period are considered invalid inputs. Subsequent time intervals with discontinuities are treated independently.

To deal with overlapping time intervals, the overlapping sample period should be the linear interpolation of the new and old sample periods, with respect to the time left in the old period:

*Overlap Period = Time left in first interval + (1 - Time left in first interval / First interval sample period) * Second interval sample period.*

Some examples:

- 0.03333 implies a constant sampling rate of 30 fps;
- 0, 100, 5 requests samples: from the time 0, in seconds, to the time 100, in seconds, with one sample every five seconds, for a total of 21 samples;
- 100, 0, 5 is an invalid input;
- 0, 100, 5, 100, 200, 10, 200, 300, 5 requests one sample every five seconds in the interval [0 s, 100 s], one sample every ten seconds in [100 s, 200 s], and one sample every five seconds in [200 s, 300 s];
- 0, 100, 5, 200, 300, 5, 100, 200, 10 is an invalid input;
- 0, 18, 8 requests three samples, at times 0 s, 8 s, and 16 s;
- 0, 18, 8, 20, 40, 12 requests five samples at time 0 s, 8 s, 16 s, 20 s, and 32 s (This is because of the discontinuity.);
- 0, 18, 8, 18, 40, 12 requests five samples, at time 0 s, 8 s, 16 s, 27 s, and 37 s (25% of the overlapping sampling period is done at a rate of 1/8 s, between 16 s and 18 s. 75% of the overlapping sampling period is done at a rate of 1/12 s after time 18 s.);
- 0, 18, 8, 18, 20, 10, 20, 24, 1 is an invalid input.

Curve-constrain sampling is a new sampling method where only the sampled times that are within the sampled curve are used. If no sampled curve is found (for example, when exporting an IK handle), the full sampling is done. You cannot constrain the sampling of transforms exported with the bake transforms export option, but it will work well with any variable animation sampling function.

Import/Export through Command Line

To run the plug-in in a batch mode using MEL, use the file command with the following arguments:

```
file -op "exportWeaklyTypedArrays=false;bakeTransforms" -typ
"COLLADA" -pr -ea "C:/path/filename.dae";
```

Options can be combined, by separating them with semicolons, as in the above example. As of now, all options are disabled by default. If an argument of false or 0 is provided, the option is kept disabled. Otherwise, it is enabled. So in the above example, the export will produce a file called `C:/path/filename.dae`. The weakly typed array option will be kept disabled. The bake transform option will be enabled. Other options are kept at default.

External References Export

Two export options allow you to tweak how external references are handled by the exporter: `exportXRefs` defaults to true, and you can unset it to filter out the external references. The `dereferenceXRefs` export option specifies the exporter's behavior when encountering an external reference. It defaults to false; if set, it will not export a COLLADA external reference but will simply step through the Maya external references as if they were a part of the exported scene.

COLLADA Physics Support

The ColladaMaya plug-in supports COLLADA Physics elements. Unfortunately, Maya itself does not have great support for physics built in. However, another plug-in, Nima, can be installed to extend Maya and add COLLADA Physics support to the ColladaMaya import/export plug-in.

Nima is basically the integration of the Novodex engine in Maya. It covers rigid body dynamics, including rigid constraints and rag dolls. It is released with source code under the MIT license to allow fellow developers to reuse and extend its functionality.

Supported Features at a Glance

The current version of Nima already supports the following major features.

- Rigid bodies (implemented through NxActor in the Novodex API) contain one or more convex or nonconvex meshes or physics shapes (i.e., capsules, boxes and spheres).
- Mesh collision shapes can be added or removed interactively. They can be positioned and oriented interactively using the regular Maya manipulators.
- Physics shapes (e.g,. capsules) have a special manipulator to position the endpoints, adjust the radius, etc.
- Rigid constraints can be created to link rigid bodies together. Almost all features of the Novodex D6 joint (NxD6Joint) are exposed through this interface (e.g., breakable force and torque, local position/orientation, etc.), with the notable exception of motors.
- Almost every parameter of rigid bodies can be key-framed and manipulated interactively, including in *interactive playback* mode. Shapes can be sculpted, and the corresponding convex or nonconvex collision mesh will be automatically updated.
- Forces exercised by fields are partially supported.
- Rag dolls can automatically be created from skinned characters.

More Samples

More samples can be found in the color plates.

- Car crash, Plate VII.
- Tornado, Plate VIII.
- Constraints, Plate IX.

More Information

- About COLLADA:
  https://collada.org/public_forum/welcome.php
- About this plug-in:
  https://collada.org/public_forum/viewforum.php?f=5
- About Maya/Alias:
  http://www.alias.com/eng/index.shtml

The binaries, source code, and all associated documents are released under the MIT license (http://www.opensource.org/licenses/mit-license.php). The official site for this plug-in is: http://sourceforge.net/projects/colladamaya.

Feeling Software (http://www.feelingsoftware.com) is also available for contract work; the Nima plug-in can also be found on this website.

Appendix:
SOFTIMAGE|XSI 5.1 Plug-In

Overview

This appendix was provided with permission to reprint by Avid Technology, Inc. It describes the support for the COLLADA 1.4.0 file format in SOFTIMAGE|XSI 5.1. Please check with Softimage for the latest version. With the release of SOFTIMAGE|XSI version 5.1, Softimage has officially endorsed and adopted COLLADA as an important supported file format. Softimage has also joined the Khronos Group to help promote and evolve the COLLADA specification.

Usage Scenarios

The first phase of the COLLADA integration into XSI was designed with three usage scenarios in mind.

XSI and the Game Pipeline

The COLLADA exporter allows the game developer to take content created in SOFTIMAGE|XSI version 5.1 and export it in a COLLADA file that can then be used and processed in a game pipeline. The primary focus is to support the basic elements, such as hierarchies, geometries, material and effect assignments, skinning, and transformation animation. In the area of effects, support for the Sony PS3 environment is enhanced by the integration of the Cg profile of the COLLADA FX specification in SOFTIMAGE|XSI shader nodes and in the COLLADA converters.

Migrating Existing dotXSI Game Pipelines to COLLADA

The integration of COLLADA in the SOFTIMAGE|FTK provides current users of the dotXSI file format a smooth transition to COLLADA. By subclassing the existing dotXSI classes and reusing the same libraries and the same import/export tools, the transition to COLLADA is essentially transparent when using XSI. As a result, tools that currently compile with the

SOFTIMAGE|FTK only require very small updates to use COLLADA as the file format. For example, the existing dotXSIConverter that ships with SOFTIMAGE|XSI did not require any modifications to support COLLADA. The only addition made was a new option in the user interface to allow for the selection of dotXSI or COLLADA as the output file format.

XSI and Interoperability with Other Digital Content Creation Tools

The COLLADA exporter and importer in XSI allows you to exchange 3D data with any digital content creation tool that supports COLLADA 1.4.0. For example, internal testing was done to validate interoperability with the ColladaMaya plug-in from FeelingSoftware and FX Composer 2 alpha 4 from NVIDIA Corporation.

COLLADA Features in SOFTIMAGE|XSI 5.1

The integration of COLLADA 1.4.0 in SOFTIMAGE|XSI 5.1 supports a subset of the entire COLLADA specification.

User Interface

Export FTK Options. See Figure C.1.

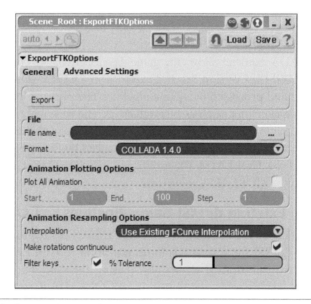

Figure C.1. Export FTK Options.

File. In the File name text box (see Figure C.1), specify a path and name for the file you want to export. You can also use the browse [...] button to select a specific location and filename from a browser.

The Format option lets you select the file format to be exported. You can choose either the dotXSI 5.0 or the COLLADA 1.4.0 file format.

Animation Plotting Options. You can enable the plotting of all animation in the scene. These options are useful when exporting advanced animation rigs, such as IK, constraints, and expressions.

Animation Resampling Options. You can specify how the plotted animation is to be sampled and filtered on export. These are useful options if you need to output animation curves using a specific type of interpolation.

Export Options

Activate "Verbose" mode to log the export progress details to the script editor history pane (see Figure C.2).

The "Export Selection Only" option takes the current selection and exports it. Otherwise, the entire scene is exported.

The "Convert Geometry To Triangles" option triangulates all polygon meshes on export.

Figure C.2. Export options.

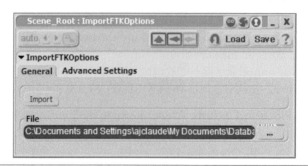

Figure C. 3. FTK Import options.

The "Apply Subdivision to Geometry" option tessellates subdivided geometries and exports the resulting polygon meshes.

In XSI, tangent data is stored in vertex colors. By default, if a vertex color property contains the string "tangent" in its name, it is exported as tangent data. The "Export Tangents as Vertex Colors" option allows you to always export vertex colors as vertex colors regardless of their name.

Shape Animation. These options are not implemented for the COLLADA exporter.

COLLADA Options. The "Export XSI Extra" option lets you export XSI-centric extra data such as visibility and custom parameter sets.

Import FTK Options. See Figure C.3.

File. You can choose to import a COLLADA or dotXSI file into XSI.

Import Options. Activate "Verbose" mode to log the import progress details to the script editor history pane (see Figure C.4).

"Import Implicit Normal" is not implemented for the COLLADA importer.

Scene Elements

Parenting information and primitive instantiating are supported. The `id` and the `name` attributes on the node drive the naming of the entity when exporting and importing data to and from COLLADA. On import, `name` has precedence over `id` for naming entities in XSI. However, since `name` is an optional attribute, `id` is used if the name attribute is not present.

The naming convention when using XSI models (known as *namespaces*) is as follows: `<model name>.<node name>`. For example, an object called

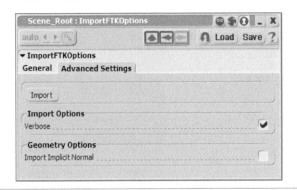

Figure C.4. Import options.

leg that is parented to an XSI model called george will have its name concatenated as george.leg.

- Transformations are partially supported. Geometry nodes use the `<scale>`, `<rotate>`, and `<translate>` elements to describe their transformations. Cameras and spot lights use the `<lookat>` element to describe their transformations.

- Material instancing is fully supported, including the binding of data to effects.

- Nodes that do not have a geometry, light, or camera instance are treated as nulls.

Known Limitations

- There is only one instance of each primitive in the hierarchy data. Multiple instantiating of the same geometry is currently not supported.

- Exporting from XSI currently reduces the transformation stack to a simple [`<translate><rotateZ><rotateY><rotateX><scale>`] stack. Importing a transformation stack other than in this specific order results in the concatenation and reduction of the stack to the [`<translate> <rotateZ><rotateY><rotateX><scale>`] components.

- Only the `<visual_scene>` elements are supported. The element `<physics_scene>` is currently not implemented.

Geometry. The supported geometry type is the polygonal mesh. Polygon lists and triangle lists are fully supported. When exporting, the `<polylist>` element is used instead of the `<polygons>` element since it is a more compact representation. However, the `<polygons>` element is supported when importing.

The supported vertex attributes include positions, normals, vertex colors, texture coordinates, and texture tangents.

Material binding per polygon or triangle list is supported.

Known Limitations

- Triangle strips are not supported.
- Texture binormals are not supported. When exporting from XSI, binormals should be recomputed by the cross product of the normals and the texture tangents.

Materials. Materials are fully supported.

Effects. The common profile is fully supported. The exporter will analyze the material render tree and guesstimate the best approximation to convert from a full-fledged shader node network to the common profile. The ProgID of the first shader attached to the surface port of the material is the one that drives the common profile description. For example, if the first shader attached to the material's surface port has a ProgID "softimage.phong.1", then the exporter will generate a <phong> element within the effect description. Textures attached to the emission, diffuse, specular, and ambient ports are also exported and imported correctly.

The Cg Profile is Supported in Two Variants. The first supported variant uses the NV_import extra which references an external CgFX file. It is used when the CgFX shader node attached to the material uses an external reference to a CgFX file. The output looks like this:

```
<effect id="check3d_fx">
  <extra type="import">
    <technique profile="NV_import">
      <import profile="cgfx"
         url="file://\\lobby\dev\CGFX\check3d.cgfx" />
  </technique>
  </extra>
</effect>
```

The second variant uses the full COLLADA FX specification for the Cg profile. The effect description must be set within the CgFX node for it to work (see Figure C.5).

Cameras

- Perspective cameras are fully supported.
- Orthographic cameras are not exported; they are converted to perspective cameras on import.

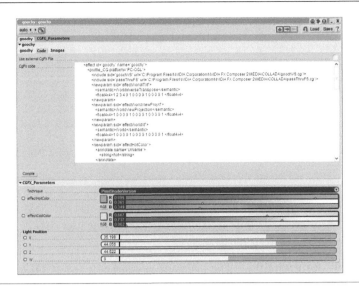

Figure C.5. Effect description set within the CGFX node.

Lights

• Point, directional, and spot lights are fully supported.

Skinning

• Skinning is fully supported. This includes bind pose matrices and envelope weights.

Animation

• Constant, linear, and spline interpolations are fully supported.
• Only animation on node transformations is currently supported.

Extras. There are two types of `<extra>` elements that are supported by the COLLADA converters in XSI.

`XSI extras` describe XSI-specific information on the COLLADA elements. For example, a scene node will have the full XSI transformation data as well as visibility flags and global material assignment data in the XSI extra:

```
<extra>
  <technique profile="XSI">
    <SI_Visibility>TRUE</SI_Visibility>
    <XSI_Transform>
    0.0 0.0 0.0 0.0 0.0 0.0 XYZ 1.0 1.0 1.0 TRUE
    0.0 0.0 0.0 0.0 0.0 0.0 0.0 0.0 0.0 1.0 1.0 1.0 0.0 0.0
```

```
0.0  0.0  0.0  0.0  1.0  1.0  1.0  0.0  0.0  0.0  0.0  0.0  0.0  1.0  1.0
1.0  0.0  0.0  0.0
     <XSI_Limit>"posx" FALSE 0.0 FALSE 0.0</XSI_Limit>
     <XSI_Limit>"posy" FALSE 0.0 FALSE 0.0</XSI_Limit>
     <XSI_Limit>"posz" FALSE 0.0 FALSE 0.0</XSI_Limit>
     <XSI_Limit>"rotx" FALSE 0.0 FALSE 0.0</XSI_Limit>
     <XSI_Limit>"roty" FALSE 0.0 FALSE 0.0</XSI_Limit>
     <XSI_Limit>"rotz" FALSE 0.0 FALSE 0.0</XSI_Limit>
   </XSI_Transform>
   <SI_GlobalMaterial>"check3d" "NODE"</SI_GlobalMaterial>
 </technique>
</extra>
```

The second type of <extra> element does not use the XSI technique profile. These extras are imported and persist as opaque user data blobs in the XSI scene. They are restored on export.

External Referencing. The current integration of COLLADA in SOFTIMAGE|XSI only supports external referencing of images and CgFX files. Other references must be resolved within the same document.

COLLADA Integration Notes

The support for COLLADA in SOFTIMAGE|XSI has been rewritten from the ground up since the COLLADA 1.3.1.3 plug-in release. The new code base now sits inside of the SOFTIMAGE|FTK, a file exchange toolkit used for most converters in SOFTIMAGE|XSI. As a result, existing FTK-based applications can now import and export COLLADA 1.4.0 files. The low-level parser (known in the FTK as the IO layer) is based on XercesC and works in SAX mode to reduce the memory footprint when importing COLLADA files. The high-level classes (known in the FTK as the Semantic Layer) have been updated with new classes that reflect the COLLADA elements.

Elements that are common to dotXSI 5.0 and COLLADA 1.4.0 have been subclassed to ease the transition between dotXSI 5.0 and COLLADA 1.4.0. As a result, the current dotXSIConverter in SOFTIMAGE|XSI also supports COLLADA 1.4.0. You can find a list of the new COLLADA classes in the FTK Reference section of the SOFTIMAGE|XSI SDK documentation.

Appendix: COLLADA FX Plug-In for Maya

Overview

This appendix was provided with permission to reprint by Feeling Software, Inc. It provides information on the installation and usage of the COLLADA FX plug-in for Maya at the time the book was written. This information is reproduced in this book for reference. First download an up-to-date plug-in and refer to its documentation if you are interested in using it.

This plug-in allows artists and developers to create, modify, assign, and visualize complex shaders written for the Cg language. It is designed to display advanced hardware rendering effects and to give immediate feedback while a shader is developed.

The plug-in has full integration with Maya's Hypershade node-based shader editor and creates dynamic GUIs for interactive parameter controls. Using the plug-in, artists can import a COLLADA document, exported from Maya or NVIDIA's FX Composer, manipulate it in Maya, then export it in the COLLADA 1.4 format.

The plug-in also supports references to legacy CgFX shader files.

In the context of this Maya plug-in, a COLLADA FX shader is a hardware shader that consists of a vertex and a fragment shader program. Shader parameters are retrieved from the programs and added to the node as dynamic attributes. Artists can tweak the parameters using the Attribute Editor and view the rendering effects in Maya's OpenGL viewport.

A screen shot of this plug-in executing an environment reflection effect is shown in Plate II.

Shader Format

COLLADA FX nodes support two types of shader formats: Cg and CgFX. Use the Attribute Editor to switch between formats. If the CgFX item is selected, an effect (.cgfx) file must be loaded in the Effect File.

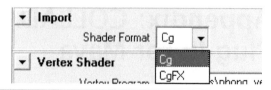

Figure D.1. Shader formats supplied by COLLADA FX.

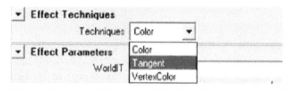

Figure D.2. CgFX effect technique.

Techniques

If a .cgfx shader is loaded, the shader node lists all techniques available in the shader option menu. (See Figure D.2.)

Parameter Types

Here are the parameter types currently supported:

Cg	Maya
bool	bool
half	float
half2	float2
half3	color
half4	color with alpha set to 1.0
half4x4	matrix
float	float
float2	float2
float3	color
float4	color with alpha set to 1.0
float4x4	matrix
sampler2D	color connected to a file pointing to a .dds texture
samplerCUBE	color connected to a file pointing to a .dds texture

Color or vector parameters are exposed as color slider controls in the Attribute Editor. Samplers are exposed as navigation bars. If any transform node is drag-and-dropped on the color slider, it will be connected to the color. A file texture node can also be connected to a sampler using drag-and-drop.

Binding Semantics

COLLADA FX shaders support binding special parameters through *binding semantics*. These were selected for backward compatibility with FX Composer and the CgFX runtime implementation.

The following semantics are currently recognized:

Name	Semantic
POSITION	vertex position
NORMAL	vertex normal vector
COLOR0	per-vertex color
TEXCOORD0-7	uv coordinate or per-vertex color
VIEWPROJ, WORLDVIEWPROJECTION	model view projection matrix
WORLDVIEWPROJECTIONINVERSE	model view projection matrix inverse
WORLDVIEWPROJECTIONINVERSETRANSPOSE	model view projection matrix inverse transpose
WORLDVIEW	model view matrix
WORLDVIEWI, WORLDVIEWINVERSE	model view matrix inverse
WORLDVIEWIT, WORLDVIEWINVERSETRANSPOSE	model view matrix inverse transpose
OBJECT	object space
OBJECTI, OBJECTINVERSE	object space inverse
OBJECTIT, OBJECTINVERSETRANSPOSE	object space inverse transpose
WORLD	world space
WORLDI, WORLDINVERSE	world space inverse
WORLDIT, WORLDINVERSETRANSPOSE	world space inverse transpose
VIEW	view matrix
VIEWI, VIEWINVERSE	view matrix inverse
VIEWIT, VIEWINVERSETRANSPOSE	view matrix inverse transpose
PROJECTION	projection matrix
PROJECTIONI, PROJECTIONINVERSE	projection matrix inverse
PROJECTIONIT, PROJECTIONINVERSETRANSPOSE	projection matrix inverse transpose

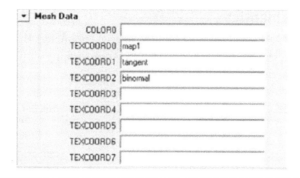

Figure D.3. Mesh Data field.

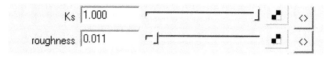

Figure D.4. Shader file editing options.

Mesh Data

Per-vertex data can be set by typing a colorSet or uvSet name in the Mesh Data fields in the Attribute Editor (see Figure D.3). By default, TEXCOORD0 is the default uvSet, and TEXCOORD0-1 is set to the per-vertex tangent and binormal vectors based on the uvSet selected in TEXCOORD0. COLOR1 is meaningless when the node is working with CgFX shaders.

Tips

Click Edit to open the loaded shader file in notepad.exe for editing (see Figure D.4).

Click Reload to reload the shader after editing. Existing parameter values and connections will be restored after the shader is reloaded, as long as the old parameter names still exist in the shader.

The COLLADA FX shader node also allows artists to change the range of sliders and to export these custom annotations through UIMin and UIMax. Click <> beside any float attribute to change this range.

Click + to switch between the color slider and the navigation bar for a color attribute (see Figure D.5). Type the name of the transform node to make the connection.

A file texture node will be created and connected to any sampler parameter right after the .cg or .cgfx shader is loaded.

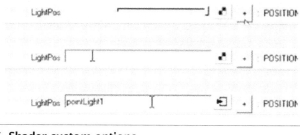

Figure D.5. Shader custom options.

Figure D.6. Sampler parameter connection options.

Passes

A COLLADA FX material can contain one or more rendering passes. Each of these passes is handled through a separate *pass node*. A COLLADA FX shader can be connected to a pass through drag-and-drop. When rendering a COLLADA FX material node, the plug-in sets the graphics state for the first pass, draws the scene geometry, sets the state for the next pass, and draws the geometry again until all the passes have been drawn. Colors from each pass are accumulated.

A screen shot is shown in Plate III.

COLLADA Translator

The ColladaMaya plugin (see Appendix B, "COLLADA Plug-In for Maya") makes it possible to export and import COLLADA FX shaders and passes in the COLLADA document (.dae) format. A typical COLLADA FX type effect will be defined and looks like this:

```
<effect>
  <profile_CG>
    <include>
    <newparam>
      <annotate>
      <semantic>
    <technique>
      <pass>
        <shader>
          <name>
          <bind>
```

If multiple `<pass>` elements are detected under the `<technique>` element, the translator will create a COLLADA FX shader for each pass and collect them in a COLLADA FX passes node.

```
<bind_material>
 <technique_common>
  <instance_material symbol="some_material" target="#material1">>
  <bind semantic="LIGHTPOS1" target="light1/translate"/>
```

When binding material to geometry instance, object connections and animation targets will be exported as shown above.

More Examples

For more examples, see the following illustrations in the color insert:

• Layered material, Plate IV.
• Fractal noise, Plate V.
• Velvet lighting model in Cg, Plate VI.

More Information

• About COLLADA:
  https://collada.org/public_forum/welcome.php
• About this plug-in:
  https://collada.org/public_forum/viewforum.php?f=5
• About Maya/Alias:
  http://www.alias.com/eng/index.shtml
• The official site for this plug-in is:
  http://www.feelingsoftware.com

Appendix: COLLADA 1.4.1

Introduction

This book has been written over a period of several months. During this time, the current release of COLLADA has been COLLADA 1.4.0. The Khronos COLLADA working group has continued improving COLLADA. The focus of the working group has been to resolve issues with the 1.4.0 schema and specification in order to produce the COLLADA 1.4.1 service release. This appendix describes the major changes between COLLADA 1.4.0 and 1.4.1.

Scope of Changes

COLLADA 1.4.1 is a service release of the COLLADA 1.4.0 schema and specification. The Khronos COLLADA working group reviewed almost 300 improvement requests. These improvement requests were divided between schema and specification issues. The schema issues were considered with respect to existing features and compatibility. The specification issues included editorial and typographical errors as well as technical clarifications and additional examples. For each schema issue that was reported, a corresponding specification issue was opened in order to synchronize changes to both the schema and specification documents. In total, of the 300 issues reported for COLLADA 1.4.0, roughly 220 of them have been fixed in the COLLADA 1.4.1 service release.

Compatibility

The COLLADA 1.4.1 schema occupies the same XML Schema namespace as the COLLADA 1.4.0 schema and therefore does not introduce new features into the schema. Furthermore, fixes applied to the 1.4.1 schema are designed to be backward compatible with the COLLADA 1.4.0 schema.

COLLADA 1.4.0 documents will validate against the COLLADA 1.4.1 schema.

Minor Changes

This section summarizes the minor changes made to the COLLADA 1.4.1 schema to correct oversights and omissions within the schema that prevented features of the schema from working correctly.

COLLADA Version

The `<COLLADA>` element version attribute now allows the value "`1.4.1`" in addition to "`1.4.0`" in accordance with the service release version.

COLLADA `xml:base`

COLLADA instance documents often contain URI values that are relative URL expressions. In order to consistently resolve these URLs to external documents, the XML specification has provided an attribute that specifies the base URL of the document. To support this XML feature, the `<COLLADA>` element now allows the `xml:base` attribute.

Input Semantics

The `<input>` element contains a semantic attribute that provides the binding information to input stream. Some of the semantics described in the specification were missing from the schema. These values have been added to the schema: `CONTINUITY`, `LINEAR_STEPS`, `MORPH_TARGET`, `MORPH_WEIGHT`, `TEXBINORMAL`, and `TEXTANGENT`.

Additionally, the legacy value `TEXTURE` has been removed as it is no longer valid.

Instance Attributes

The ability to instantiate objects in COLLADA 1.4 is extremely powerful and useful. The design allows these objects to be animated as well. In order to fully enable animated instances, the entire family of `<instance_*>` elements now allows the `name` and `sid` attributes to complete the targeting information. The `name` and `sid` attributes are optional.

COLLADA FX Changes

Changes described in this section center around the powerful COLLADA FX portion of the schema. As developers continue to implement the full set of features, they have also reported issues that required changes to the schema in order to enable capabilities that were intended to exist in COLLADA 1.4.0 but could not be implemented without additional schema support.

Color Targets

The rendering surface targets within COLLADA FX were underspecified for the operations they are designed to support. To correct the problems found by developers, several attributes are now available to the `<color_target>`, `<depth_target>`, and `<stencil_target>` elements. These new attributes are:

- The `index` attribute provides the ordinal for the target.
- The `mip` attribute provides the MIP level of the target.
- The `slice` attribute provides the slice index of the target.
- The `face` attribute provides the surface face orientation of the target.

Surface Initialization

The COLLADA 1.4 FX design includes powerful rendering surface configuration and initialization features. The `<surface>` element can be initialized from external texture files in varying degrees of complexity. It was found during development of NVIDIA's FX Composer 2.0 that the schema was insufficient to describe the most complex use cases such as initialization of a cube map from a DDS file. Additional schema was required to enable the use cases, and these fixes are in COLLADA 1.4.1.

The `<surface>` element now has optional initialization child elements that enable the following:

- `<init_as_null>` to create an uninitialized surface that can be fully initialized later by the runtime engine.
- `<init_as_target>` to create a render-to-texture or similar surface.
- `<init_cube>` to create a cube map texture.
- `<init_volume>` to create a volumetric texture.
- `<init_planar>` to create a simplified planar texture from a more complex external file.

This set of changes to the `<surface>` element constitutes the most significant changes in the 1.4.1 schema.

Surface Formatting

In conjunction with surface initialization, complex surface formatting was not properly enabled by the existing `<format>` element. To correct the problems encountered by tool developers, the `<surface>` element now has an optional `<format_hint>` child element. In addition, the `<format>` element has been made optional.

Usertype Extensions

The ability to create user-defined types within an effects profile was hampered by the inability to set parameters. This oversight has been fixed by allowing the `<usertype>` element to have `<setparam>` child elements. Furthermore, the `<usertype>` element has a source attribute to complete the declaration of the type.

Profile Assets

The various effects profiles are themselves objects that can be asset managed by the appropriate software. To enable this as intended, the profile elements (`<profile_COMMON>`, `<profile_GLES>`, `<profile_GLSL>`, and `<profile_CG>`) now allow an `<asset>` child element.

COLLADA Physics Changes

Changes described in this section center around the unique COLLADA Physics portion of the schema.

Velocity Default Values

The COLLADA Physics schema defines rigid body elements that are instantiated into the physical simulation. The instantiation process is often automated by physics runtime engines with regard to the initial velocity of objects. Therefore, the schema now provides default values for these parameters to simplify COLLADA instance documents. The `<velocity>` and `<angular_velocity>` child elements of the `<instance_rigid_body>` element now have default values of zero, indicating that the objects are initially at rest.

Rigid Constraint Default Values

The COLLADA Physics schema defines rigid body constraint parameters that are part of the physical simulation. In order to minimize the complexity of these definitions, several parameters now have default values consistent with the automation provided by physics runtime engines. Physics elements that now have default values include:

- `<limits>` children `<swing_cone_and_twist>` and `<linear>`.
- `<spring>` children `<angular>` and `<linear>`.

Notes and References

Chapter 1: Introduction to COLLADA

[1]   The authors received an e-mail from a Lead Systems Engineer on a US Army simulator program mentioning their interest to use COLLADA as a database format.

[2]   The Lunar Module Mission Simulator was used at the Kennedy Space Center between 1968 and 1972. It was used by every Apollo astronaut to train prior to their mission. Cameras controlled by a computer, filming a model of the lunar surface, projected the image in front of the four windows so the astronauts would feel as if they were actually maneuvering for a landing on the Moon. In this early real-time image generator, the database was in hardware!

[3]   There are over 700 bibliographic references on ray-tracing techniques. Andrew S. Glassner's book, *An Introduction to Ray Tracing*, first published in 1989 by Morgan Kaufmann is a good reference book. PovRay (Persistence of Vision Raytracer) is a free ray-tracing tool available for many platforms and also in source code (http://www.povray.org/).

[4]   Pixar Animation Studios created the RenderMan rendering technology to generate their own feature film productions. Since its introduction in the 1990s, it has become a standard tool in many computer graphics studios (http://renderman.pixar.com/).

[5]   Computer-aided design (CAD) is a very large market. Originally created for the automobile and the aerospace industries, these DCC tools are now ubiquitous in the manufacturing industry. Pierre Bézier, a French mathematician who died November 25, 1999, was one of the early pioneers. While working at Renault, a French automaker, he invented a method of describing any 2nd degree curve using only four points, which is now referred to as the Bézier curve.

[6]   General Electric was a pioneer in terrain paging capability for their IMAGE series. Terrain paging is a complex feature that requires specific hardware such as direct DMA engines from disk to main memory and fast disk array systems. A lot of information on terrain paging and related algorithms can be found on the World Wide Web (http://www.vterrain.org/).

[7]   Christopher C. Tanner, Christopher J. Migdal, and Michael T. Jones. "The Clipmap: A Virtual Mipmap." In *Proceedings of SIGGRAPH 98, Computer Graphics Proceedings, Annual Conference Series*, edited by Michael Cohen, pp. 151–242, Reading, MA: Addison Wesley, 1998.

[8] In complexity theory, the NP-complete problems are the most difficult problems in NP (nondeterministic polynomial time).

[9] Google Earth lets you browse the Earth from your computer, paging both terrain and satellite images in real time from the Internet. It is freely available (http://earth.google.com/).

[10] Christopher Tanner and Rémi Arnaud created a prototype of this technology as a demonstration when looking for venture money to finance the Intrinsic Graphics start-up. Once Intrinsic Graphics was financed, it focused on middleware for the game market. The original technology was so compelling that Keyhole was created as a separate entity to create a product. This company was later bought by Google, and the product became Google Earth.

[11] Iris Performer, a very popular scene graph, was developed at Silicon Graphics and is still in use today. J. Rohlf and J. Helman. "IRIS Performer: A High Performance Multiprocessing Toolkit for Real-Time 3D Graphics." In *Proceedings of SIGGRAPH 94, Computer Graphics Proceedings, Annual Conference Series*, edited by Andrew Glassner. pp. 381—395, New York: ACM Press, 1994. OpenSceneGraph was first created as an open-source equivalent, since Performer was originally not available on any other platform than the SGI computer. Industry-standard database formats, such as Multigen OpenFlight, were created and are still in use today in the simulation industry.

[12] Binary space partition (BSP) trees were first used in the early flight simulators' visual systems to determine a hidden part removal algorithm. The idea is to determine the drawing order of all the geometry so that the hidden parts are covered by the visible parts. Also known as the painter's algorithm, this was used in early 3D games before the hardware accelerated Z-buffer was widely available in graphics hardware accelerators.

[13] DotXSI and the FTK (File Transfer Toolkit) were created by Softimage (http://softimage.com/products/xsi/pipeline_tools/dot_xsi_format/).

[14] Historical information on the creation of OpenGL and DirectX can be found on Wikipedia (http://en.wikipedia.org/wiki/Opengl#History) (http://en.wikipedia.org/wiki/Direct_x#History).

[15] The name COLLADA was coined by the engineers in R&D, since several projects had code names that were named after winds. A collada is a strong north or northwest wind blowing in the upper part of the Gulf of California, but blowing from northeast in the lower part of the Gulf. The acronym COLLAborative Design Activity was then created by Attila Vass, senior manager in the SCE US R&D department.

[16] Unfortunately, this relies on the capability of the DCC tools to be flexible enough to store the extra data in their internal representation. A discussion on this project is available on the World Wide Web (https://collada.org/public_forum/viewtopic.php?t=312).

[17] Criterion has since been acquired by Electronic Arts. EA has made RenderWare their main tool. Although the product was still available as a middleware on the market, the loss of independence rapidly impacted their ability to sell.

The other game developers could not afford to depend on their competitor's technology.

[18] Vicarious Vision was later purchased by Activision, eliminating another independent middleware vendor.

[19] The Emdigo website (http://www.emdigo.com/).

[20] AGEIA acquired Novodex in 2004, which gave them the PhysX SDK. In September 2005, they acquired Meqon Research AB, consolidating the market for the physics engine for game development.

[21] Discreet and Autodesk offer a wide range of products for the media and entertainment market (http://www.discreet.com/) (http://www.autodesk.com/).

[22] Alias had been owned by Silicon Graphics, Inc. since 1995. It was acquired by Accel-KKR, an equity investment firm, for $57M in April 2004. It was sold back to Autodesk in January 2006 for $197M. Autodesk now has both 3ds Max and Maya DCC tools, representing close to 80% of the tools used in the game industry (http://www.alias.com/) (http://www.autodesk.com/).

[23] Softimage, an Avid company, is the maker of the XSI DCC tool (http://www.softimage.com/) (http://www.avid.com/).

[24] R. Arnaud, M. Barnes. "COLLADA: An Open Interchange File Format for the Interactive 3D Industry." SIGGRAPH '04 Exhibitor Tech Talk, 2004.

[25] X3D has also decided to use XML as the base technology (http://www.web3d.org/). Unfortunately, X3D design is not very popular among game developers, since it was designed for a different domain of application: 3D for the Web. Later on, the X3D community created a document that shows that the two designs are very different (http://realism.com/Web3D/Collada/Nodes).

[26] COLLADA 1.1 was published in December 2003. COLLADA 1.2 was published in January 2004 as a patch release. COLLADA 1.3 was released in March 2005, introducing only a few features such as skinning but improving the conformance test and the quality of plug-ins. There was a COLLADA 1.3.1 patch release in August 2005. The specification stayed quite stable between 1.1 and 1.3.1, waiting for DCC vendors to create quality tools and developers to start using the technology. All those releases were done under an SCE copyright and licensing. COLLADA 1.4 was released in January 2006 under the Khronos umbrella, introducing major features such as COLLADA FX, COLLADA Physics, and a new design philosophy based on strong typing. Once again, the specification is in a stable phase, waiting for good implementations to be available. With the additional interest from developers, the cycle will be much shorter this time.

[27] ATI website (http://www.ati.com/).

[28] NVIDIA website (http://www.nvidia.com/).

[29] 3Dlabs website (http://www.3dlabs.com/). In February 2006, 3Dlabs decided to drop their desktop division and concentrate on the mobile embedded market space.

[30] Nokia website (http://www.nokia.com/).

[31] At the 2005 PlayStation press conference, Masami Chatani (CTO) announced that the PS3's development environment will support COLLADA. This raised the interest in COLLADA from game developers.

[32] Khronos Group. "COLLADA Approved by the Khronos Group as Open Standard." Press Release, July 29, 2005 (http://www.scei.co.jp/corporate/release/pdf/050729e.pdf).

Chapter 2: COLLADA Document

[33] The W3C eXtensible Markup Language (XML) specification can be found on the World Wide Web (http://www.w3.org/TR/REC-xml/).

[34] Robin Green (SCEA) coined a statement that summarizes the major considerations and design decisions for the COLLADA project: "*COLLADA is your data in motion.*" This has since been refined to "*COLLADA is your asset in motion.*"

[35] Game developers also expressed the concern that text encoding could not retain the precision of a floating-point number. In numerical-computing circles, this issue has been studied exhaustively and the findings published in papers. David Goldberg published an informative paper in the March 1991 issue of *Computing Surveys:* David Goldberg. "What Every Computer Scientist Should Know About Floating Point Arithmetic." *ACM Computing Surveys* 23:1, 1991. Available on World Wide Web (http://docs.sun.com/source/806-3568/ncg_goldberg.html). The conclusion is that such concerns are unfounded and that nine decimal digits are sufficient to retain the precise value of any IEEE 754 single precision floating-point value (see also https://collada.org/public_forum/viewtopic.php?t=366).

[36] This method was demonstrated at the SIGGRAPH '05 COLLADA tech talk by Alias.

[37] Discussion on this subject is available on the World Wide Web (https://collada.org/public_forum/viewtopic.php?t=25).

Chapter 3: COLLADA Geometry

[38] The stream processing model is a central technology behind the exceptional performance exhibited by modern graphics processing units (GPUs) manufactured by companies such as ATI, Inc. and NVIDIA Corporation.

[39] The COLLADA schema is the natural place for metadata. Taking advantage of the features of the chosen XML technologies contributes to smaller instance documents.

[40] Access to external, non-XML source data was considered an important feature by game developers during the initial requirements-gathering phase. Interestingly, all source data has been in XML documents after two years of existence.

[41] Complex polygons with holes are not possible for every DCC tool or tool chain to handle. The flexibility is provided because it is often the approach desired by artists when modeling many everyday objects.

[42] COLLADA geometry does not use the technique extensibility mechanism because the design identifies the level of multirepresentation as a higher-level asset management issue.

Chapter 4: COLLADA Scenes

[43] The term "shader" was also considered as the highest-level concept instead of "material." In COLLADA 1.0, there was a one-to-one relationship between the two elements of the same name. With the introduction of "effects," this third high-level concept complicated matters, but "material" still remained the central abstraction.

[44] Lights as objects in the scene, or more precisely nodes in the scene graph, are considered anachronistic by proponents of global illumination–based designs. The distinct light source object type is a relic of the fixed function graphics pipeline that we have not moved completely away from yet.

[45] Artists and developers hold different opinions about the common usage and importance of "area" lights. A consensus was not reached so they are not included in the common profile.

[46] A common definition of the <imager> element was attempted during the design of COLLADA 1.2, but a consensus was not reached so it was left out of the schema.

[47] The <node> element can contain the number and order of transformation elements to accommodate all manner of software tools, not only those used in existing DCC tools.

[48] The flexibility given by allowing multiple <visual_scene> elements is possible using the <node> element to perform the compositions instead. This addition may be unnecessary.

[49] COLLADA strives to avoid a scripting solution for rendering and pipeline configuration that would take it out of the structured XML domain.

Chapter 5: COLLADA Effects

[50] Bui Tuong Phong was a computer graphics researcher and pioneer. He invented the Phong reflection model, an illumination technique widely used in computer graphics. This algorithm was published in 1973 in his PhD thesis, "Illumination for Computer Generated Images." It is a simplified model applied at each pixel, combining a *specular* reflection component, a *diffuse* reflection component, an *ambient* reflection component, and a *shininess* component.

[51] Cook and Torrance proposed their shading algorithm in "A Reflectance Model for Computer Graphics."(R. L. Cook and K. E. Torrance. "A Reflection Method for Computer Graphics." ACM *Transactions on Graphics* 1:1 (1982), 7–24.) It is based on a physical model of real materials. Specifically, it bases reflection on the properties of many "microfacets" that make up the surface of a material. The formulation includes a microfacet distribution function, which determines scattering based on a statistical approximation of the variation of the angles of

the microfacets. There is also a geometrical attenuation term, which models how much the microfacets shadow and block the light from each other. There is also a Fresnel term, which alters the amount of reflection based on the outgoing angle. This Fresnel term is wavelength dependent and causes the color of the reflected light to change based on the outgoing angle.

[52] Gouraud shading is used to achieve smooth lighting on low-polygon surfaces without the heavy computational requirements of calculating lighting for each pixel. The technique was first presented by Henri Gouraud in "Continuous Shading of Curved Surfaces." (H. Gourand. "Continuous Shading of Curved Surfaces." *IEEE Transactions on Computers.* 20:6 (1971), 623–628.) This technique has many visible artifacts compared to a per-pixel method. It used to be quite popular since it produced better images than uniform colored polygons (flat shading) without the need for per-pixel computation. This method is no longer used, unless the goal is to produce images with a vintage look!

[53] James F. Blinn. "Models of Light Reflection for Computer Synthesized Pictures." *Proc. SIGGRAPH '77, Computer Graphics* 11:2 (1977), 192–198. This model differs from previous models in that the intensity of the highlight changes with the direction of the light source.

[54] There are many books that explain how to write shaders and many sample shaders available. *Advanced Game Development with Programmable Graphics Hardware* by Alan Watt and Fabio Policarpo (A K Peters, 2005) is a good reference for game developers. *GPU Gems,* edited by Randima Fernando (Addison-Wesley, 2004), *GPU Gems 2,* edited by Matt Pharr (Addison-Wesley, 2005), *OpenGL Shading Language (the Orange Book)* by Randi J. Rost (Addison-Wesley, 2004), and *The Cg Tutorial: The Definitive Guide to Programmable Real-Time Graphics* by Randima Fernando and Mark J. Kilgard (Addison-Wesley, 2003) are also excellent sources.

[55] FX Composer is an application for Windows freely available from the NVIDIA developer website that is used to create, debug, and tune shaders (http://developer.nvidia.com/). The latest version, FX Composer 2.0, which should be available at the time this book is published, is designed to create COLLADA FX files and can handle both OpenGL and DirectX API programming models.

Chapter 7: COLLADA Physics

[56] John F. Jacobs, *The SAGE Air Defense System: A Personal History* (MITRE Corporation, 1986) is recommended if you want to learn everything about the Whirlwind, but unfortunately it is out of print. Fortunately, there is an entry on Wikipedia: (http://en.wikipedia.org/wiki/Whirlwind_(computer)).

[57] Ivan Sutherland. "Sketchpad, A Man-Machine Graphical Communication System." Ph.D. diss., 1963.

[58] More information about *Half-Life 2* is available on the World Wide Web (http://half-life2.com/).

[59] AGEIA, a semiconductor company that specializes in physics processing, announced a physics processing unit (PPU) in March 2005. It operates in a similar

way to other processing units like graphics processing units (GPUs) by offloading physics data onto a dedicated chip, leaving the main CPU free to carry out other tasks. The new chip is called the PhysX and claims to offer substantially greater physics processing compared to conventional CPUs.

[60] Stephane Redon. "Algebraic Solution to the Problem of Collision Detection of Rigid Polyhedral Objects", (http://i3d.inrialpes.fr/people/redon/), 2000,

[61] Open Dynamic Engine (ODE) is an open source project that is available on the World Wide Web (http://ode.org/).

[62] For more information on Havok, see World Wide Web (http://www.havok.com/).

[63] For more information about AGEIA NovodeX Physics SDK, consult the World Wide Web (http://www.ageia.com/).

[64] Chris Hecker, "Rigid Body Dynamics." Available from the World Wide Web (http://www.d6.com/users/checker/dynamics.htm.) See also V-collide (http://www.cs.unc.edu/~geom/V_COLLIDE/) and I-Collide (http://www.cs.unc.edu/~geom/I_COLLIDE/).

[65] Bullet has its own forum for physics simulation on the World Wide Web (http://www.continuousphysics.com/Bullet/phpBB2/).

[66] Display system frequencies are not the same everywhere. Typically 60 Hz is used in the USA and Japan, and 50 Hz in most of Europe. Commercial displays offer frequency doublers: 100 Hz in Europe. There are now prototypes of commercial displays running at 120 Hz, and even at 240 Hz!

[67] Continous collision detection technology has been part of SIGGRAPH courses since 2004.

[68] Nima is an AGEIA PhysX engine plug-in for Alias that can be dowloaded from the World Wide Web (http://www.feelingsoftware.com/).

[69] Havok Complete™ is one of the first physics middleware that combines a game physics SDK (Havok Physics) with an animation system (Havok Animation), in order to attempt to solve the problem of giving more control to the animator while keeping all the advantages of real-time physics.

Chapter 8: COLLADA Content Pipeline

[70] The classic tool for automating software builds is the Unix *make* program, which was invented around 1974 to reduce software build times for C programs on the Unix operating system. *Make* programs decide whether source files need rebuilding by using text *makefiles* that contain dependency trees and by comparing time stamps on source files and object files.

[71] Ant, a build system written in Java, is available from the World Wide Web (http://ant.apache.org/).

[72] MSBuild reference documentation is available on the World Wide Web (http://msdn2.microsoft.com/en-us/library/0k6kkbsd.aspx).

[73] The Concurrent Versions System (CVS) is an open-source product that keeps track of all work and all changes in a set of files (http://www.nongnu.org/cvs/).

[74] Subversion (SVN) is a more recent open-source versioning system that enables concurrent check-ins and versioning of directories (http://subversion.tigris.org/).

[75] Perforce is a popular commercial versioning system tool (http://www.perforce.com/).

[76] Alienbrain is a commercial product from NXN (http://www.alienbrain.com/).

[77] In order to participate in the design of COLLADA, one has to become a Khronos contributor member. For more information, consult the World Wide Web (http://www.khronos.org/).

[78] This chapter is about the COLLADA DOM 1.4.0 that was about to be released at the time of this writing. The COLLADA DOM API may have changed in subsequent releases.

[79] The W3C publishes the Document Object Model requirements, available from World Wide Web (http://www.w3.org/DOM/). The COLLADA DOM is not fully compliant with those requirements.

[80] Doxygen is a documentation system for C++, C, Java, Objective-C, Python, IDL (Corba and Microsoft flavors), and to some extent PHP, C#, and D (http://www.stack.nl/~dimitri/doxygen/).

[81] The OpenSceneGraph is an open-source high-performance 3D graphics toolkit, used by application developers in fields such as visual simulation, games, virtual reality, scientific visualization, and modeling. Written entirely in Standard C++ and OpenGL, it runs on all Windows platforms, OSX, GNU/Linux, Solaris, and FreeBSD operating systems (http://www.openscenegraph.org/).

Index

T - #0123 - 111024 - C66 - 229/152/12 - PB - 9780367446291 - Gloss Lamination